بسم الله الرحمن الرحيم

To the Reader

● A special chapter is devoted to the collapse of the theory of evolution because this theory constitutes the basis of all anti-spiritual philosophies. Since Darwinism rejects the fact of creation—and therefore, the existence of Allah—over the last 140 years it has caused many people to abandon their faith or fall into doubt. It is therefore an imperative service, a very important duty to show everyone that this theory is a deception. Since some readers may have the chance to read only one of our books, we think it appropriate to devote a chapter to summarize this subject.

● All the author's books explain faith-related issues in the light of Qur'anic verses, and invite readers to learn Allah's words and to live by them. All the subjects concerning Allah's verses are explained so as to leave no doubt or room for questions in the reader's mind. The books' sincere, plain, and fluent style ensure that everyone of every age and from every social group can easily understand them. Thanks to their effective, lucid narrative, they can be read at one sitting. Even those who vigorously reject spirituality are influenced by the facts these books document and cannot refute the truthfulness of their contents.

● This and all the other books by the author can be read individually, or discussed in a group. Readers eager to profit from the books will find discussion very useful, letting them relate their reflections and experiences to one another.

● In addition, it will be a great service to Islam to contribute to the publication and reading of these books, written solely for the pleasure of Allah. The author's books are all extremely convincing. For this reason, to communicate true religion to others, one of the most effective methods is encouraging them to read these books.

● We hope the reader will look through the reviews of his other books at the back of this book. This rich source material on faith-related issues is very useful, and a pleasure to read.

● In these books, unlike some other books, you will not find the author's personal views, explanations based on dubious sources, styles that are unobservant of the respect and reverence due to sacred subjects, nor hopeless, pessimistic arguments that create doubts in the mind and deviations in the heart.

SIGNS OF
THE END TIMES
IN SURAT AL-KAHF

HARUN YAHYA

GOODWORD BOOKS

About the Author

Now writing under the pen-name of HARUN YAHYA, he was born in Ankara in 1956. Having completed his primary and secondary education in Ankara, he studied arts at Istanbul's Mimar Sinan University and philosophy at Istanbul University. Since the 1980s, he has published many books on political, scientific, and faith-related issues. Harun Yahya is well-known as the author of important works disclosing the imposture of evolutionists, their invalid claims, and the dark liaisons between Darwinism and such bloody ideologies as fascism and communism.

His pen-name is a composite of the names *Harun* (Aaron) and *Yahya* (John), in memory of the two esteemed Prophets who fought against their people's lack of faith. The Prophet's seal on the his books' covers is symbolic and is linked to the their contents. It represents the Qur'an (the final scripture) and the Prophet Muhammad (peace be upon him), last of the prophets. Under the guidance of the Qur'an and the Sunnah (teachings of the Prophet), the author makes it his purpose to disprove each fundamental tenet of godless ideologies and to have the "last word," so as to completely silence the objections raised against religion. He uses the seal of the final Prophet, who attained ultimate wisdom and moral perfection, as a sign of his intention to offer the last word.

All of Harun Yahya's works share one single goal: to convey the Qur'an's message, encourage readers to consider basic faith-related issues such as Allah's Existence and Unity and the hereafter; and to expose godless systems' feeble foundations and perverted ideologies.

Harun Yahya enjoys a wide readership in many countries, from India to America, England to Indonesia, Poland to Bosnia, and Spain to Brazil. Some of his books are available in English, French, German, Spanish, Italian, Portuguese, Urdu, Arabic, Albanian, Russian, Serbo-Croat (Bosnian), Polish, Malay, Uygur Turkish, and Indonesian.

Greatly appreciated all around the world, these works have been instrumental in many people recovering faith in Allah and gaining deeper insights into their faith. His books' wisdom and sincerity, together with a distinct style that's easy to understand, directly affect anyone who reads them. Those who seriously consider these books, can no longer advocate atheism or any other perverted ideology or materialistic philosophy, since these books are characterized by rapid effectiveness, definite results, and irrefutability. Even if they continue to do so, it will be only a sentimental insistence, since these books refute such ideologies from their very foundations. All contemporary movements of denial are now ideologically defeated, thanks to the books written by Harun Yahya.

This is no doubt a result of the Qur'an's wisdom and lucidity. The author modestly intends to serve as a means in humanity's search for Allah's right path. No material gain is sought in the publication of these works.

Those who encourage others to read these books, to open their minds and hearts and guide them to become more devoted servants of Allah, render an invaluable service.

Meanwhile, it would only be a waste of time and energy to propagate other books that create confusion in people's minds, lead them into ideological chaos, and that clearly have no strong and precise effects in removing the doubts in people's hearts, as also verified from previous experience. It is impossible for books devised to emphasize the author's literary power rather than the noble goal of saving people from loss of faith, to have such a great effect. Those who doubt this can readily see that the sole aim of Harun Yahya's books is to overcome disbelief and to disseminate the Qur'an's moral values. The success and impact of this service are manifested in the readers' conviction.

One point should be kept in mind: The main reason for the continuing cruelty, conflict, and other ordeals endured by the vast majority of people is the ideological prevalence of disbelief. This can be ended only with the ideological defeat of disbelief and by conveying the wonders of creation and Qur'anic morality so that people can live by it. Considering the state of the world today, leading into a downward spiral of violence, corruption and conflict, clearly this service must be provided speedily and effectively, or it may be too late.

In this effort, the books of Harun Yahya assume a leading role. By the will of Allah, these books will be a means through which people in the twenty-first century will attain the peace, justice, and happiness promised in the Qur'an.

The works of the author include *The New Masonic Order, Judaism and Freemasonry, Global Freemasonry, Knight Templars, Islam Denounces Terrorism, Terrorism: The Ritual of the Devil, The Disasters Darwinism Brought to Humanity, Communism in Ambush, Fascism: The Bloody Ideology of Darwinism, The 'Secret Hand'in Bosnia, Behind the Scenes of The Holocaust, Behind the Scenes of Terrorism, Israel's Kurdish Card, The Oppression Policy of Communist China and Eastern Turkestan,Palestine, Solution: The Values of the Qur'an, The Winter of Islam and Its Expected Spring, Articles 1-2-3, A Weapon of Satan: Romanticism, Signs from the Chapter of the Cave to the Last Times, Signs of the Last Day, The Last Times and The Beast of the Earth, Truths 1-2, The Western World Turns to God, The Evolution Deceit, Precise Answers to Evolutionists, The Blunders of Evolutionists, Confessions of Evolutionists, The Qur'an Denies Darwinism, Perished Nations, For Men of Understanding, The Prophet Musa (as), The Prophet Yusuf (as), The Prophet Muhammad (saas), The Prophet Sulayman (as), The Golden Age, Allah's Artistry in Colour, Glory is Everywhere, The Importance of the Evidences of Creation, The Truth of the Life of This World, The Nightmare of Disbelief, Knowing the Truth, Eternity Has Already Begun, Timelessness and the Reality of Fate, Matter: Another Name for Illusion, The Little Man in the Tower, Islam and the Philosophy of Karma, The Dark Magic of Darwinism, The Religion of Darwinism, The Collapse of the Theory of Evolution in 20 Questions, Allah is Known Through Reason, The Qur'an Leads the Way to Science, The Real Origin of Life, Consciousness in the Cell, Technology Imitates Nature, A String of Miracles, The Creation of the Universe, Miracles of the Qur'an, The Design in Nature, Self-Sacrifice and Intelligent Behaviour Models in Animals, The End of Darwinism, Deep Thinking, Never Plead Ignorance, The Green Miracle: Photosynthesis, The Miracle in the Cell, The Miracle in the Eye, The Miracle in the Spider, The Miracle in the Gnat, The Miracle in the Ant, The Miracle of the Immune System, The Miracle of Creation in Plants, The Miracle in the Atom, The Miracle in the Honeybee, The Miracle of Seed, The Miracle of Hormone, The Miracle of the Termite, The Miracle of the Human Body, The Miracle of Man's Creation, The Miracle of Protein, The Miracle of Smell and Taste, The Miracle of Microworld, The Secrets of DNA.*

The author's childrens books are: *Wonders of Allah's Creation, The World of Animals, The Glory in the Heavens, Wonderful Creatures, Let's Learn Our Islam, The World of Our Little Friends: The Ants, Honeybees That Build Perfect Combs, Skillful Dam Builders: Beavers.*

The author's other works on Quranic topics include: *The Basic Concepts in the Qur'an, The Moral Values of the Qur'an, Quick Grasp of Faith 1-2-3, Ever Thought About the Truth?, Crude Understanding of Disbelief, Devoted to Allah, Abandoning the Society of Ignorance, The Real Home of Believers: Paradise, Knowledge of the Qur'an, Qur'an Index, Emigrating for the Cause of Allah, The Character of the Hypocrite in the Qur'an, The Secrets of the Hypocrite, The Names of Allah, Communicating the Message and Disputing in the Qur'an, Answers from the Qur'an, Death Resurrection Hell, The Struggle of the Messengers, The Avowed Enemy of Man: Satan, The Greatest Slander: Idolatry, The Religion of the Ignorant, The Arrogance of Satan, Prayer in the Qur'an, The Theory of Evolution, The Importance of Conscience in the Qur'an, The Day of Resurrection, Never Forget, Disregarded Judgements of the Qur'an, Human Characters in the Society of Ignorance, The Importance of Patience in the Qur'an, General Information from the Qur'an, The Mature Faith, Before You Regret, Our Messengers Say, The Mercy of Believers, The Fear of Allah, Jesus Will Return, Beauties Presented by the Qur'an for Life, A Bouquet of the Beauties of Allah 1-2-3-4, The Iniquity Called "Mockery", The Mystery of the Test, The True Wisdom According to the Qur'an, The Struggle with the Religion of Irreligion, The School of Yusuf, The Alliance of the Good, Slanders Spread Against Muslims Throughout History, The Importance of Following the Good Word, Why Do You Deceive Yourself?, Islam: The Religion of Ease, Enthusiasm and Excitement in the Qur'an, Seeing Good in Everything, How do the Unwise Interpret the Qur'an?, Some Secrets of the Qur'an, The Courage of Believers, Being Hopeful in the Qur'an, Justice and Tolerance in the Qur'an, Basic Tenets of Islam, Those Who do not Listen to the Qur'an, Taking the Qur'an as a Guide, A Lurking Threat: Heedlessness, Sincerity Described in the Qur'an.*

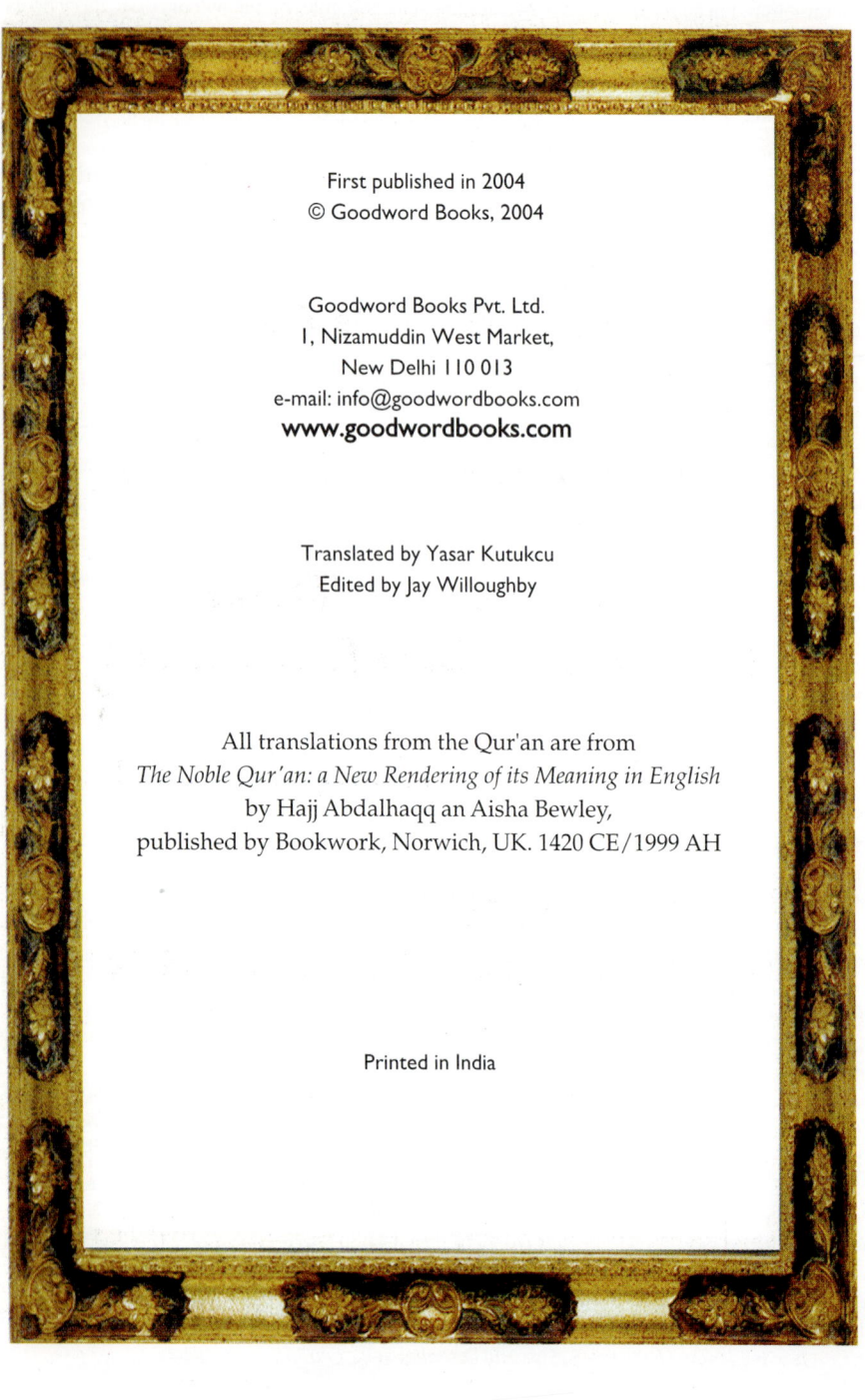

First published in 2004
© Goodword Books, 2004

Goodword Books Pvt. Ltd.
1, Nizamuddin West Market,
New Delhi 110 013
e-mail: info@goodwordbooks.com
www.goodwordbooks.com

Translated by Yasar Kutukcu
Edited by Jay Willoughby

All translations from the Qur'an are from
The Noble Qur'an: a New Rendering of its Meaning in English
by Hajj Abdalhaqq an Aisha Bewley,
published by Bookwork, Norwich, UK. 1420 CE/1999 AH

Printed in India

Contents

Introduction 8

Signs of the End Times
in Surat al-Kahf 10

Conclusion 221

The Deception
of Evolution 223

Introduction

The Qur'an contains all the commands and information necessary for the believer's life. It is Allah's book of revelation, valid until the Day of Judgment. One of its greatest miracles is it has retained its relevance to all people, regardless of when they live, since Allah first revealed it as a guide to wisdom and the righteous path.

Its narratives concerning past nations provide guidance to people in so many ways. The lives of the Prophets, their calls to their nations, and their actual practices are examples for the believers to follow. Furthermore, the Qur'an contains signs for the future and some mysteries upon which the believers must reflect. Such is the case with Surat al-Kahf, one of its suras.

Prophet Muhammad (saas) and many Muslim scholars have pointed out Surat al-Kahf for this reason. The Qur'an's account of the Companions of the Cave (Ashab al-Kahf) and Ar-Raqim, Prophet Musa's (as) experiences with Khidr (as) (the person of knowledge), and the account of Dhu'l-Qarnayn (as) contain many secrets and expressions hinting at the End Times.

Many prophetic hadiths connect Surat al-Kahf with the End Times. Some of them are as follows:

Related by an-Nawwas ibn Sam'an: He who among you will survive to see him (the Dajjal) should recite over him the opening verses of Surah al-Kahf. (Sahih Muslim)

Related by Abu Umamah al-Bahili: Whoever enters his (the Dajjal's) Hell, let him seek refuge with Allah and recite the opening verse of Surat al-Kahf, and it will become cool and peaceful for him, as the fire became

cool and peaceful for Abraham. (Ibn Kathir)

One reason why the Prophet (saas) recommended reading Surat al-Kahf is that it contains very important signs pointing to the End Times. Surat al-Kahf contains the signs required for the believers' defense and fight against the Dajjal and the irreligious movements bringing so much evil to humanity, which he wants to spread around the world, as well as many lessons from which the Muslims can learn. Our Prophet's (saas) recommendation to memorize and read this sura attentively is a clear indication of this. As we will see throughout this book, the experiences of Ashab al-Kahf in an unbelieving world, the lessons Prophet Musa (as) learned from Khidr (as), and Dhu'l-Qarnayn's (as) rule over the world, established to disseminate Islam's values, are matters upon which the believers need to reflect.

We will explain the reasons behind these events so that readers can ponder and meditate upon Surat al-Kahf, which contains very important signs for today, in order to gain insight into these secrets and to abide by the Prophets' (saas) advice. Attentive readers will see that this sura bears the signs of the End Times, a time near the Hour, during which the practices of systems of unbelief and falsehood become widespread and Allah sends forth the truth to destroy them.

By Allah's will, this time is very near, so much so that it has become crucial for people to reflect upon this matter. Thus, Muslims must ponder Surat al-Kahf carefully, bear its verses in mind, and analyze each verse in light of the Qur'an's other verses.

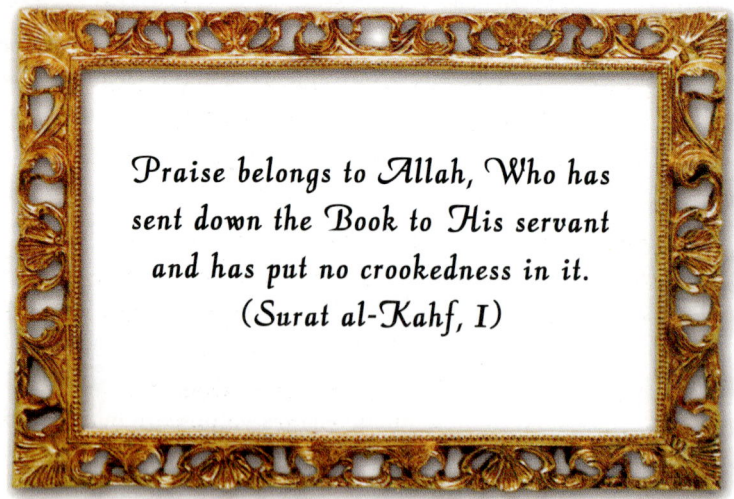

Praise belongs to Allah, Who has sent down the Book to His servant and has put no crookedness in it. (Surat al-Kahf, 1)

The sura's first verse indicates the importance of being grateful to Allah, Who gave humanity everything: a perfectly functioning body, an environment suitable for life on Earth, the order in the universe, food, water, and much more. Allah's generosity is infinite, for He gave us so much that we cannot list His blessings even in general terms. We are reminded of this reality in the following verse:

> If you tried to number Allah's blessings, you could never count them. Allah is Ever-Forgiving, Most Merciful. (Surat an-Nahl, 18)

One of the believers' foremost characteristics is to be in a state of gratefulness for all that Allah has given them and to remember that His gifts are a trial for humanity. As Surat an-Nisa' 147 states, Allah **"is always responsive to gratitude."** However, in spite of this, most people are ungrateful for what they are given. Prophet Sulayman's (as) words are reported in Surat an-Naml:

> "This is part of my Lord's favor to test me, to see if I will give thanks or show ingratitude. Whoever gives thanks only does so to his own gain. Whoever is ungrateful, my Lord is Rich Beyond Need, Generous." (Surat an-Naml, 40)

In the End Times, people are totally removed from gratefulness. Having forgotten that Allah gives all that they have, they are completely absorbed in their worldly lives and consider all of their wealth and possessions to be the result of their own effort and mind. Such people have to know that they are being ungrateful to Allah, because only He gives everything. This reality is revealed in the following verses:

He has given you everything for which you have asked Him. If you tried to number Allah's blessings, you could never count them. Man is indeed wrongdoing, ungrateful. (Surah Ibrahim, 34)

Any blessing you have is from Allah. Then when harm touches you, it is to Him that you cry for help. But when He removes the harm from you, a group of you associate others with their Lord, ungrateful for what We have given them. Enjoy yourselves. You will soon know! (Surat an-Nahl, 53-55)

As these verses state, people do not realize that Allah gives them everything and they deny this truth by associating others with Him. Satan, who follows this strategy, seeks to push people away from thankfulness and toward ungratefulness for Allah's gifts so that they will begin to deny this truth and then go astray. The Qur'an exposes Satan's wicked strategy and real purpose, as follows:

[Satan said:] "Then I will come at them from in front of them and behind them, from their right and from their left. You will not find most of them thankful." He [Allah] said: "Get out of it, reviled and driven out. As for those who follow you, I will fill up Hell with every one of you." (Surat al-A`raf, 17-18)

Naturally, there are consequences in this world for people's ungratefulness. The fact of people's forgetfulness and ungratefulness is at the bottom of all the poverty, destitution, decadence, deprivation, spiritual decline and similar problems that we see all around us. While being grateful opens up blessings, well-being, and peace, ungratefulness brings great sorrow. Allah says:

And when your Lord announced: "If you are grateful, I will cer-

tainly give you increase, but if you are ungrateful, My punishment is severe." (Surah Ibrahim, 7)

As this verse reveals, people who do not thank Allah for what He gives earn a severe punishment: sorrow in this world and in the Hereafter.

Past events can teach us many valuable lessons. In the twentieth century, the world was ruled by anti-religious people, such as those who followed communism and fascism, who distanced the people from true religion's goodness by portraying denial as an attractive substitute. Their followers denied Allah, and so forgot about thankfulness and encountered great tragedies over many long years. In return for their ungratefulness, Allah withheld some of His gifts. The Qur'an reveals that the "reward" for ungratefulness is the following:

Allah makes an example of a city that was safe and at peace, its provision coming to it plentifully from every side. Then it showed ingratitude for Allah's blessings, so He made it wear the robes of hunger and fear for what it did. (Surat an-Nahl, 112)

The cause for the famine, poverty, fear, and suffering that we saw during the twentieth century is the people's ungratefulness. The Qur'an reveals that such people will be punished:

[By] that We repaid them, because they did not believe. And [thus] do We repay except the ungrateful? (Surah Saba', 17)

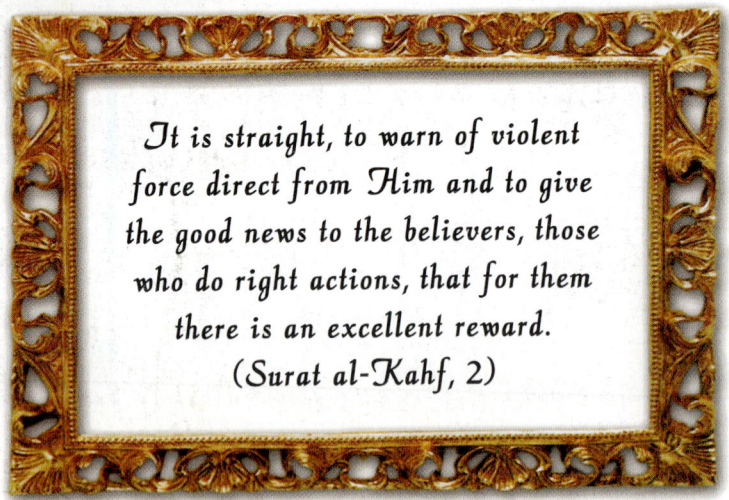

It is straight, to warn of violent force direct from Him and to give the good news to the believers, those who do right actions, that for them there is an excellent reward.
(Surat al-Kahf, 2)

This verse points out the Qur'an's importance and that it is the true book. The Qur'an guides humanity, reminds people of their eternal life, and shows them the righteous path. It is a revelation and the only path that shows us how to win Allah's good pleasure and mercy, and Paradise. It is the absolute measure for right and wrong. As Surat al-Baqara 120 states, **"Allah's guidance is the true guidance."** Our Lord reveals that the believers must hold on tightly to the Qur'an's guidance, as follows:

> **So hold fast to what has been revealed to you. You are on a straight path. It is certainly a reminder to you and to your people, and you will be questioned. (Surat az-Zukhruf, 43-44)**

Surat al-Kahf 2 indicates the importance of abiding by Allah's revelation. All believers have the life-long responsibility of obeying His injunctions, orders, and recommendations, and no difficulty, pressure, or hardship can cause them to be distracted or careless in this matter. Regardless of the circumstances, they are meticulous, diligent, and determined.

The verse also draws our attention to the obligation of warning oth-

ers. Allah frequently reminds the faithful of this important obligation and indicates the necessity of commanding the right and forbidding the wrong. He instructs us to do this as an act of worship, and gives the good news of salvation to those who do so:

> **Those who repent, those who worship, those who praise, those who fast, those who bow, those who prostrate, those who command the right, those who forbid the wrong, those who preserve the limits of Allah: give good news to the believers. (Surat at-Tawba, 112)**

As with everything else, the best examples of this are the Prophets. The Messengers whom Allah willed to fulfill this honorable obligation warned their people in a variety of ways, invited them to the true faith, reminded them of Hell, and warned them about eternal suffering. Allah reveals this reality, as follows:

I have warned you of a Fire that rages, in which only the most wretched will roast. (Surat al-Layl, 14-15)

Surat al-Kahf 2 also points out the importance of right action, defined as good deeds done with a true heart in order to win Allah's good pleasure, and grace, and Paradise. Another verse with the same message is the following:

If anyone seeks glory, let him know that glory is Allah's alone. To Him ascends good speech, and righteous work raises it. But people who plot evil deeds will suffer a harsh punishment. The plotting of such people is profitless. (Surah Fatir, 10)

In many other verses, our Lord points out the importance of doing right actions and the rewards that He will give in return. Some of them are given below, as follows:

Give the good news to those who believe and do right actions, that they will have Gardens with rivers flowing under them. When they are given fruit there as provision, they will say: "This is what we were given before." But they were only given a simulation of it. They will have there spouses of perfect purity, and will remain there timelessly, forever. (Surat al-Baqara, 25)

Those who believe, those who are Jews, and the Christians and Sabaeans, all who believe in Allah and the Last Day and act rightly, will have their reward with their Lord. They will feel no fear and will know no sorrow. (Surat al-Baqara, 62)

As for those who believe and do right actions and humble themselves before their Lord, they are the Companions of the Garden, remaining in it timelessly, forever. (Surah Hud, 23)

Surat al-Kahf 2 touches upon another important issue: giving the believers the good news of Paradise. Many verses order the Messengers to do this, for the believers draw great comfort from being told that all of their troubles, difficulties and shortcomings in this life are only temporary, and that Allah's help, grace, and mercy are always with them. The nearness of the Hereafter's blessings increases the believers' motivation, zeal, and effort. As one verse says:

We have made it easy on your tongue so that you can give good news to those who guard against evil and warn stubbornly hostile people by it. (Surah Maryam, 97)

All of the issues touched upon in Surat al-Kahf 2 are subjects upon which Muslims living near to or in the End Times need to reflect carefully. As this verse indicates, holding fast to the Qur'an will protect people from the evil flowing from evil and anti-religious ideologies, as well as the trials and tribulations of the End Times. Conscientious Muslims of the End Times must do right actions under the guidance of the Qur'an, urge people to do right, give them the good news of the blessings of Paradise, and warn them of the punishment of Hell and not to make compromises with Allah's law.

A place in which they will remain forever.
(Surat al-Kahf, 3)

Some people deny Allah's existence and the nearness of the eternal life of Paradise or Hell. For them, death means entering nothingness, for there is no Day of Judgment. Others believe in Hell, but think that its suffering will last only a number of days. According to this view, people will remain there for a short period of time to pay for their sins, and then will leave it behind for the blessings of Paradise. However, the Qur'an does not mention any such temporary punishment, and Allah reveals the following truth:

That is because they say: "The Fire will only touch us for a number of days." Their inventions have deluded them in their religion. (Surah Al 'Imran, 24)

Surat al-Kahf 3 points out people's incorrect understanding of Hell and reveals that it is an eternal resting place for those who persist in unbelief. People who get so absorbed in their worldly lives that they forget about Allah's existence, who do not follow the righteous path of Allah's Messenger (saas), and who do not obey the Qur'an will be in Hell forever, unless Allah wills otherwise, for such is His justice. The Qur'an also reveals that those who persist in unbelief will continue their insolence in Hell:

The evildoers will remain timelessly, forever, in the punishment of Hell. It will not be eased for them. They will be crushed there by despair. We have not wronged them; it was they who were wrongdoers. They will call out [addressing the keeper of Hell]: "Malik, let your Lord put an end to us!" He will say: "You will stay the way you are." (Surat az-Zukhruf, 74-77)

As seen in the above verses, not even in Hell will the unbelievers comprehend the fact that they are dependent on Allah; rather, they will continue in their conceit by not turning to Him but, instead, calling out to an angel to "let your Lord put an end to us." By doing so, they prove that they are still transgressors. Allah reveals that the unbelievers who ask: "Can we be sent back so that we can do something other than what we did?" (Surat al-A`raf, 53) are liars:

If only you could see when they are standing before the Fire and saying: "Oh! If only we could be sent back again, we would not deny the Signs of our Lord, and we would be among the believers." No, it is simply that what they were concealing before has been shown to them. If they were sent back, they would merely return to what they were forbidden to do. Truly, they are liars. (Surat al-An`am, 27-28)

Other verses state that people are given enough time on Earth, but that they do not abandon their conceit:

Or lest he should say, when he sees the punishment: "If only I could have another chance so that I could be a good-doer!" "No, the fact is that My Signs came to you, but you denied them and were arrogant and one of the unbelievers." (Surat az-Zumar, 58-59)

From all of this, we understand that such people will not mend their ways. Since Allah is most merciful with the believers, He does not let such evil people enter Paradise and be with the believers. Paradise, with all that it contains and its inhabitants, is a place of goodness, and nothing that

Allah disapproves of can be found there. This is one of the consequences of His mercy and justice to His devout servants.

The eternal blessings of Paradise are only for the believers. Allah says:

Their recompense is forgiveness from their Lord, and Gardens with rivers flowing under them, remaining in them timelessly, forever. How excellent is the reward of those who act! (Surah Al 'Imran, 136)

As for those who disobey Allah and His Messenger and overstep His limits, We will admit them into a Fire, remaining in it timelessly, forever. They will have a humiliating punishment. (Surat an-Nisa', 14)

Do they not know that whoever opposes Allah and His Messenger will have the Fire of Hell, remaining in it timelessly, forever? That is the great disgrace. (Surat at-Tawba, 63)

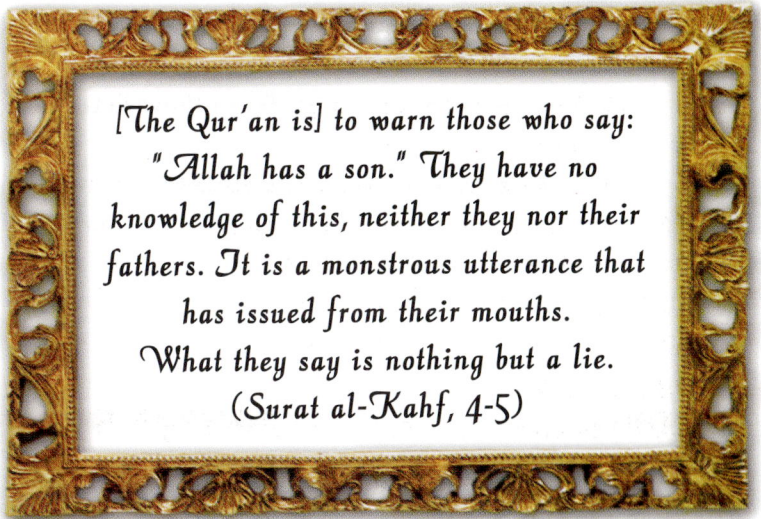

[The Qur'an is] to warn those who say: "Allah has a son." They have no knowledge of this, neither they nor their fathers. It is a monstrous utterance that has issued from their mouths. What they say is nothing but a lie. (Surat al-Kahf, 4-5)

These two verses deal with the Christians' seriously mistaken understanding of Allah. By devising the doctrine of the Trinity, the Christians deviated from their true religion. The following verses explain how they did this:

O People of the Book, do not go to excess in your religion. Say nothing but the truth about Allah. The Messiah, `Isa son of Maryam, was only the Messenger of Allah and His word, which He cast into Maryam, and a Spirit from Him. So believe in Allah and His Messengers. Do not say: "Three." It is better that you stop. Allah is only One God. He is too Glorious to have a son! Everything in the heavens and in Earth belongs to Him. Allah suffices as a Guardian. (Surat an-Nisa', 171)

They say: "Allah has a son." Glory be to Him! He is the Rich Beyond Need. Everything in the heavens and on Earth belongs to Him. Have you authority to say this, or are you saying about Allah that which you do not know? (Surah Yunus, 68)

That is `Isa son of Maryam, the word of truth about which they are in doubt. It is not fitting for Allah to have a son. Glory be to Him! When He decides on something, He just says to it, "Be!" and it is. (Surah Maryam, 34-35)

There can be no doubt that this mentality is the faith of those who associate others with Allah. As the Qur'an reveals, Allah has no partners, equals, or children. He is the sole Governor of all that exists, as well as the Lord of the heavens and Earth. Those Muslims living in the End Times are obliged to explain such mistaken beliefs to all who hold them.

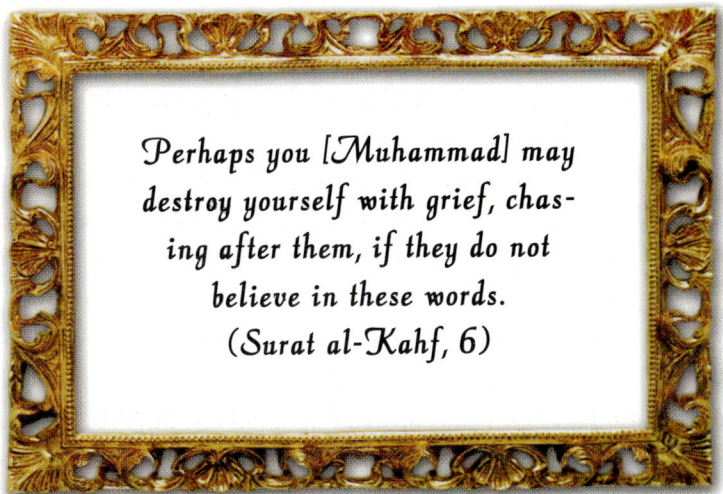

Perhaps you [Muhammad] may destroy yourself with grief, chasing after them, if they do not believe in these words.
(Surat al-Kahf, 6)

This verse deals with those who do not respond to the calls to faith made by the Prophet (saas) and the believers. Devout believers abide by Allah's order to command right and forbid evil, invite people to believe in Allah, and inform them of the truth contained in the Qur'an. However, most people turn away from the Messengers' calls and persist in denial, as revealed by: **"The Hour is coming—there is no doubt about it. But most of mankind do not believe"** (Surah Ghafir, 59).

The unbelievers respond to such calls in many ways. Some demand miracles from the Messengers, as in: **"We will not believe you until you make a spring gush out from the earth for us"** (Surat al-Isra', 90), while others simply mock the believers. An an example of the latter is given below:

> **When they are told: "Believe in the way that the people believe," they exclaim: "What! Are we to believe in the way that fools believe?" No indeed! They are the fools, but they do not know it. (Surat al-Baqara, 13)**

Every Prophet was greeted by his nation with similar mockery and often was subjected to various forms of oppression. For instance, Prophet Nuh (as) used all methods to call his people to faith, but they responded negatively, as follows:

> He said: "My Lord, I have called my people night and day, but my calling has only made them more evasive. Indeed, every time I called them to Your forgiveness, they put their fingers in their ears, wrapped themselves up in their clothes, and were overweeningly arrogant. Then I called them openly. Then I addressed them publicly and privately." I said: "Ask forgiveness of your Lord. Truly He is Endlessly Forgiving." (Surah Nuh, 5-10)

As we can understand from these verses, most people, regardless of time or place, respond negatively to the calls to true religion. However, it must not be forgotten that such reactions never demoralize the believers, for they know that only Allah can bestow faith. No matter how well they speak, how moving and wise their words are, the believers cannot put faith into someone's heart unless Allah wills it. Other verses also reveal this truth:

> We sent a Messenger among every people saying: "Worship Allah and keep clear of all false deities." Among them were some whom Allah guided, but others received the misguidance they deserved. Travel about the land and see the final fate of the unbelievers. However eager you are for them to be guided, Allah will not guide those whom He misguides. They will have no helpers. (Surat an-Nahl, 36-37)

As these verses reveal, no one can make anyone else believe. Therefore, the believers are responsible only for calling to faith. After they have fulfilled this obligation, they must leave it to Allah to give faith. Trusting Allah, being patient, and inviting to His religion in the most pleasant manner will have a great effect upon people's hearts. Allah says:

So remind them. You are only a reminder. You cannot compel them [to believe]. But as for anyone who turns away and is an unbeliever, Allah will punish him with the greatest punishment. Certainly it is to Us that they will return. Then their reckoning is Our concern. (Surat al-Ghashiya, 21-26)

Only Allah can bestow faith and make someone a believer. Many other verses, some of which are listed below, state this fact:

If your Lord had willed, all people on Earth would have believed. Do you think that you can force people to be believers? No one can believe except with Allah's permission. (Surah Yunus, 99-100)

You cannot guide those whom you would like to guide, but Allah guides those whom He wills to guide. He knows best those who are guided. (Surat al-Qasas, 56)

Surah Yusuf also discusses this subject. Irrespective of how genuine the call to faith is, people who have not been guided cannot believe. The Muslims are responsibile for calling and advising, and after doing this are to leave the person's status as a believer or an unbeliever to Allah. All of their efforts in this respect will be recorded and rewarded by Allah's will, while those who persist in their opposition to the truth will be punished. Allah reveals this truth in Surah Yusuf:

But most people, for all your eagerness, are not believers. You do not ask them for any wage for it. It is only a reminder to all beings. How many Signs there are in the heavens and Earth! Yet they pass them by, turning away from them. Most of them do not believe in Allah without associating others with Him. Do they feel so secure that the all-enveloping punishment of Allah will not come upon them, or that the Last Hour will not come upon them all of a sudden, when they least expect it? Say: "This is my way. I call to Allah with inner sight, I and all who follow me. Glory be to Allah! I am not one of the idolaters!" (Surah Yusuf, 103-108)

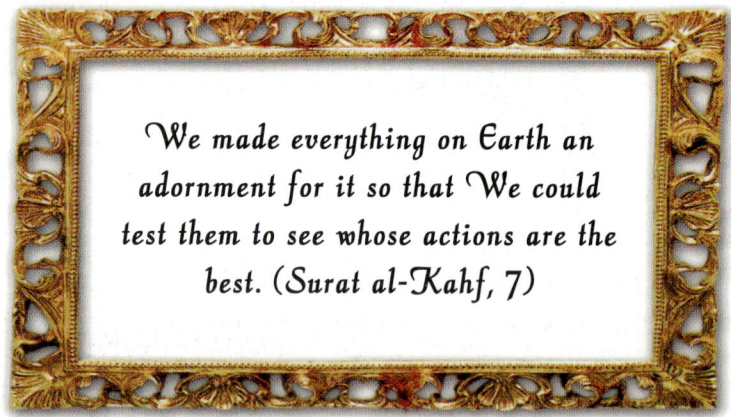

We made everything on Earth an adornment for it so that We could test them to see whose actions are the best. (Surat al-Kahf, 7)

Most people either do not know that their present life in this world is a trial to determine their true value in Allah's sight, or else they know this truth but choose to ignore it. This is why they are so dedicated to the worldly life and do not want to think about death and an eternal life in the Hereafter. But Allah reveals that people are tried while on Earth: **"We will test you with a certain amount of fear and hunger, and loss of wealth and life and fruits. But give good news to the steadfast"** (Surat al-Baqara, 155). He also reveals the purpose of life on Earth and death, as follows:

> He Who created death and life to test which of you is best in action. He is the Almighty, the Ever-Forgiving. (Surat al-Mulk, 2)

Just saying "I believe" is never enough to win Allah's good pleasure and grace, and Paradise; people have to prove the soundness of their faith and dedication to His revelation throughout their lives and in every situation. One must always turn to Allah and adhere strictly to His commands, whether in hardship, illness, suffering, and hunger or in wealth, power, and influence, for:

> Do people imagine that they will be left to say: "We believe," and will not be tested? We tested those before them, and Allah will surely make evident those who are truthful and and He will surely make evident the liars. (Surat al-`Ankabut, 2-3)

But most people prefer the pleasures of this life over the life of the Hereafter. To own the latest sports car, a luxurious villa, jewels, or designer cloths are thought, mistakenly, to be the purpose of life. They race to become richer, more beautiful, or more famous, and spend their lives chasing these goals. However, nothing will benefit them unless they use it appropriately, as the following verses reveal:

To mankind, the love of worldly appetites is painted in glowing colors: women and children, and heaped-up mounds of gold and silver, and horses with fine markings, and livestock and fertile farmland. All that is merely the enjoyment of the life of this world. The best homecoming is in the presence of Allah. Say: "Shall I tell you of something better than that?" Those who do their duty will have Gardens with their Lord, with rivers flowing under them, remaining in them timelessly, forever, and purified wives, and Allah's good pleasure. Allah sees His servants. (Surah Al `Imran, 14-15)

As these verses make clear, this life is temporary and its pleasures are misleading. In the End Times, as it has always been throughout history, all that exists (e.g., palaces, huge factories, bridges, gold and jewelry, money piled up in the bank, stock shares, cars, speed boats, and planes) is created to test people. While owning or not owning such things has specific connotations in human societies, in the eyes of Allah they mean nothing.

What really matters is one's faith in Allah, sincerity, and good character. Every person will die and realize that the eternal life of the Hereafter is true. Therefore, it is very unwise to be misled by the pleasures of this life. The believers, who realize this truth, exchange their lives and property for the eternal life in the Hereafter and enjoy this deal. Allah says to the believers:

Allah has bought from the believers their selves and their wealth in return for Paradise. They fight in the Way of Allah, and they kill and are killed. It is a promise binding upon Him

in the Torah, the Gospel, and the Qur'an, and who is truer to his contract than Allah? Rejoice, then, in the bargain you have made. That is the great victory. (Surat at-Tawba, 111)

SIGNS OF THE END TIMES IN SURAT AL-KAHF

We will certainly make everything on it a barren wasteland.
(Surat al-Kahf, 8)

All beauty and wealth are created to test humanity, as mentioned earlier. In this verse, our Lord reminds us that no matter how beautiful, grand, or valuable our possessions, eventually all of them will become dust.

If Allah wills, He can unexpectedly remove those cherished things that make people forget His existence, thereby leaving them destitute. Allah is All-powerful; He gives wealth and poverty and, as the owner of everything, gives it to whomsoever He wills. The Qur'an mentions this in many verses, several of which are given below:

> The Keys of the heavens and Earth belong to Him. He expands the provision of anyone He wills or restricts it. He has knowledge of all things. (Surat ash-Shura, 12)

> Do they not see that Allah expands provision for whoever He wills and also restricts it? There are certainly Signs in that for people who believe. (Surah Rum, 37)

> Allah expands the provision of any of His servants He wills and restricts it. Allah has knowledge of all things. (Surat al-Ankabut, 62)

SIGNS OF THE END TIMES IN SURAT AL-KAHF

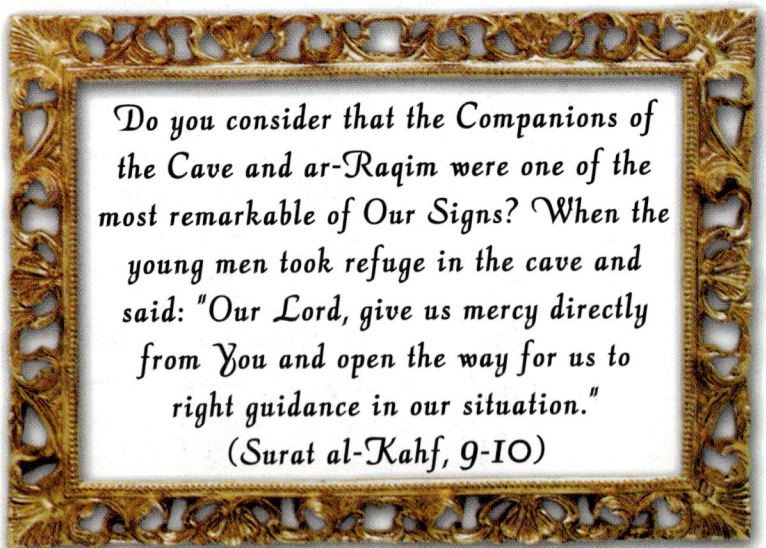

Do you consider that the Companions of the Cave and ar-Raqim were one of the most remarkable of Our Signs? When the young men took refuge in the cave and said: "Our Lord, give us mercy directly from You and open the way for us to right guidance in our situation."
(Surat al-Kahf, 9-10)

These verses touch upon this group's extraordinary situation. As the narrative unfolds, we see that their experiences are of an unusual and metaphysical nature. Their entire life is full of miraculous developments. Some of our Prophet's (as) hadiths make a connection between them and the End Times. This indicates that people living in the End Times may have supernatural experiences.

The continuation of the verse might be suggesting that the youth of the End Times will take on great responsibilities, for they will play an important role in the ideological struggle against anti-religious philosophies, presenting true religion, and ending oppression. Other verses state the importance of youth in informing people about religion. For example, in Surat al-Kahf, we are told of Musa's (as) "young servant," and another verse says that only some young people of Musa's (as) nation believed in him:

No one believed in Musa except some children of his people, out of fear that Pharaoh and the elders would persecute them...
(Surah Yunus, 83)

Surat al-Kahf 10 tells us that those young people sought refuge in the cave from the existing oppressive system, which did not allow them to express their views, tell the truth, and call to Allah's religion. Thus, they distanced themselves from their people.

This verse might be signaling the creation of similar totalitarian regimes in the End Times, for regimes founded upon communism, fascism, or other ideologies seek to curb people's freedoms and oppress those who want to lead a religious life. The Companions of the Cave left their people and sought refuge because of similar oppression. Muslims living in the End Times probably will have to remain out of sight and hidden in order to escape the oppression of communist and fascist systems. Those who do this successfully will distance themselves from society and will be seen only rarely.

However, this should not be understood as an idle period, for they took refuge there while asking for Allah's grace and help. They also sought to improve and develop themselves. Muslims of the End Times who live under oppressive regimes will conceal themselves and hope for Allah to increase His grace upon them, and also to make their lives and struggle against anti-religious movements easier.

The Companions of the Cave's prayer to Allah (verse 10) also draws our attention to the fact that the believers must never forget that only Allah wills something to happen. All people are forever needy, helpless, and dependent upon Him, and cannot achieve anything through their own intellect, effort, and power unless Allah wills it. How can they see anything through to its conclusion when they cannot even lift a hand, walk, or breathe, except by His will? Many verses remind people that they must always depend upon Allah's help, support, and grace due to their incapacity and the fact that only Allah can will something to happen. For example:

You did not kill them; it was Allah Who killed them. And you did not throw, when you threw; it was Allah Who threw, so that He might test the believers with this excellent trial from Him.

Allah is All-Hearing, All-Knowing. (Surat al-Anfal, 17)

Allah creates and does all things; humanity, on the other hand, is tested in the areas of sincerity and submission. The Companions of the Cave, aware of this reality, immediately turned to Allah after finding refuge and expressed their submission by praying to Him. Knowing that Allah would increase their wisdom and make things easier for them in every respect, the first thing that they did was to seek His help. As this situation shows, what matters most is for people to be genuine Muslims who pray to our Lord and ask Him for everything.

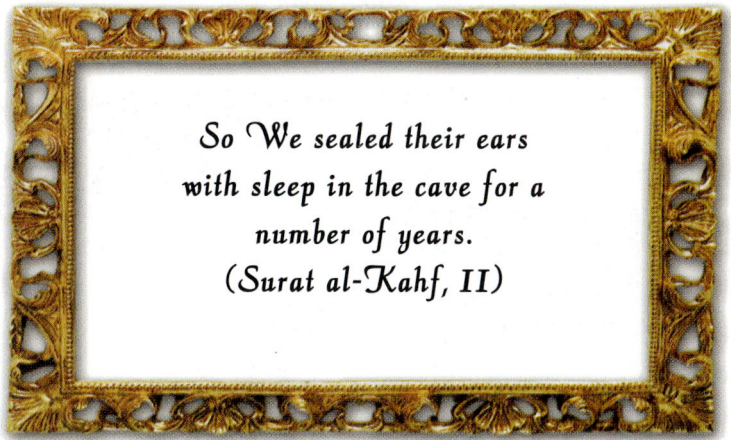

So We sealed their ears with sleep in the cave for a number of years.
(Surat al-Kahf, 11)

Just as the Companions of the Cave sought refuge from the oppression of the prevailing godless system, the believers in the End Times will choose to conceal themselves, for their own protection, from such oppressive systems as communism, fascism, and other enemies of religion and moral values. Their existence will resemble that of the Companions of the Cave: they will be oppressed, will not have freedom of thought, and will not be able to speak their minds.

However, this period of concealment is not about worrying and suffering. Quite the contrary; it is a waiting period in peace and contentment. The expression **"We sealed their ears with sleep in the cave for a number of years"** suggests that the believers' time of concealment will pass in inner peace, as if they were asleep.

For the Muslims, this is a period of personal development, education, acquiring knowledge, and growing stronger in faith. They will not be affected by the violence, oppression, injustice, and cruelty unleashed upon society by those who do not believe and are enemies of moral values. The believers will be away from all of this hardship, as if they were in a cave, and, by Allah's grace, this situation will protect them.

These people are still living under the oppression of anti-religious systems. This chaos and injustice is a sign of the End Times. However, the Muslims know that, Allah willing, this difficult period is about to end. This realization gives them great joy.

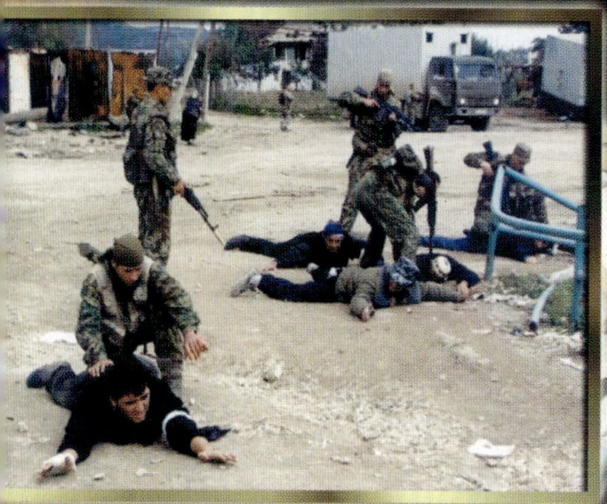

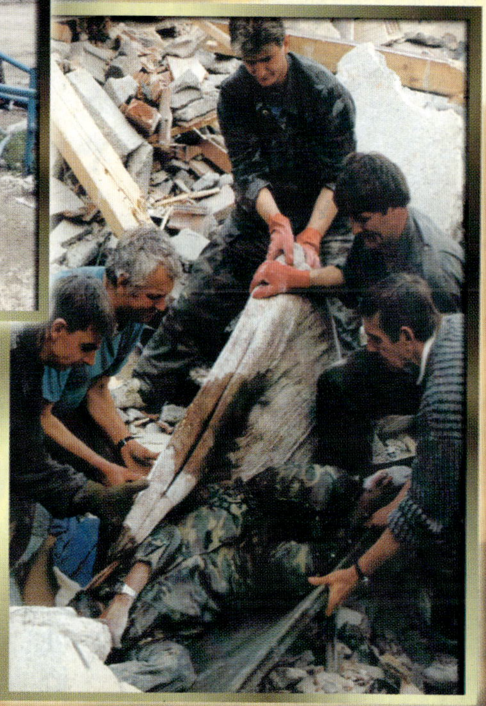

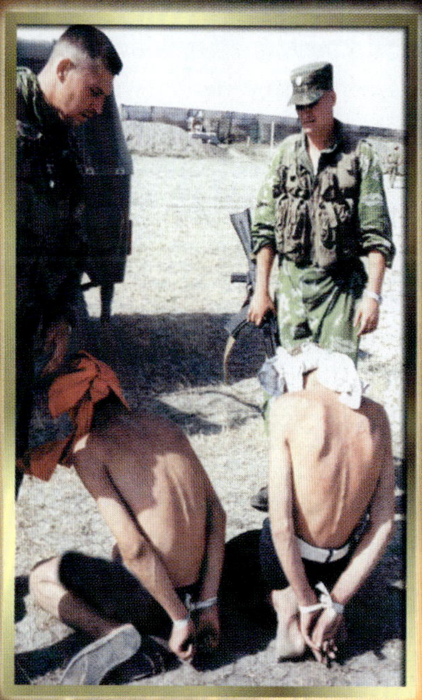

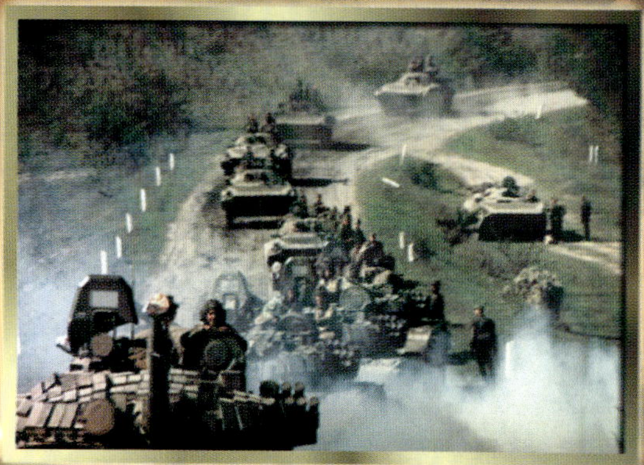

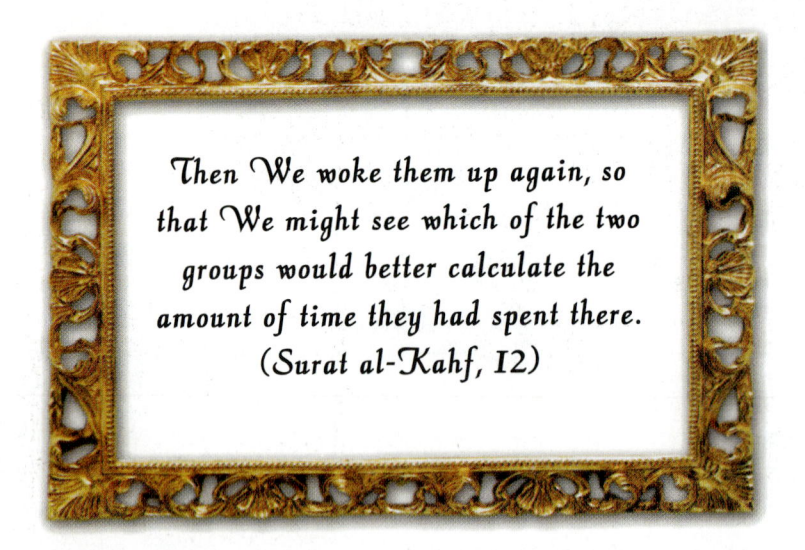

> *Then We woke them up again, so that We might see which of the two groups would better calculate the amount of time they had spent there. (Surat al-Kahf, 12)*

As this verse indicates, the Companions of the Cave's concealment lasted for a certain period, after which they awoke at a time of Allah's willing and by His will. The people of faith's concealment in the End Times will continue until the destined time by Allah comes. Then, all secrecy will be abandoned, and the believers will mix with the people freely and tell them the truth about faith, Allah's existence, and the Qur'an's morality.

Only Allah knows how long this period will last, for as this verse indicates, the number of years, days, and hours of this period is within His knowledge. Surat al-Jinn reveals Allah's attribute of *Al-Muhsi* (The Reckoner, The One Who knows the number of everything even though infinite):

> **So that He may know that they have indeed transmitted the Messages of their Lord. He encompasses what is in their hands, and has counted the exact number of everything. (Surat al-Jinn, 28)**

> *We will relate their story to you with truth. They were young men who believed in their Lord, and We increased them in guidance.*
> *(Surat al-Kahf, 13)*

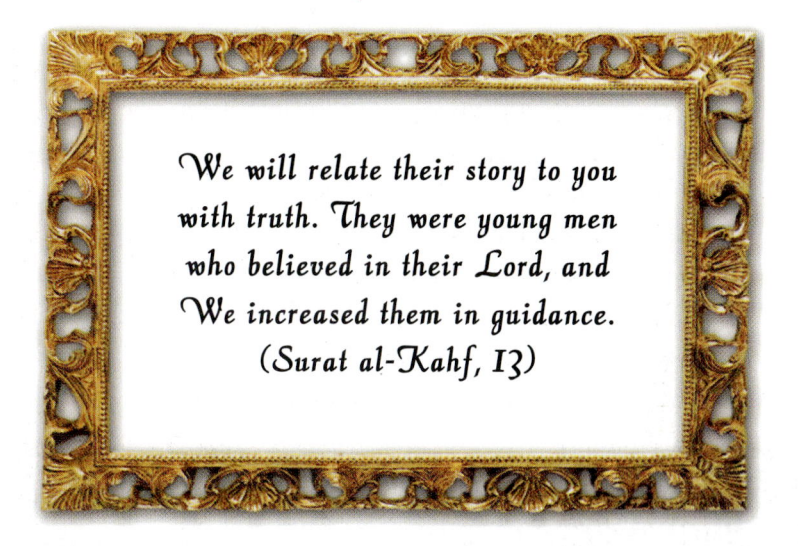

This verse underlines the importance of a strong faith and guidance, because in Allah's presence the great job that one has done might count for nothing if one did not comply strictly with the Qur'an and follow the Prophet's (saas) path. One's financial success, career, or fame here is of no help in the Hereafter, because what truly matters is faith and obedience to Allah, Who describes His guided devotees in the following terms:

> That is the Book, without any doubt. It contains guidance for those who guard against evil: those who believe in the Unseen, establish prayers, and spend from what We have provided for them; those who believe in what has been sent down to you and what was sent down before you, and are certain about the Hereafter. They are the people guided by their Lord. They are the ones who have success. (Surat al-Baqara, 2-5)

In another verse, our Lord gives the good tidings to His guided devotees that they will not experience any fear or sorrow:

> We said: "Go down from it, every one of you! Then when guid-

ance comes to you from Me, those who follow My guidance will feel no fear and will know no sorrow." (Surat al-Baqara, 38)

These verses reveal that Allah eases the way of Muslims to success in their actions. If they are experiencing hardship, Allah helps them out of it. This truth is stated in the following verse:

Allah is the Protector of those who believe. He brings them out of the darkness into the light. But those who do not believe have false deities as protectors. They take them from the light into the darkness. Those are the Companions of the Fire, remaining in it timelessly, forever. (Surat al-Baqara, 257)

> *We put courage into their hearts when they stood up and said: "Our Lord is the Lord of the heavens and Earth, and We will not call on any deity apart from Him. We would, in that case, have uttered an abomination."*
> *(Surat al-Kahf, 14)*

This verse states the importance of patience, determination, and willpower for believers. Only people who trust in Allah have these qualities. The expression "We put courage" indicates that Allah decrees everything and gives the believers the strength to meet all hardships and difficulties with determination and patience.

No one can exceed the destiny that Allah has written for him or her, either in word or in deed. Therefore, those who are aware that only Allah does everything within destiny and know that they have no power to do anything will be naturally patient. Their knowledge that Allah creates everything in the best and most beneficial way for His steadfast servants gives them peace and comfort. Allah gives the news of salvation and a great reward for His servants who adopt this fine morality and are patient in the following verses:

What is with you runs out, but what is with Allah goes on forever. Those who were steadfast will be recompensed according to the best of what they did. Anyone who acts rightly, male or female, being a believer, We will give them a good life and recompense them according to the best of what they did. (Surat an-Nahl, 96-97)

Obey Allah and His Messenger, and do not quarrel among yourselves lest you lose heart and your momentum disappear. And be steadfast. Allah is with the steadfast. (Surat al-Anfal, 46)

... If there are twenty of you who are steadfast, they will overcome two hundred; and if there are a hundred of you, they will overcome a thousand of those who do not believe, because they are people who do not understand. (Surat al-Anfal, 65)

Among the believers' attributes are determination and willpower, along with faith and awareness of, and trust in, Allah. Those who believe in destiny and trust Allah will not lose heart or inspiration when faced with hardship and difficulty, because they know that, ultimately, it is Allah Who does everything. Therefore, they welcome every opportunity as a chance to earn a reward and do good deeds with joy and excitement.

The verse also states that the Companions of the

Palestinian Muslims worshipping under the oppression of Israeli soldiers.

Cave entered the king's presence after their time of concealment ended. At this time, idolatry and the denial of Allah were still widespread, the people were still far from religion's morality, and the Muslims were still being oppressed. In spite of all of this, the Companions of the Cave told the king that they would never abandon their belief in, and worship of, Allah as the only Being worthy of their worship, and that it would be a crime against Allah to say anything to the contrary, even if only for the sake of protocol.

Such courage and determination in the presence of an authoritarian and tyrannical king proves that they were sincere Muslims. Allah creates everything in destiny to bring the best benefits to believers. Thus, unless He wills it, nothing can harm anyone. Since the Companions of the Cave knew this fact, they were able to display this exemplary trust in Him and determination.

In the End Times, people will adopt idols and spread their mistaken ideas and fantasies. This verse indicates that sincere Muslims must preserve their belief with the same degree of courage and determination when faced with oppressive and totalitarian regimes.

Muslims of East Turkestan have been crushed by the repressive communist system for more than half a century.

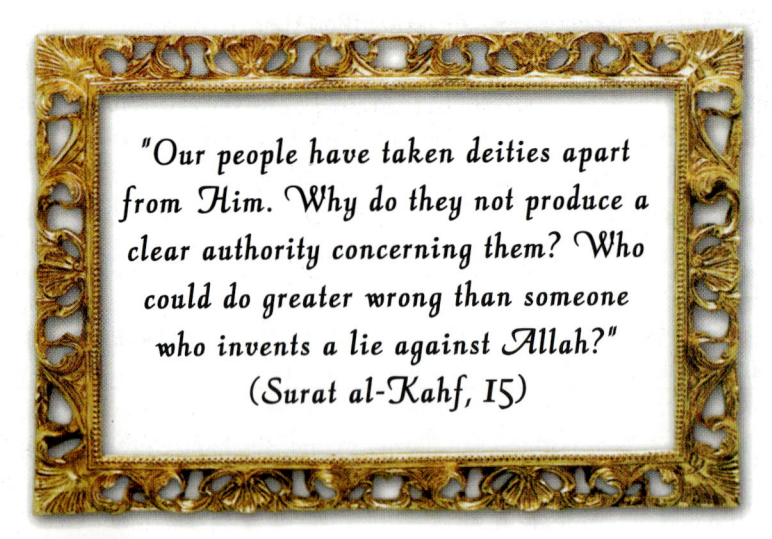

> *"Our people have taken deities apart from Him. Why do they not produce a clear authority concerning them? Who could do greater wrong than someone who invents a lie against Allah?"*
> *(Surat al-Kahf, 15)*

As this verse states, the Companions of the Cave called their idolatrous people to faith, invited them to Allah's religion, asked them to stop associating others with Allah, and demanded that they bring forth the evidence upon which they based their denial. When they could not do this, they exposed their idolatrous people as liars and slanderers.

Today, Muslims also demand proof from those who take idols besides Allah. In the End Times, there exists an idolatrous belief that idolizes matter and chance: Darwinism.

Darwinism claims that the universe has no purpose, was formed by random occurrences, and that only the fittest members of nature survive. This anti-religious system is based upon conflict and violence. In reality, these claims of random occurrences being responsible for everything are no more than acts of slander by the Darwinists against Allah, Who is All-Powerful and has created everything that ex-

Charles Darwin

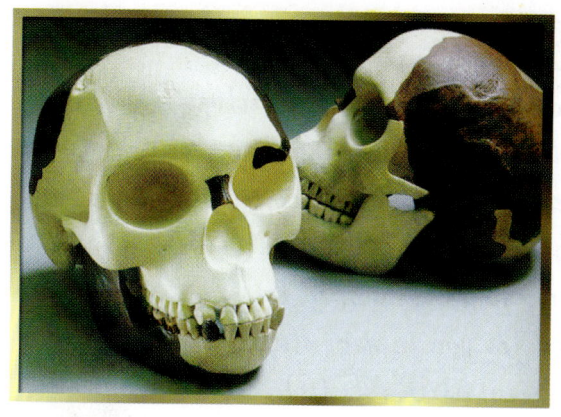

> One of the best-known evolutionist hoaxes is this so-called Piltdown man skull and its subsequent portrayal as one of man's ancestors. This hoax was eventually exposed as a fabrication made by fusing an orangutan's jaw bones to a man's skull.

ists. To support their slanderous claims, they cheat, lie, and offer faked evidence. The history of Darwinism is full of such frauds as the Piltdown man, the Nebraska man, the recapitulation theory, which maintains that the stages in an organism's embryonic development correspond to the stages of the species' characteristic evolutionary development, and *Archaeoraptor* (the faked dinosaur-bird). Darwinism manipulates and fabricates evidence, and produces imaginary drawings and scenarios to persuade people that humanity is the product of past evolutionary processes. To this end, it misconstrues scientific evidence without the slightest hesitation.

As a result, Darwinism is one of the largest and most anti-religion systems of thought facing the Muslims of the End Times. Today's Muslims, like the Companions of the Cave, are demanding evidence from the Darwinists, who deny Allah but idolize chance, to prove their case. In response, the Darwinists present yet more lies and frauds, but never any clear-cut evidence, by all sorts of demagogy because they have no evidence to support their claims. (For detailed information, see Harun Yahya, *The Evolution Deceit*, London: Ta-Ha Publishers, 2003, 8th ed.)

Darwinism's claim that everything is the product of chance is a clear slander directed against Allah. The expression **"Who could do greater wrong than someone who invents a lie against Allah?"** (Surat al-Kahf, 15) indicates this wrongdoing.

> *When you have separated yourselves from them and everything they worship except Allah, take refuge in the cave, and your Lord will unfold His mercy to you and open the way to the best for you in your situation.*
> (Surat al-Kahf, 16)

This verse states that the Companions of the Cave distanced themselves completely from the unbelievers' system of thought. This created an ideological conflict between the believers and the unbelievers, who were oppressing them.

Due to the unbelievers' oppression, the Companions of the Cave felt the need for total segregation. Thus, they severed all links with the unbelievers by seeking refuge in the cave. During this period, Allah's grace descended upon them, and He made things easier for them in many respects. The most important aspect of His help and support was sparing them from the negative impact of the unbelievers.

Irreligious societies habitually attack Muslims' sacred values and mock and insult their beliefs and practices. For these reasons, it is a great comfort and ease for the believers to keep apart from such people, because this allows them to find more opportunities to serve religion instead of always meeting with hostility. This also means more time for personal development, acquiring deeper knowledge, and engaging in cultural and social activities. Thanks to this opportunity, which Allah gives them, they can work harder to help their people have a better life and inform them of the only path to salvation: adopting the values of the Qur'an.

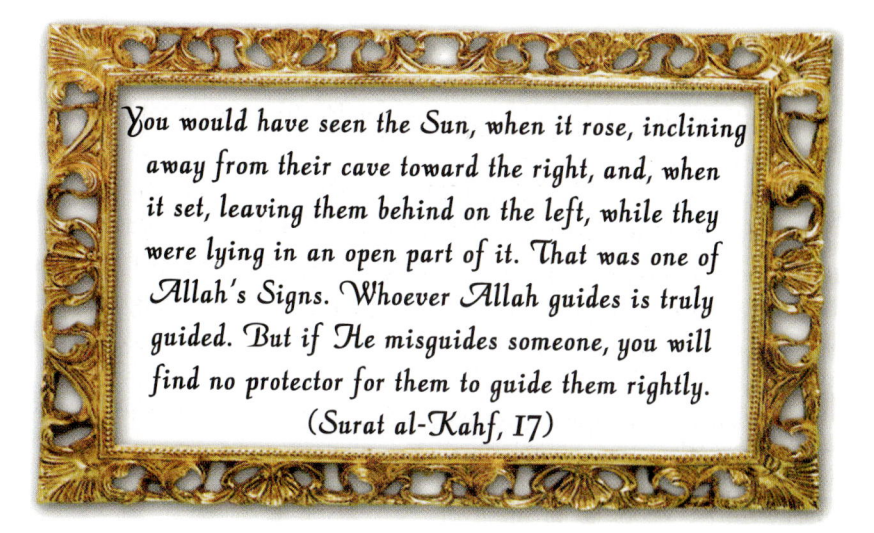

> *You would have seen the Sun, when it rose, inclining away from their cave toward the right, and, when it set, leaving them behind on the left, while they were lying in an open part of it. That was one of Allah's Signs. Whoever Allah guides is truly guided. But if He misguides someone, you will find no protector for them to guide them rightly.*
> (Surat al-Kahf, 17)

This verse might be suggesting that the Muslims' homes should receive sunlight. A house, as far as possible, should receive sunlight at dusk as well as dawn, so that its inhabitants can derive the positive effects of sunlight, which creates a healthier atmosphere. Or, it might be suggesting that homes should be spacious and cozy, so that it will be a pleasure to live in them. Muslims should make their homes, as far as they can, spacious, airy, calming, and full of light.

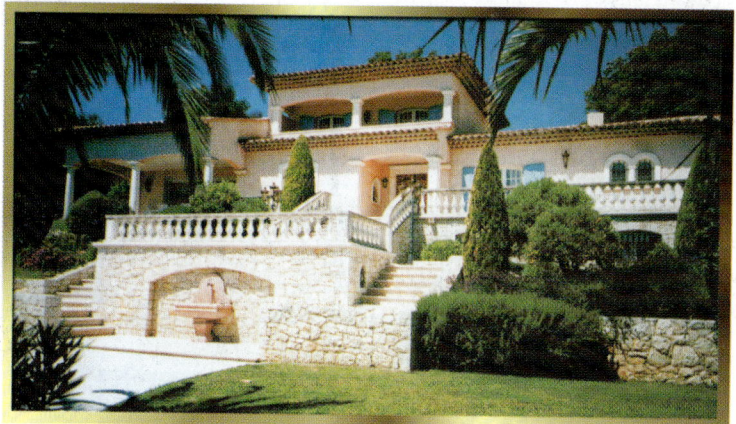

As mentioned earlier, this verse proclaims the importance of guidance by Allah. It states that only those to whom Allah gives guidance will find salvation, and that those to whom He does not give it will find only eternal suffering.

Surat al-Kahf 17 emphasizes that those who call others to faith must do so with serenity, patience, calmness, and in a non-confrontational manner. They must not forget that only Allah gives faith, as He states in: **"There is no compulsion where religion is concerned. Right guidance has become clearly distinct from error. Anyone who rejects false deities and believes in Allah has grasped the Firmest Handhold, which will never give way. Allah is All-Hearing, All-Knowing"** (Surat al-Baqara, 256). If those who are invited to belief choose to reject the invitation, those who made the call must trust in Allah and not pressure the other party.

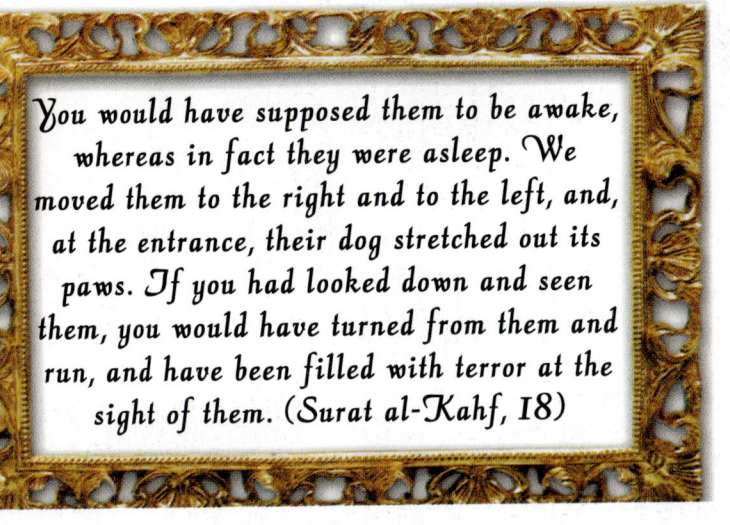

> *You would have supposed them to be awake, whereas in fact they were asleep. We moved them to the right and to the left, and, at the entrance, their dog stretched out its paws. If you had looked down and seen them, you would have turned from them and run, and have been filled with terror at the sight of them.* (Surat al-Kahf, 18)

Today, some Muslims are enveloped in a similar type of slumber, and thus are not affected by the evil flowing from materialist ideologies, all of which seek to distance people from religion. They continue to live a life of Qur'anic morality without being influenced by the moral degeneration, chaos, and oppression engendered by materialism.

Perhaps the Companions of the Cave's state of sleep was the result of the inner peace and trust they experienced by submitting to destiny, because Allah creates everything according to a preordained decree and directs all events to the believers' advantage. Our Lord states that **"… Allah will not give the unbelievers any way against the believers"** (Surat an-Nisa', 141). This is surely good news and a cause for serenity for all believers, for it is a sign that everything is positive and beneficial for the Muslims.

Another cause for the Muslims' sense of safety and inner peace is Allah's promise that He will lead His sincere servants to success. The following verse delivers this good news to the believers:

Allah has promised those of you who believe and do right actions that He will make them successors in the land, just as He

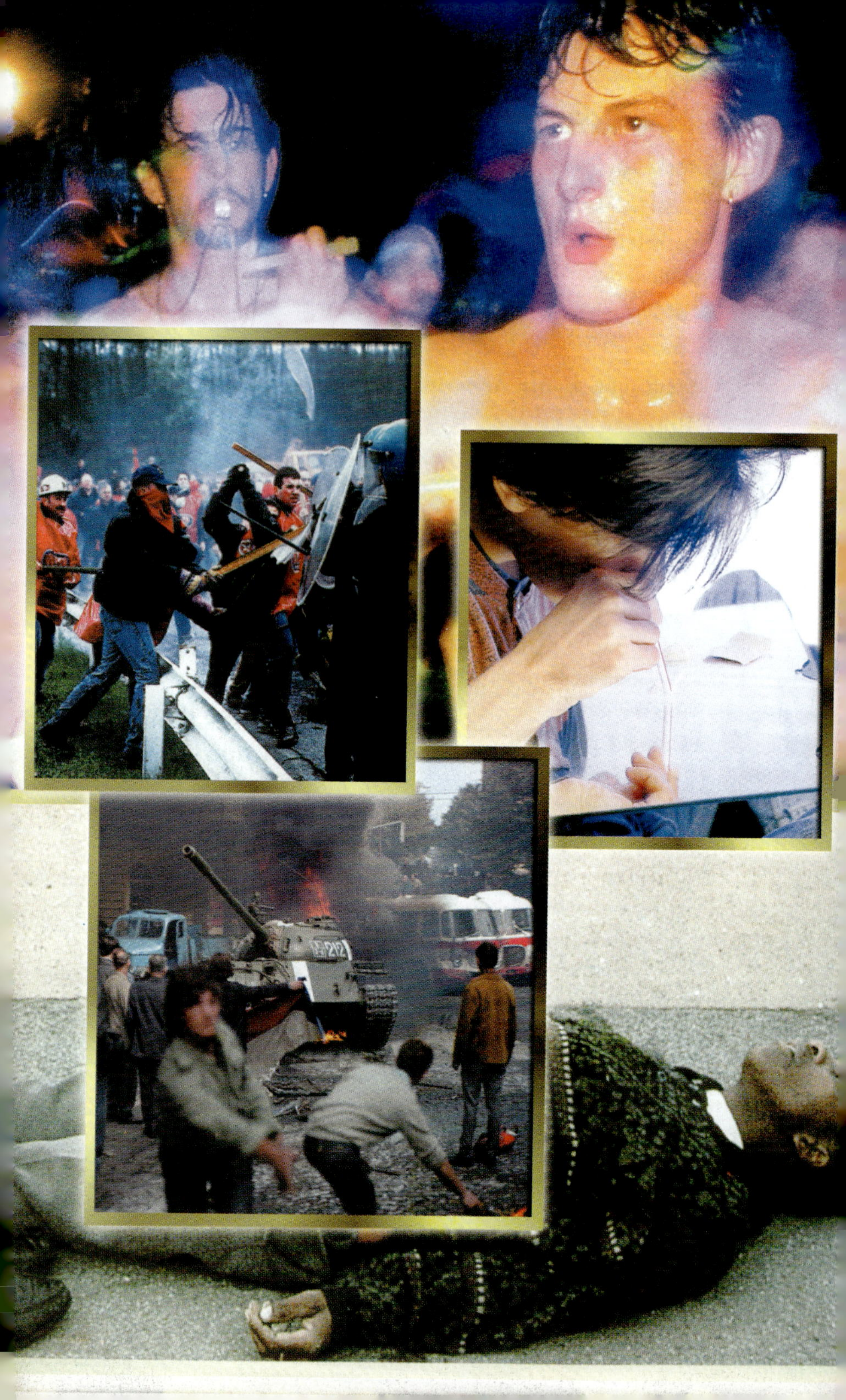

made those before them successors, and will firmly establish for them their religion with which He is pleased, and give them, in place of their fear, security. "They worship Me, not associating anything with Me." Any who do not believe after that, such people are deviators. (Surat an-Nur, 55)

In other words, Allah will lead His committed servants to security regardless of the difficulties they are facing. This is one reason for today's Muslims, like the Companions of the Cave, to continue their work in peace.

The Muslims also know and draw comfort from the fact that only Allah can will something to happen to them. Allah draws our attention to the determination of those believers who submit to Him, believe in destiny, and trust Him completely with the following verse:

Say: "Nothing can happen to us except what Allah has ordained for us. He is Our Master. It is in Allah that the believers should put their trust." (Surat at-Tawba, 51)

All over the world, we see conflict, people struggling against hunger and poverty, and dramatic increases in moral degeneration. The only way out of this negative situation is to tell people, with patience and compassion, about how adhering to the values of the Qur'an will bring about goodness and well-being.

... their dog stretched
out its paws...
(Surat al-Kahf, 18)

Surat al-Kahf 18 also mentions the love of animals and that, possibly, Muslims can keep a dog in their garden for safety reasons. Dogs are friendly and dependable animals, loyal to their owner, and sensitive enough to recognize and respond to danger immediately. Therefore, Muslims can acquire a guard dog as a precaution, but first must put their trust in Allah.

The verse also might be suggesting that believers can keep animals because of love and care for them. Prophet Sulayman (as) is given as an example, as seen in the following verse:

When swift horses, champing at the bit, were displayed before him [Prophet Sulayman] in the afternoon, he said: "Truly do I love the love of good with a view to the glory of my Lord"— [repeating these words as the steeds raced away,] until the they were hidden by the veil [of distance—whereupon he would command], "Return them to me." And he set about stroking their shanks and necks. (Surah Sad, 31-33)

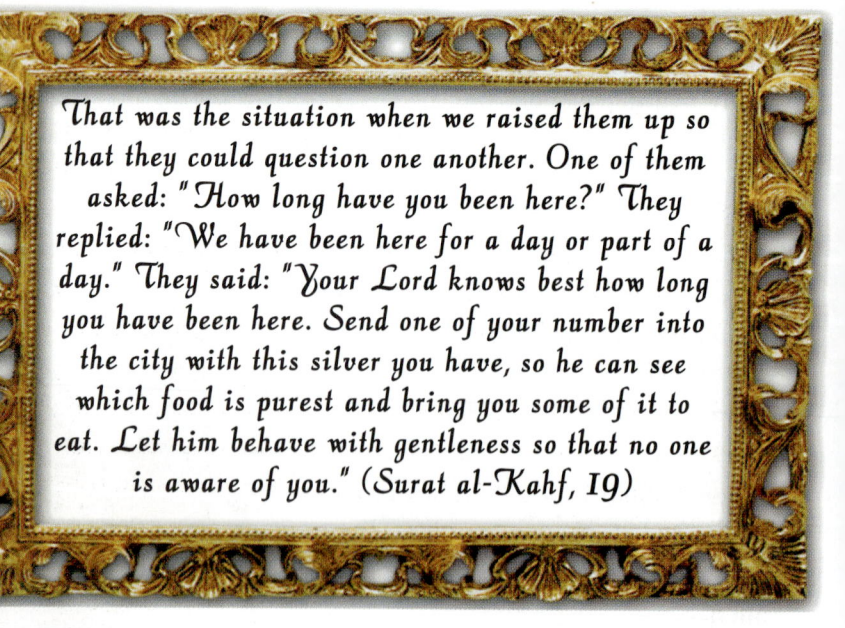

> *That was the situation when we raised them up so that they could question one another. One of them asked: "How long have you been here?" They replied: "We have been here for a day or part of a day." They said: "Your Lord knows best how long you have been here. Send one of your number into the city with this silver you have, so he can see which food is purest and bring you some of it to eat. Let him behave with gentleness so that no one is aware of you." (Surat al-Kahf, 19)*

In this verse, the Muslims discuss their current situation before reaching a decision. The verse also relates their discussion as to how long they had been in the cave. They said: "Your Lord knows best how long you have been here." This indicates that when there is no agreement or final decision, believers say "Allah knows best" and leave the outcome to Him, for only He knows the unknown. For this reason, it is not a sign of trust in Him to argue about something that cannot be known, for this only causes disturbance among the people. What is important in such a case is to submit to Allah and remember destiny.

This verse also contains other messages for the believers. First, the Companions of the Cave ask the believer they send to town to get only the purest food for them. The believers' sensitivity in matters of cleanness is related in many verses, such as when Allah's Messenger made: **"... good things lawful for them and bad things forbidden for them"** (Surat al-A`raf, 157) and Allah commanded believers: **"Purify your** clothes" (Surat al-Muddaththir, 4).

The following two verses also mention good and clean foods:

So eat from what Allah has provided for you, lawful and good, and be thankful for His blessing, if it is Him you worship. (Surat an-Nahl, 114)

Eat of the good things We have provided for you, but do not go to excess in it, or My anger will be unleashed on you. Anyone who has My anger unleashed on him has plunged to his ruin. (Surah Ta Ha, 81)

Surat al-Kahf 19 also points out that believers prefer to buy their food in cities. Perhaps this is because they can find a greater variety of foods there. Cities also have another benefit for believers, for the call to faith begins in the cities:

This is a Book We have sent down and blessed, confirming what came before it, so that you can warn the Mother of Cities [Makka] and the people around it. Those who believe in the Hereafter believe in it and safeguard their prayer. (Surat al-An`am, 92)

Surat al-Kahf 19 also reminds believers to be gentle and courteous at all times, for this is a requirement of the Qur'an's morals.

Another possible understanding of this account of the Companions of the Cave is that the Muslims of the End Times generally will stay at home to avoid attracting attention to themselves at a time of great wickedness and rule by such anti-religious ideologies as fascism or communism. Or, it might be suggesting that believers, when required, will be at home for long periods of time in order to develop in science and knowledge. It is related that the Prophet (saas) advised those who sought his views on the End Times to "stay at home." (*Abu Dawud*)

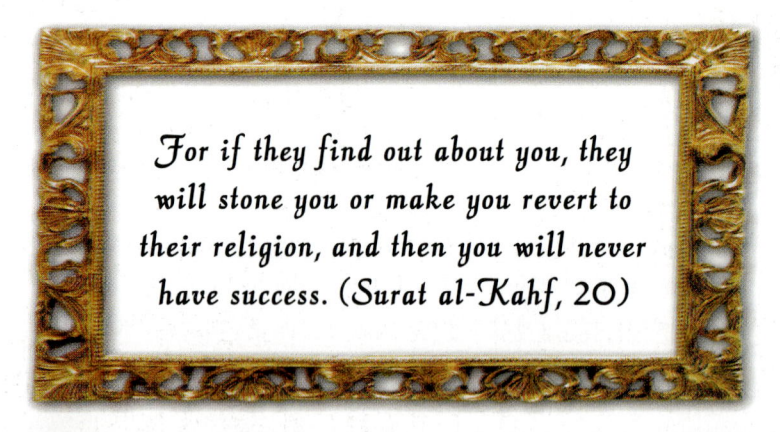

> *For if they find out about you, they will stone you or make you revert to their religion, and then you will never have success. (Surat al-Kahf, 20)*

The expression "They will stone you" describes a form of terror. This character trait is clearly recognizable today in people who are under the influence of godless ideologies. For example, terrorists who subscribe to communism are led by their hostility to the state to throw stones and attack its officials, as well as at the police forces. These attacks aim to weaken and demoralize them so that the communists can realize their anti-religious ideals and establish their rule by dragging the country into chaos and conflict.

Once they succeed, they seek to indoctrinate people loyal to faith with their system of thought, which considers recurring conflict between people inevitable. They want to see all of the people rebel against the state, take to the streets and fight one another. But such anarchist movements will lead to nothing, and their followers will not succeed, for Allah says:

> **But as for those who break Allah's contract after it has been agreed upon, and sever what Allah has commanded to be joined, and cause corruption in the land, the curse will be upon them. They will have the Evil Abode. (Surat ar-Ra`d, 25)**

Given this, it is vital for the people of the End Times to stay clear of the bloodstained ideologies that have brought nothing but evil to the world, not to side with those who corrupt others, and not to be influenced by the provocations of anti-religious ideologies or their agitations.

People influenced by godless ideologies see the solution in violence, hostility, and rebellion. This terrorist characteristic leads society into chaos. The only way to prevent this is to explain to the people why they should fear Allah and how they can avert His punishment.

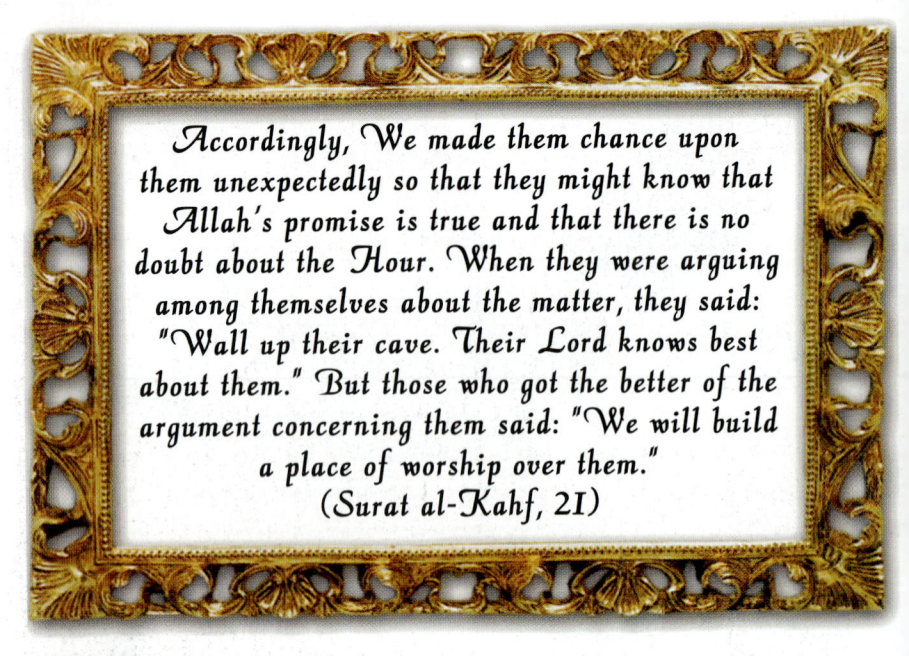

> *Accordingly, We made them chance upon them unexpectedly so that they might know that Allah's promise is true and that there is no doubt about the Hour. When they were arguing among themselves about the matter, they said: "Wall up their cave. Their Lord knows best about them." But those who got the better of the argument concerning them said: "We will build a place of worship over them."*
> *(Surat al-Kahf, 21)*

This verse contains clear signs of the End Times and the Hour. The discovery of the Companions of the Cave could be a sign for the good, that even if they exist far apart from one another, one day they will definitely meet each other. Allah reveals this truth with **"so race each other to the good. Wherever you are, Allah will bring you all together. Truly Allah has power over all things"** (Surat al-Baqara, 148).

The verse also mentions the decision to build a place of worship on the site where the Companions of the Cave were found, which means that such places of worship can be built where good and righteous devotees of Allah have spent their lives so that they will be remembered. Also, such places can serve as centers of learning and worship, which will help to spread beneficial ideas and good character. These places will then become meeting points for the believers who come together to remember Allah's name.

Many verses underline the importance of places of worship in which only Allah is remembered. Some of them are as follows:

Those who were expelled from their homes without any right, merely for saying: "Our Lord is Allah." If Allah had not driven some people back by means of others, monasteries and churches, synagogues and mosques, where Allah's name is mentioned much, would have been pulled down and destroyed. Allah will certainly help those who help Him—Allah is All-Strong, Almighty. (Surat al-Hajj, 40)

All mosques belong to Allah, so do not call on anyone else besides Allah. (Surat al-Jinn, 18)

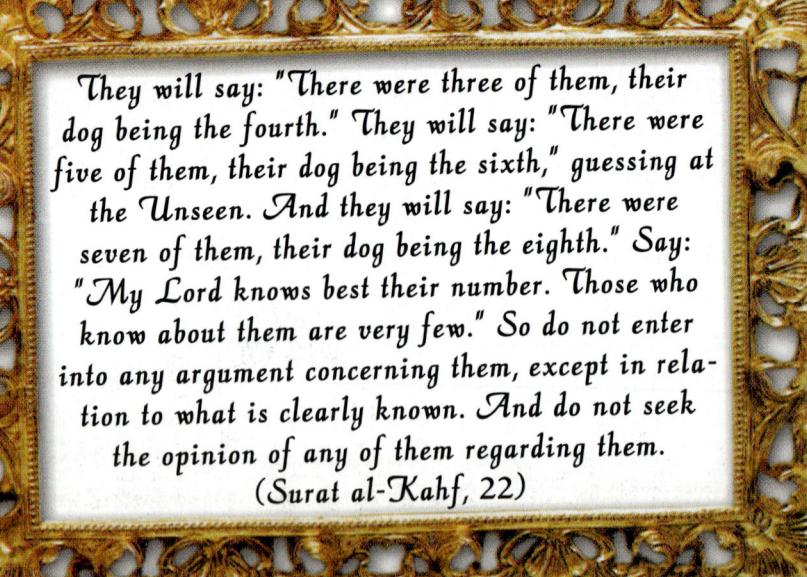

> They will say: "There were three of them, their dog being the fourth." They will say: "There were five of them, their dog being the sixth," guessing at the Unseen. And they will say: "There were seven of them, their dog being the eighth." Say: "My Lord knows best their number. Those who know about them are very few." So do not enter into any argument concerning them, except in relation to what is clearly known. And do not seek the opinion of any of them regarding them.
> (Surat al-Kahf, 22)

As this verse states, some people speculated about how many Companions of the Cave there actually were. However, the verse states that their actual number is known only to our Lord, for only He knows the Unseen and can reveal part of it to His chosen few.

The continuation of the verse stipulates that such speculation is wrong. Such disputes are termed "guessing at the Unseen" and are referred to in other verses as well:

> They will say: "We believe in it," but how can they reach out for it from a distant place, when beforehand they had rejected it, *shooting forth about the Unseen from a distant place*? A barrier will be set up between them and the thing that they desire, just as was done with their kind before. They too were in a state of crippling doubt. (Surah Saba', 52-54)

All Muslims ought to refrain from such useless arguments and just say: "Allah knows best." They should respond in the following terms: **"You** know what is in my self but I do not know what is in Your Self. You are the Knower of all unseen things" (Surat al-Ma'ida, 116), because many verses state that only Allah knows the Unseen. One such verse is as follows:

> The keys of the Unseen are in His possession. No one knows them but Him. He knows everything in the land and sea. No leaf falls without His knowing it. There is no seed in the darkness of the ground, and nothing moist or dry, which is not in a Clear Book. (Surat al-An`am, 59)

In these types of arguments, people's views usually are based upon hearsay. Obviously, there is no point in listening to arguments based solely upon conjecture and ignorance. As **"Do not pursue what you have no knowledge of. Hearing, sight and hearts will all be questioned"** (Surat al-Isra', 36) makes clear, people should avoid any talk based upon hearsay.

"Those who know about them are very few" also indicates that a few people could have this knowledge. For instance, one such person could be Khidhr (as), whose miraculous circumstances we will explore shortly. It is also possible that Khidhr's disciples might have this knowledge, with Allah's will and revelation. The Qur'an reveals that Allah reveals some of the Unseen to His Messengers.

> He is the Knower of the Unseen, and does not divulge His Unseen to anyone—except a Messenger with whom He is well pleased, and then He posts sentinels before him and behind him. (Surat al-Jinn, 26-27)

Allah revealed some knowledge of the Unseen to our Prophet (saas) and then told him that:

> This is news of the Unseen that We reveal to you [O Muhammad]. You were not with them when they decided what to do and devised their scheme. (Surah Yusuf, 102)

Allah informed Prophet Nuh (as) about some of the future events that he would experience:

It was said: "Nuh, descend with peace from Us and with blessings on you and on the nations that will issue from those who are with you. But there are nations to whom we will give enjoyment, and then a painful punishment from Us will afflict them." That is some of the news of the Unseen that We reveal to you. Neither you nor your people knew it before this time. So be steadfast. The best end-result is for those who do their duty. (Surah Hud, 48-49)

Surat al-Kahf 22 reveals the appropriate methods of argument: "… **do not enter into any argument concerning them, except in relation to what is clearly known.**" When arguing with others, believers must provide evidence that is compatible with the Qur'an, whereas those who reject religion do the contrary, for they seek to create disputes in order to display their hostility to the believers and their religion. Allah states in **"just for argument's sake…"** (Surat az-Zukhruf, 58), that the deniers use blasphemous arguments because they are **"a disputatious people"** who have an argumentative and hostile nature. This is why people living the Qur'an's morality must distance themselves from all of this and behave in the way that earns Allah's good pleasure. Allah provides an example as to how they should speak with the unbelievers:

So call and go straight, as you have been ordered to. Do not follow their whims and desires, but say: "I believe in a Book sent down by Allah and am ordered to be just between you. Allah is our Lord and your Lord. We have our actions and you have your actions. There is no debate between us and you. Allah will gather us all together. He is our final destination." (Surat ash-Shura, 15)

The phrase "do not seek the opinion of any of them regarding them" at the end of Surat al-Kahf 22 advises all believers to refrain from seeking views other than that of Revelation, because only Allah knows the Unseen. Thus, believers believe that arguments based only upon people's faulty speculation, knowledge, presumptions, and interpretations are worthless. Therefore, giving any credence to such "information" is forbidden.

> *Never say about anything:
> "I will do it tomorrow."*
> *(Surat al-Kahf, 23)*

The lives of people who have forgotten destiny's reality pass in planning for tomorrow, next month, next year, and after retirement. Some people plan their career at the workplace, what they will do after their children get married, or how they will acquire wealth and property. However, this verse reminds all people that they do not know what will happen to them tomorrow.

People who map out their lives have forgotten destiny, for only Allah determines each person's destiny. Therefore, whatever Allah has "written" for one's tomorrow, whether or not the person in question has "planned" it, will occur. This fact is stated in the following verse:

You do not engage in any matter, recite any portion of the Qur'an, or do any action without Our witnessing you while you are occupied with it. Not even the smallest speck eludes your Lord, either on Earth or in heaven. Nor is there anything smaller than that, or larger, which is not in a Clear Book. (Surah Yunus, 61)

Destiny is Allah's knowledge of everything that has happened in the past and will happen in future. Many people ask how Allah can know what will happen to us. The answer is as follows: Allah is not subject to time and space, both of which He created, and so what we call the past, present, and future are all the same to Him. Just as we see the beginning, middle, and end of a ruler and all of its units in between, Allah sees and knows the "time" of our existence as one whole, from its beginning to its end. However, we only experience a particular event, all of which He already knows, when its time has come and thus witness the destiny that Allah has created for us.

Saying that something definitely will happen is, in fact, growing arrogant toward Allah, something that will result in ultimate loss, as the following verse proclaims:

As for those who believe and do right actions, He will pay them their wages in full and will give them increase from His favor. As for those who show disdain and grow arrogant, He will punish them with a painful punishment. They will not find any protector or helper for themselves besides Allah. (Surat an-Nisa', 173)

For the person marked by the red circle, the way behind him is where he was in the past, and the street ahead is where he will be in future. Someone with a bird's-eye view of the street can see that the person's past, present, and future at the same instant. Allah, the sole Creator of everything, is beyond time and space and therefore knows all of these stages as one time.

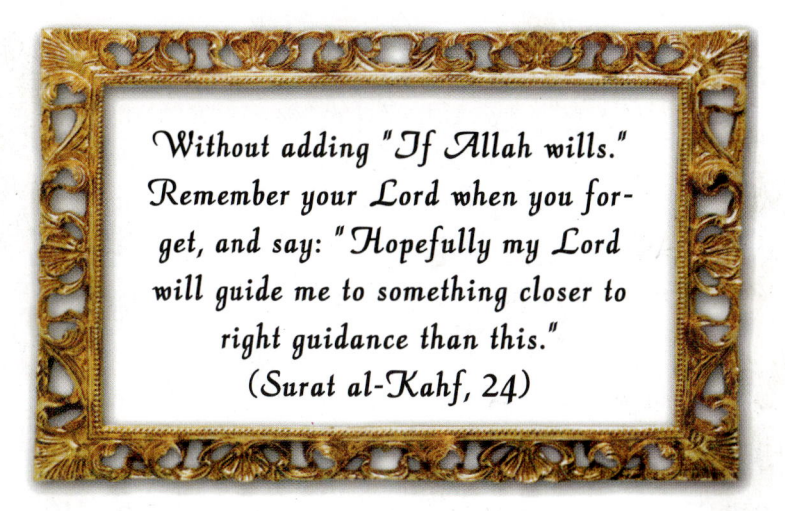

> *Without adding "If Allah wills." Remember your Lord when you forget, and say: "Hopefully my Lord will guide me to something closer to right guidance than this."*
> *(Surat al-Kahf, 24)*

When the believers forget something, they should remember Allah's name, for there is a positive aspect to remembering, if Allah has willed it to be in that person's best interests to be so. Remembering His name can be a healing in a situation of forgetfulness, but one can remember only if Allah wills it because some benefit will result.

Then, the verse orders the Prophet (saas) to pray to Allah for a victory close at hand. Success in our worldly lives is sometimes achieved in the long-term, while at other times it is a short-term thing. Sometimes one works really hard and puts much effort into a project without seeing any short-term success. Thus, it is necessary to remain determined and patient for a long time. Such perseverance contains a multitude of good and much educational value. However, believers also can ask Allah for success in the short term. The important thing is to turn to Allah with a true heart, as did Prophet Shu`ayb (as), who said: **"My success is with Allah alone. I have put my trust in Him, and I turn to Him"** (Surah Hud, 88). Those who trust Allah, knowing that He has created all things, can expect His support at all times. Allah reminds the Prophet (saas) that only He can lead someone to an easy success: **"We will ease you to the Easy Way."** (Surat al-A`la, 8)

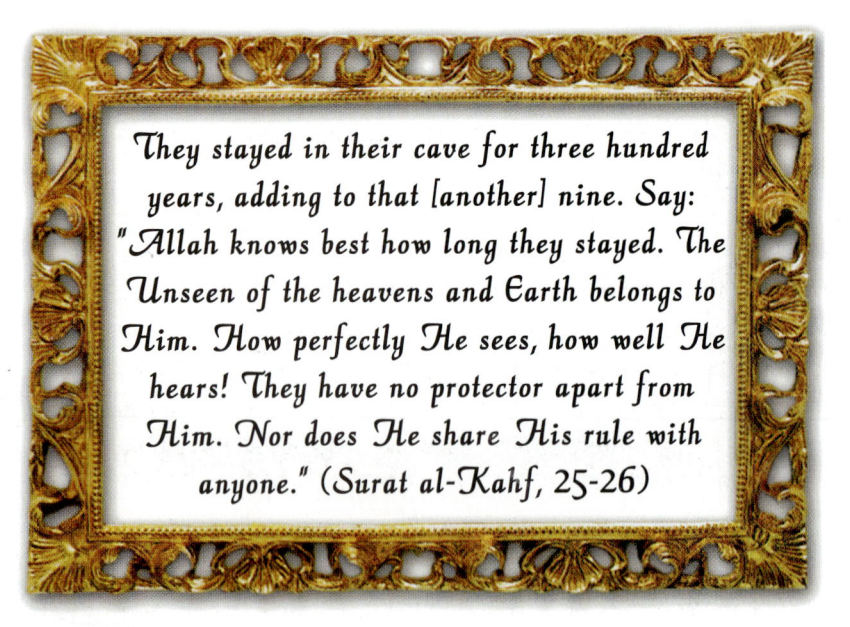

> *They stayed in their cave for three hundred years, adding to that [another] nine. Say: "Allah knows best how long they stayed. The Unseen of the heavens and Earth belongs to Him. How perfectly He sees, how well He hears! They have no protector apart from Him. Nor does He share His rule with anyone." (Surat al-Kahf, 25-26)*

These verses reveal that the Companions of the Cave's state of sleep lasted for 300 years, and that a further 9 years were added toward the end of this period. Thus, their state of sleep lasted for 309 years.

Surat al-Kahf 26 states that Allah's rule and control of the Unseen is total, because He creates all things in the heavens and Earth. This attribute of our Lord is described in the following verses:

> **The Unseen of the heavens and Earth belongs to Allah, and the whole affair will be returned to Him. So worship Him and put your trust in Him. Your Lord is not unaware of what you do. (Surah Hud, 123)**
>
> **Allah, there is no god but Him, the Living, the Self-Sustaining. He is not subject to drowsiness or sleep. Everything in the heavens and Earth belongs to Him. Who can intercede with Him except with His permission? He knows what is before them and what is behind them, but they cannot grasp any of**

His knowledge, except for what He wills. His Footstool encompasses the heavens and Earth, and their preservation does not tire Him. He is the Most High, the Magnificent. (Surat al-Baqara, 255)

As the Creator cannot be bound by His creation, Allah is independent of what we consider to be time. A million or even a billion years of human time means nothing to Him, for everything exists in His presence as if it were only one moment. Allah sees and hears everything, regardless of how far in the past or in the future it is, and He sees it all perfectly, from every aspect, and with or without direction. He also perceives sound with all of its aspects, known to us or else in the best way, as the following verse states:

My Lord knows what is said in Heaven and on Earth. He is the All-Hearing, the All-Knowing. (Surat al-Anbiya', 4)

As all people are subject to time and space, they cannot know anything of the Unseen unless Allah reveals it to them. Only our Lord, the Creator of time and space, sees and hears the past, present, and future in their entirety. He governs absolutely the infinitely past and future of time, history, events, matter, destiny, and everything, whether living or non-living, for:

Both East and West belong to Allah, so wherever you turn, the Face of Allah is there. Allah is All-Encompassing, All-Knowing. (Surat al-Baqara, 115)

He is the only protector and helper of all living beings, for there is none other. Humanity is truly helpless and therefore exposed to hardship at all times. And, the only way to escape material as well as spiritual suffering is to seek refuge with Allah, our only friend and helper, by acknowledging Him as our sole protector. The following verses reveal this truth:

... Do you not know that Allah has power over all things? Do you not know that to Allah belong the kingdom of the heavens and Earth, and that, besides Him, you have no protector and no

helper? (Surat al-Baqara, 106-107)

To Allah belong the kingdom of the heavens and Earth. He gives life and causes to die. You have no protector or helper besides Him. (Surat at-Tawba, 116)

My Protector is Allah, Who sent down the Book. He takes care of the righteous. (Surat al-A`raf, 196)

The concluding part of verse 26 states that our Lord has no partners. Allah has power over everything and is the only governor of time, space, and all dimensions, whether they are known to us or not. He has no associates, and such a thought is not even conceivable, as the following verse makes clear:

Say: "He is Allah, Absolute Oneness, Allah, the Everlasting Sustainer of all. He has not given birth and was not born. And no one is comparable to Him." (Surat al-Ikhlas, 1-4)

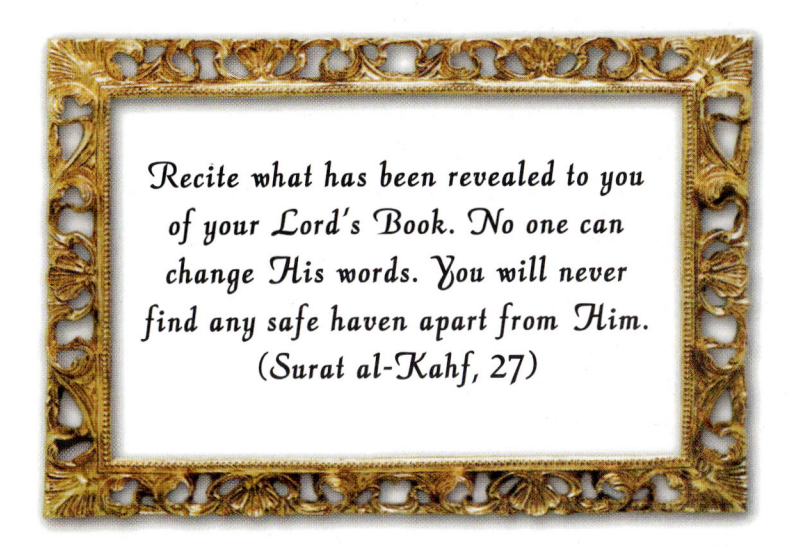

> *Recite what has been revealed to you of your Lord's Book. No one can change His words. You will never find any safe haven apart from Him.*
> *(Surat al-Kahf, 27)*

The most reliable resource from which we can learn about true religion is the Qur'an, because it is the Creator's word, and naturally the Creator knows the ultimate truth of everything. In the Qur'an, Allah reveals everything that humanity needs to know. Furthermore, in this verse He orders the Prophet (saas) to recite the revelations contained in the Qur'an.

A little further on, the verse states that these revelations are immune to change. The Qur'an informs us that the earlier holy books were all falsified, added to, or deleted from, but this is not the case with the Qur'an. As Allah reveals in Surat al-Hijr 9, the Qur'an is under His protection: **"We have sent down the Reminder, and We will preserve it."** This fact is elaborated upon in the following verses:

The words of your Lord are perfect in truthfulness and justice. No one can change His words. He is the All-Hearing, the All-Knowing. (Surat al-An`am, 115)

Falsehood cannot reach it from before it or behind it—it is a revelation from One Who is All-Wise, Praiseworthy. (Surah Fussilat, 42)

The expression: **"No one can change His words. You will never find any safe haven apart from Him"** points to a great error by those people who do not appreciate Allah's infinite might. They acquire protectors and friends other than Allah in the belief that they will be of some help and support in times of hardship. But, we should never forget that those with whom they seek refuge are themselves only creations and helpless servants of Allah. All beings whom they exalt are no more than manifestations of Allah and receive their power, if they have any, from Him, for every being and thing moves only because of His will.

Those you call on besides Allah are servants just like yourselves. Call on them and let them respond to you, if you are telling the truth. Do they have legs with which they can walk? Do they have hands with which they can grasp? Do they have eyes with which they can see? Do they have ears with which they can hear? Say: "Call on your partner-deities, try all your wiles against me, and grant me no reprieve. My Protector is Allah, Who sent down the Book. He takes care of the righteous." Those you call on besides Him cannot help you. They cannot even help themselves. (Surat al-A`raf, 194-97)

As these verses make clear, those people chosen to be guardians and protectors are themselves helpless beings who have a degree of power only if Allah wills it. They cannot save anyone from hardship, suffering, or catastrophe. Another verse expresses this reality:

They worship, instead of Allah, what can neither harm them nor help them, saying: "These are our intercessors with Allah." Say: "Would you inform Allah of something about which He does not know, either in the heavens or on Earth?" May He be glorified and exalted above what they associate with Him! (Surah Yunus, 18)

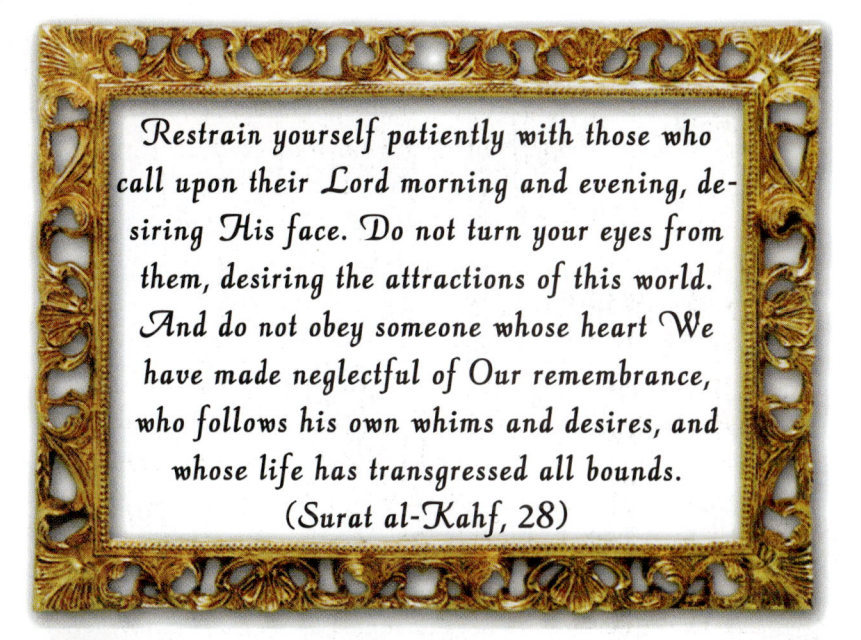

> *Restrain yourself patiently with those who call upon their Lord morning and evening, desiring His face. Do not turn your eyes from them, desiring the attractions of this world. And do not obey someone whose heart We have made neglectful of Our remembrance, who follows his own whims and desires, and whose life has transgressed all bounds.*
> *(Surat al-Kahf, 28)*

This verse points out the importance of always calling upon Allah, every morning and evening, seeking only His good pleasure. Prayer is a great gift, for it is a way to draw closer to Allah. People can pray at any time of day and wherever they are. Allah reveals the value of prayer in: **Say: "What has My Lord to do with you if you do not call upon Him?"** (Surat al-Furqan, 77). In another verse, He informs people that:

> **If My servants ask you about Me, I am near. I answer the call of the caller when he calls upon Me. Therefore, they should respond to Me and believe in Me, so that hopefully they will be rightly guided. (Surat al-Baqara, 186)**

The verse then reminds people once more that this world's temporary possessions should not affect them, because life in this world is no more than a trial. Surat al-Kahf reveals why this world's desirable commodities (e.g., houses, cars, yachts, mansions, gold, silver, and fashionable clothes) were created:

We made everything on Earth adornment for it so that We could test them to see whose actions are the best. (Surat al-Kahf, 7)

After a specific number of years, each person will find himself or herself suddenly appearing before Allah on the Day of Judgment, for life passes rather quickly. Allah reminds us of this reality: **"These people love this fleeting world and have put the thought of a Momentous Day behind their backs"** (Surat al-Insan, 27). The life of the Hereafter, which many people neglect while living in this world, is an eternal reality that no one can escape. This is why being led astray by this world's temporary attractions and thus forgetting the eternal life in the Hereafter is such a serious mistake. Allah reveals that:

> The life of this world is nothing but a game and a diversion. The Hereafter is better for those who guard against evil. So will you not use your intellect? (Surat al-An'am, 32)
>
> Know that the life of this world is merely a game and a diversion, an ostentation and a cause of boasting among yourselves, and trying to outdo one another in wealth and children, like the plant-growth after rain that delights the cultivators, but then withers and you see it turning yellow, and then it becomes broken stubble. In the Hereafter, there is terrible punishment but also forgiveness from Allah and His good pleasure. The life of this world is nothing but the enjoyment of delusion. (Surat al-Hadid, 20)

Further on in the same verse, the importance of the believers being together is stated. Remembering Allah, praying to Him, and doing everything for His good pleasure is the behavior of all devout believers. The vital need of being together with them, with people who remember Allah at all times, is obvious. Believers derive many benefits from spending time with one another, for they remind each other of the Qur'an's verses and remember Allah, and are less likely to miss prayers or be led astray, which has a greater chance of happening when people are alone or during times when such meetings are rare. They recite Allah's name together, advise people to do good and avoid evil, and benefit from one another in terms of knowledge and culture. Engaging in such activities will enable them to live in an atmosphere of joy, contentment, purity, trust, and safety. The believers' relationship with each other is described in the following verse:

> The believing men and women are friends of one another. They command what is right and forbid what is wrong, establish prayer and give alms, and obey Allah and His Messenger. They are the people upon whom Allah will have mercy. Allah is Almighty, All-Wise. (Surat at-Tawba, 71)

On the other hand, staying with unbelievers has many negative aspects. For example, such people are always slandering and displaying aggression toward Allah and the believers' sacred values, voicing their animosity, and mocking the believers. Allah forbids the believers to be in such an environment:

It has been sent down to you in the Book that when you hear Allah's Signs being rejected and mocked by people, you must not sit with them until they start talking of other things. If you do, you are just the same as them. Allah will gather all the hypocrites and unbelievers into Hell. (Surat an-Nisa', 140)

Another negative aspect of being together with unbelievers, who chase after their base instincts and keep away from Allah's word, is the probability that those with weak faith will be influenced in a negative way. Devout Muslims who have strong faith, Allah willing, cannot be influenced by unbelievers; however, those believers who are new Muslims or who do not yet completely live the Qur'an's morality, can be influenced by the unbelievers' misleading conversation and display of knowledge, and even end up following their example. If this happens, they are the losers in both this world and the next.

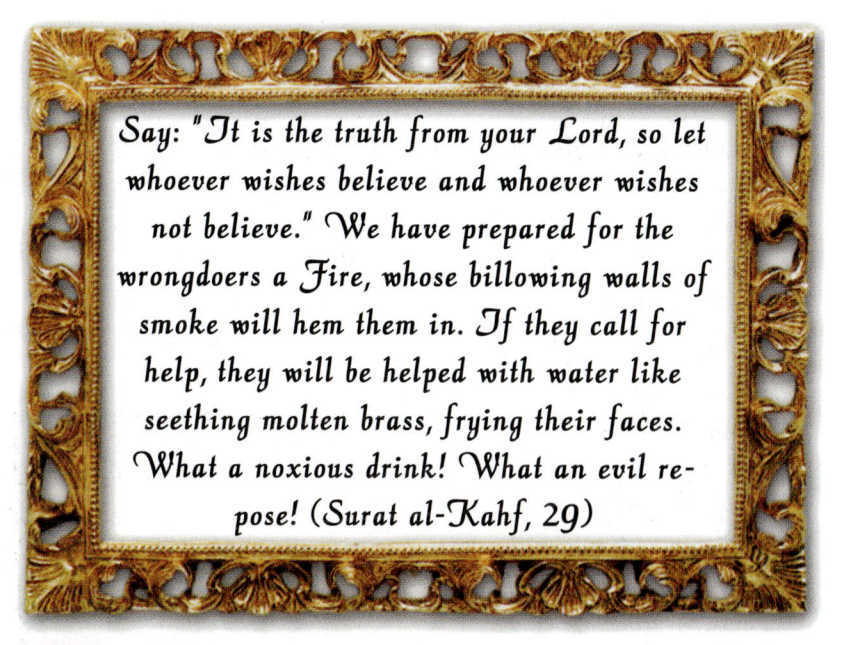

> Say: "It is the truth from your Lord, so let whoever wishes believe and whoever wishes not believe." We have prepared for the wrongdoers a Fire, whose billowing walls of smoke will hem them in. If they call for help, they will be helped with water like seething molten brass, frying their faces. What a noxious drink! What an evil repose! (Surat al-Kahf, 29)

Once the believers have explained Allah's religion and the Qur'an's verses to the unbelievers, they must not pressure them to embrace it. As we explained earlier, only Allah can give faith. The attitude of the believers toward unbelievers is described, as follows:

I do not worship what you worship, and you do not worship what I worship. Nor will I worship what you worship, nor will you worship what I worship. You have your religion, and I have my religion. (Surat al-Kafirun, 2-6)

The believers' only responsibility is to warn the unbelievers of the sufferings in Hell following death and the great danger that this poses for them if they continue to reject belief. This verse describes the eternal suffering in Hell that awaits all unbelievers. On that day, they will have no helpers or intercessors.

Allah reveals in **"the Day they are shoved roughly into the Fire of**

Hell" (Surat at-Tur: 13), how those who have earned Hell will be degraded. Those who were arrogant because of their wealth, status, and their ability to oppress other people will realize their sorry state and helplessness in Hell. They will be **"flung into a narrow place in it, shackled together in chains"** (Surat al-Furqan, 13), and rest in the murk of its thick black smoke. They will hear the incessant seething and gasping of the Fire and hear continuous sounds of moaning and groaning. They will be led from one suffering to another and, despite their pleading, their pain will not be eased, because Hell is **"a sealed vault of Fire"** (Surat al-Balad, 20) from which no one can escape.

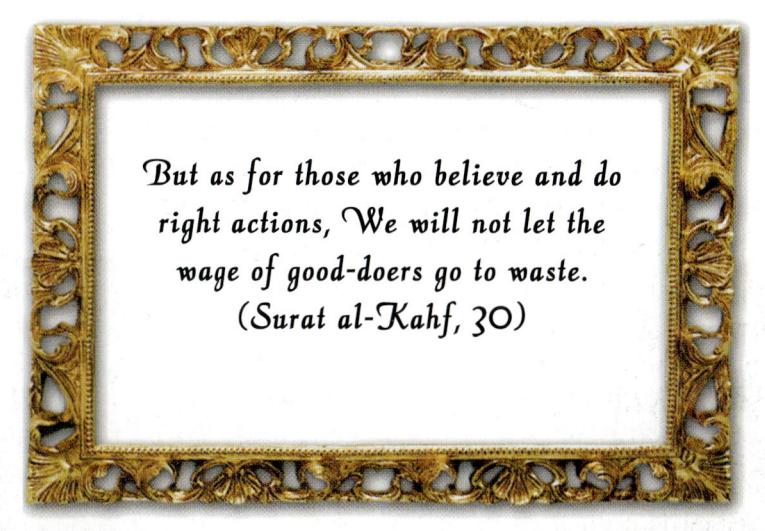

> *But as for those who believe and do right actions, We will not let the wage of good-doers go to waste. (Surat al-Kahf, 30)*

We have already explained the importance of right actions. In this verse, Allah draws our attention to the importance of doing truly good deeds. The best deed, the one that pleases Him the most, is the one done in complete compliance with the Qur'an's morality and out of genuine devotion. Allah points out the importance of good behavior in the following verse:

Everything in the heavens and everything in Earth belongs to Allah, so that He can repay those who do evil for what they did, and repay those who do good with the Very Best. (Surat an-Najm, 31)

These verses proclaim the importance of doing good deeds that are pleasing to Allah. Our Lord informs us that those who do good can look forward to an even better reward, and that they must expect their reward only from Him.

Allah encompasses everything that humanity does. It is enough for Him to be aware of our good deeds, for He knows what our hearts contain and rewards those deeds. Allah states that He gives a just reward for those good deeds that comply with the Qur'an's morality and gives the righteous the good tidings of Paradise, as follows:

Yes, the friends of Allah will feel no fear and will know no sorrow. Those who believe and guard against evil, there is good news for them in the life of this world and in the Hereafter. There is no changing the words of Allah. That is the great victory! (Surah Yunus, 62-64)

> *They will have Gardens of Eden, with rivers flowing under them. They will be adorned in them with bracelets made of gold, and will wear green garments made of the finest silk and rich brocade, reclining there on couches. What an excellent reward! What a wonderful repose!*
> *(Surat al-Kahf, 31)*

This verse describes the endless gifts of Paradise that are given as a reward to those believers who strive to please Allah by doing good. Allah has promised Paradise to the believers in many verses. For instance, the following verse informs us that the believers will be welcomed warmly and sent in companies to Paradise:

Gardens of Eden that they enter, with rivers flowing under them, where they have whatever they desire. That is how Allah repays those who do their duty, those whom the angels take in a virtuous state. They say: "Peace be upon you. Enter the Garden for what you did." (Surat an-Nahl, 31-32)

Following this honorable welcome, Allah bestows upon them countless gifts. But above all of these gifts will be the believers' spiritual joy of having won Allah's good pleasure and Paradise. While the unbelievers will be suffering in the punishing Fires of Hell and enduring inexplicable remorse, the believers will be leading their lives as servants having won His good pleasure and love. Contrary to Hell, which will

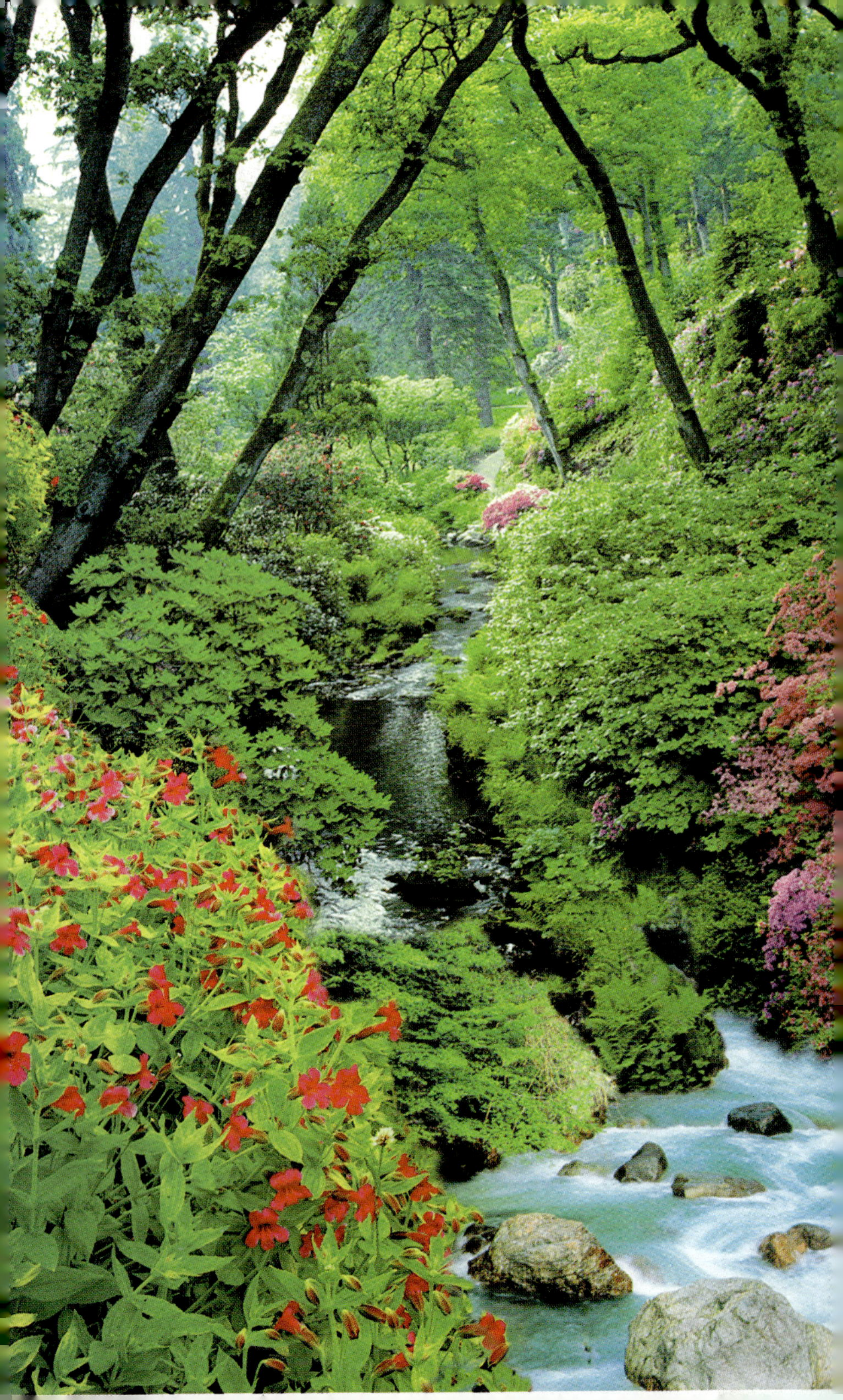

be tight and crowded, the believers will rest in **"a Garden whose breadth is like that of Heaven and Earth combined"** (Surat al-Hadid, 21) in Paradise, where they will see beauty and a great kingdom all around. They will recline on couches lined with rich brocade, enjoy easily picked fruit, reside in palaces with rivers flowing under them, sit on high-raised thrones, and converse with one another. There will be cool shades in Paradise, which Allah describes as a place that is neither too cool nor too hot.

As described in Surat al-Kahf 31, the green clothing worthy of the people of Paradise is made of the finest silk and rich brocade. In addition, they will wear golden bracelets. Besides beautiful clothing, the people of Paradise will be provided with delicious foods and drinks. Specifically, the Qur'an mentions a variety of fruit, the flesh of any fowl that they may desire, tasty drinks, dates and pomegranates without equal, fruit-laden lote trees, and bananas piled bunch on bunch. And these are just some of Allah's promised gifts.

Furthermore, there will be only beauty in Paradise, for people of Paradise will no longer need to endure anything with patience, as we do in this world. There will be an environment full of endless beauty without any tiredness, fear, sorrow, or any other conceivable trouble. Allah reveals Paradise's beauty, as follows:

An image of the Garden promised to those who guard against evil: In it are rivers of water that will never spoil, rivers of milk whose taste will never change, rivers of wine that are delightful to all who drink it, and rivers of honey of undiluted

purity. In it they will have fruit of every kind and forgiveness from their Lord... (Surah Muhammad, 15)

Allah has detailed the gifts of Paradise and the sufferings of Hell in the Qur'an. Those who pretend not to understand the truth will be losers in both worlds. For this reason, people should seriously prepare and strive for the Hereafter in order to win our Lord's unique gifts, as the following verse makes clear:

That abode of the Hereafter—We grant it to those who do not seek to exalt themselves in the land or to cause corruption in it. The successful outcome is for those who guard against evil. (Surat al-Qasas, 83)

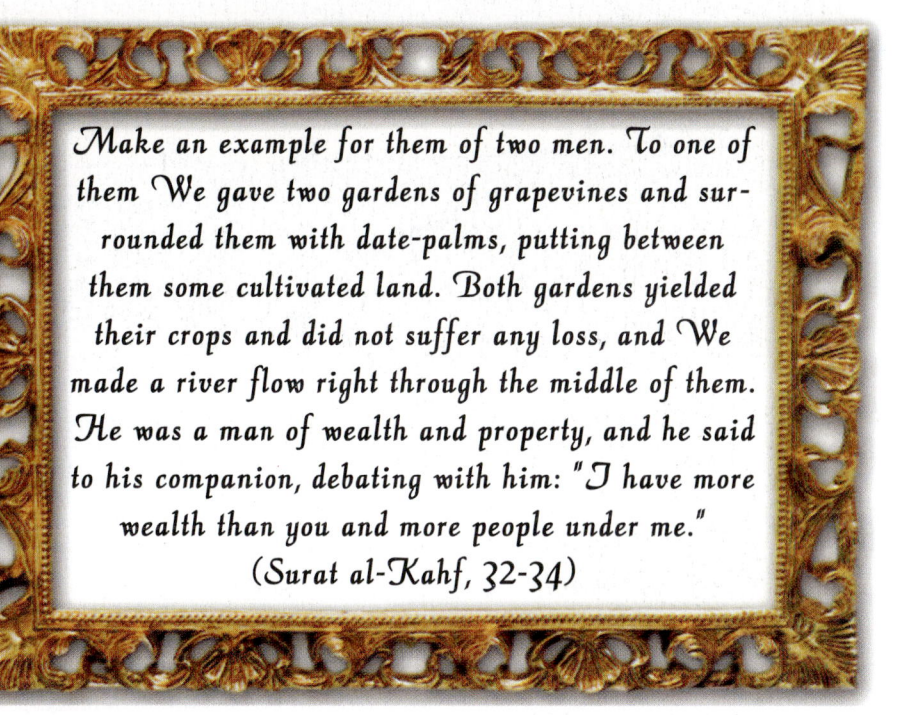

> *Make an example for them of two men. To one of them We gave two gardens of grapevines and surrounded them with date-palms, putting between them some cultivated land. Both gardens yielded their crops and did not suffer any loss, and We made a river flow right through the middle of them. He was a man of wealth and property, and he said to his companion, debating with him: "I have more wealth than you and more people under me."*
> (Surat al-Kahf, 32-34)

By relating this parable, Allah wants people to compare a believer with someone who claims to believe in Allah but who is, in reality, an unbeliever. One of the garden owners is richer than the other, a "superiority" that caused him to become arrogant and proud toward Allah.

But Allah, Who created everything out of nothing, is the sole owner of all that exists and tests some people by giving them wealth and property. Some people become ungrateful because they consider this wealth and property to be the fruit of their own effort and intellect. They exult in their possessions and make them a source of pride and prestige among people. On the other hand, sincere believers behave in the following manner:

Say: "O Allah! Master of the Kingdom. You give sovereignty to whoever You will, and You take sovereignty from whoever You will. You exalt whoever You will, and You abase whoever You will. All good is in Your hands. You have power over all things. (Surah Al `Imran, 26)

The ungrateful garden owner claimed that the gardens and their produce belonged to him, forgetting that they were only a gift and a test from Allah. He succumbed to a fierce pride and a blatant arrogance, as revealed in the following verses:

> Do not strut arrogantly about the land. You will certainly never split the land apart, nor will you ever rival the mountains in height. All of that is evil action and hateful in the sight of your Lord. (Surat al-Isra', 37-38)

In many verses, Allah describes what will happen to such people, such as:

> Fierce competition for this world distracted you until you went down to the graves. No indeed, you will soon know! Again, no indeed, you will soon know! No indeed, if you only knew with the Knowledge of Certainty, you will certainly see the Blazing Fire! Then you will certainly see it with the Eye of Certainty. Then you will be asked that Day about the pleasures you enjoyed. (Surat at-Takathur, 1-8)

> *He entered his garden and wronged himself by saying: "I do not think that this will ever end. I do not think the Hour will ever come. But if I should be sent back to my Lord, I will definitely get something better in return."*
> *(Surat al-Kahf, 35-36)*

This ungrateful person clearly displayed his disrespect for Allah by asserting that no disaster would ever touch his gardens. In short, he claimed a kind of godhood for himself.

But only Allah, Who created time and space and is beyond them, is endless. Allah's name *Al-Khaliq* (the Creator) has the inherent meaning of: the One Who creates everything from nothing and creates all things with the knowledge of what will happen to them. Every stage of each person, from the first moment of existence until the moment death, exists in Allah's presence. In Allah's guardianship (*hifz*), everything remains as it is, for He created everything that each person experienced or saw, and every detail of their lives. Nothing is ever lost, as the following verse informs us: **"That is so you will know that Allah knows what is in the heavens and in Earth, and that Allah has knowledge of all things"** (Surat al-Ma'ida, 97).

Since Allah is not subject to time, everything occurs for Him and meets its destination all at once. But people, who are subject to time, divide their lives into past, present, and future. However, such a division applies only

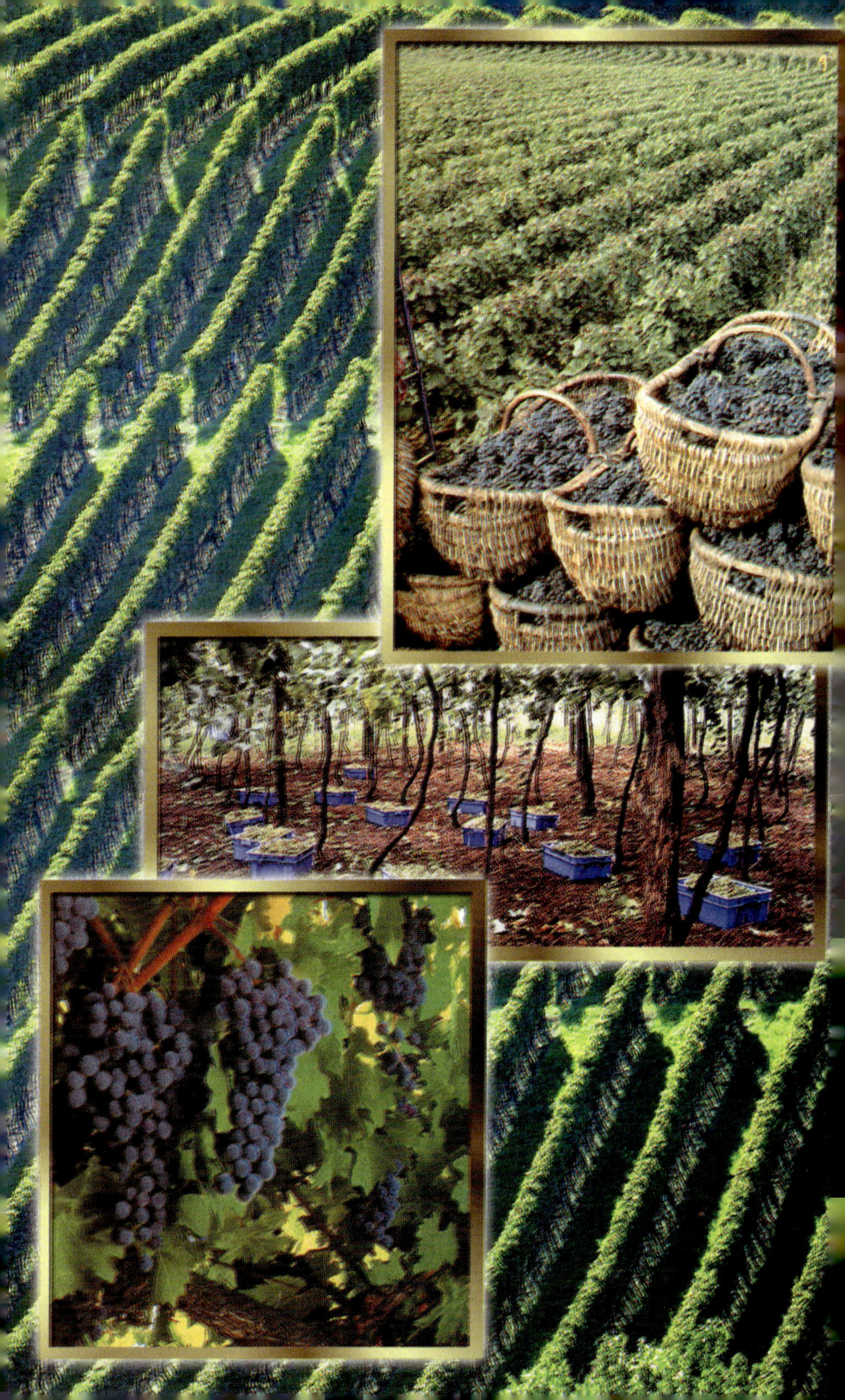

to humanity, for what we consider the "past" is the "past" only to us, and what we consider the "unknowable future" is the "unknowable future" only to us. Given that Allah is our Creator, our ordering of time cannot be applied to Him, a fact revealed by the following verse:

> [Luqman said:] "My son, even if something weighs as little as a mustard-seed and is inside a rock or anywhere else in the heavens or Earth, Allah will bring it out. Allah is All-Pervading, All-Aware. (Surah Luqman, 16)

For Allah, all events occur in one moment. The examples given from the lives of Musa (as), the Companions of the Cave, Khidhr (as), Dhu'l-Qarnayn (as), Muhammad (saas), and all of the other Prophets, as well as of our own time, are all like one moment in His presence. Our grandchildren, even their grandchildren, and the lives of all the people who will come after them also occur in the same moment. In Allah's presence, the Hour has taken place and the people have gone to their eternal abode already. Those who believe in Allah are in Paradise, and those who do not are suffering in Hell.

According to a widespread but false belief, Allah has created humanity, given its members a certain amount of time, awaits the results of their trials, and will continue to wait until the universe dies. (We hold Allah above this.) But in reality, it is inconceivable for Allah to wait, for waiting is a human characteristic whereas Allah is beyond and above all imperfections of humanity. Allah's name *Al-Quddus* (The Holy) means that He is free from all error, weakness, shortcoming, heedlessness and from any kind of defect. He encompasses all people's past and future, and the details of all their life experiences. But people believe that time, as they understand it here, flows from the past (before) toward the future (after), whereas in Allah's presence such words and concepts do not exist. Everything, all people and all living beings, live all at once. All times, eras, periods, histories, and even all days, hours, and minutes, are present in the same moment. Even if the limited intellectual capacity of people prevents them from seeing this truth, this reality is clear.

This is the main reason why believers appreciate Allah's might and so submit to and trust in Him. They know that Allah encompasses them and everything else, that they are totally dependent upon Him, and that they are small next to His greatness.

Being able to appreciate Allah's greatness and power, and to comprehend the wisdom behind events and their fine details, believers submit to Allah willingly.

The verse **"But if I should be sent back to my Lord, I will definitely get something better in return"** (Surat al-Kahf, 36) describes people who believe that they will enter Paradise without observing the boundaries established by Allah or obeying His commands. Such people consider themselves exempt and are arrogant with Allah.

Many people say that they believe in Allah and the Qur'an, although they have no fear of Him. They do not obey Allah's commands, abide by what is lawful and unlawful, and do not follow the Messenger's (saas) path. And yet they have a strong faith that they will go to Paradise after they die.

On the other hand, the believers hope for Paradise but fear Hell: **"those who affirm the Day of Judgment, those who are fearful of the punishment of their Lord (no one is safe from the punishment of his Lord)"** (Surat al-Ma`arij, 26-28). This attitude is pointed out in: **"Call on Him fearfully and eagerly. Allah's mercy is close to the good-doers"** (Surat al-A`raf, 56). Believers behave in this way because no one can be certain that he or she will not enter Hell, but all of them know that the unbelievers will certainly suffer its fierce punishment:

> Do they feel secure that the all-enveloping punishment of Allah will not come upon them, or that the Last Hour will not come upon them all of a sudden, when they least expect it? (Surah Yusuf, 107)
>
> Do those who plot evil actions feel secure that Allah will not cause the land to swallow them up or that a punishment will not come upon them from where they least expect? (Surat an-Nahl, 45)

> *His companion, with whom he was debating, said to him: "Do you not, then, believe in Him Who created you from dust, then from a drop of sperm, and then formed you as a man?*
> *(Surat al-Kahf, 37)*

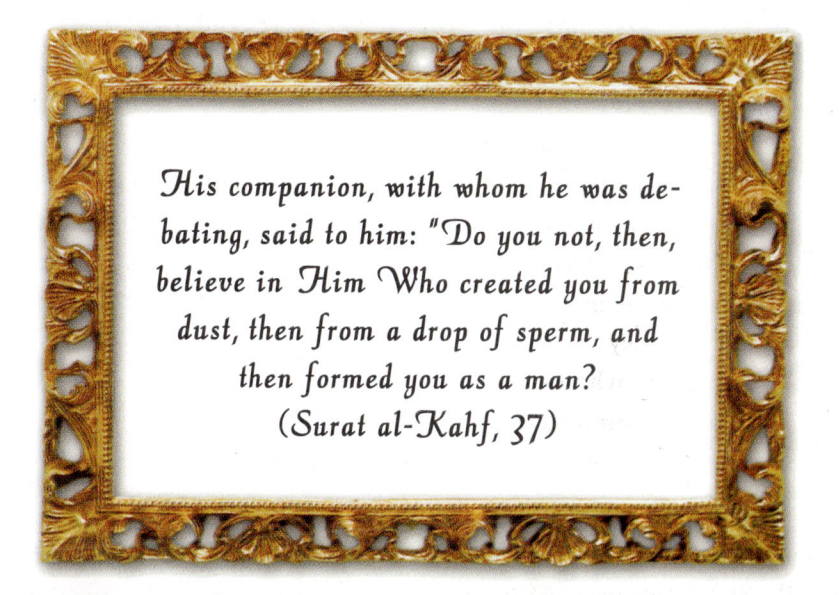

This verse provides guidance on how believers should behave when inviting others to good morality or when reminding people of Allah. If the people with whom they are talking have forgotten their helplessness before Allah and have become arrogant, the best thing to do is to remind them of their helplessness.

The other garden owner, being a man of faith, invites the arrogant owner to faith by reminding him that he was "created from dust and a drop of sperm." Clearly, if Allah wills it, this invitation could have a positive effect on this person. The faithful garden owner realized his neighbor's weak faith and perceived the need to provide support. To explain Allah's signs in nature is one of the best ways to strengthen another person's faith.

The speech of the arrogant garden owner differs from the speech of a Muslim. In fact, it evokes the style of an unbeliever. This is why the faithful garden owner begins his question with "Do you not, then, believe in Him?" The other person might not be openly proclaiming his unbelief, but his words clearly show that he does not believe with certainty. Although he professes belief with his words, and yet he does not actually abide by Allah's law. This contradiction means that he denies Allah.

One often meets these self-contradicting people. Most people say they believe in Allah, but they do not lead a life that pleases Him. Instead, they act contrary to the Qur'an's morality and do not follow in the Prophet's (saas) footsteps. Despite their words and deeds, which amount to denial, they consider themselves righteous and destined for Paradise. But they are only deceiving themselves, for Allah says that:

As for those who denied Our Signs and the encounter of the Hereafter, their actions will come to nothing. Will they be repaid except for what they did? (Surat al-A`raf, 147)

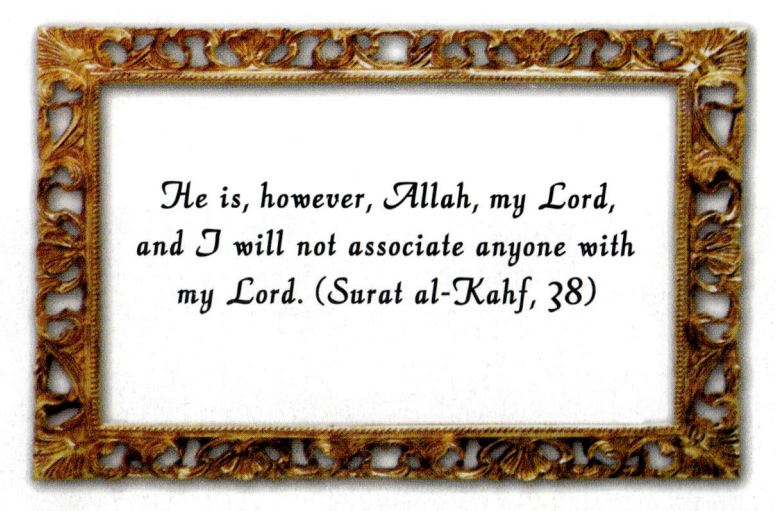

> *He is, however, Allah, my Lord, and I will not associate anyone with my Lord. (Surat al-Kahf, 38)*

Throughout Surat al-Kahf, Allah points out that the majority of people ascribe partners to Him. In the Qur'an, denial by association means to prefer anybody, anything, or any idea over Allah, or to consider them equal and to act accordingly. The Qur'an calls this "setting up other gods together with Allah." In truth, this means to choose a purpose in life contrary to Allah's good pleasure, to seek salvation from or the pleasure of any other being, or to hold anything in higher esteem than Allah.

People need to refrain from such a sin, for Allah warns humanity that while He will forgive all other sins, if He wills to do so, He will never forgive this particular sin (Surat an-Nisa', 116). Obviously, Muslims will want to avoid such a great sin at all costs. Prophet Luqman (as) advised his son as follows: **"My son, do not associate anything with Allah. Associating others with Him is a terrible wrong"** (Surah Luqman, 13). Another reason why this sin is so great is that it causes good deeds to be erased, which leads to ultimate loss. The Qur'an reveals this:

> It has been revealed to you and those before you: "If you associate others with Allah, your actions will come to nothing, and

you will be among the losers." (Surat az-Zumar, 65)

Given the above, all who ascribe partners to Allah will end up in Hell, unless they sincerely repent and embrace, and then adhere to, His religion. This is why those who are in awe of Allah's glory must be aware of this danger.

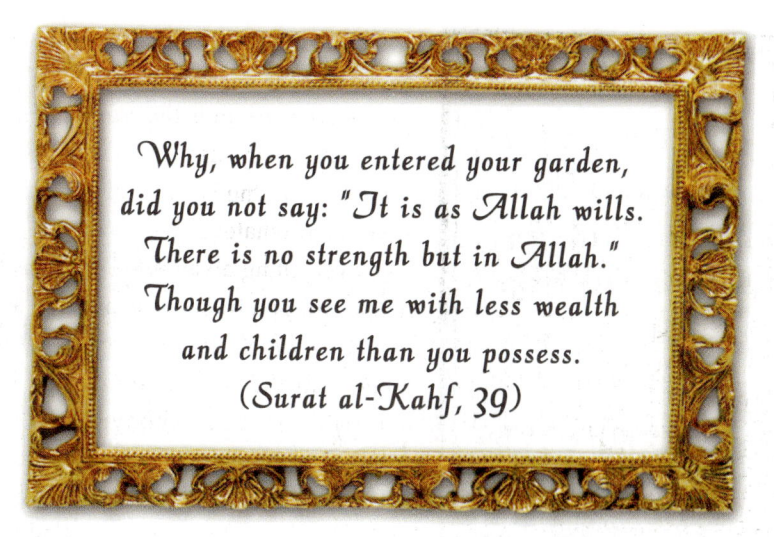

> *Why, when you entered your garden, did you not say: "It is as Allah wills. There is no strength but in Allah." Though you see me with less wealth and children than you possess.*
> (Surat al-Kahf, 39)

This verse indicates the importance of "ma sha' Allah" (It is as Allah wills). Believers use it to express their respect when regarding the superior art and power of Allah's creation.

Using this expression in a heartfelt manner reminds others that Allah owns all things, that everything happens in according to destiny, and that only He can will anything to happen. No doubt, such reminders are beneficial, for people easily forget their own helplessness and descend into ignorance.

For example, the unbelieving garden owner is ascribing partners to Allah by stating that he owns all of the property. Even though he does not clearly express his denial, "hidden association" is inherent in his words and behavior. Thus his friend warns him about ascribing partners to Allah and reminds him that everything belongs to Allah.

Especially in our own time, people must always be aware of this danger, for such situations occur frequently. For instance, *Al-Ghani* (The Rich, He Who is free from need) is one of Allah's attributes, but the same word is used to describe people. There is no objection in using this term to describe someone's financial status, but it can turn into association if one considers his or her self, intellect, or effort to be the cause of this wealth.

> *[Turn, then, away from all that is false], turning to Him alone. Heed Him and establish prayer. Do not be one of those who associate [others with Him].* (Surah Rum, 31)

This being the case, people easily forget, as did the unbelieving owner of the garden, that Allah is the true owner of all wealth. They also forget that just as He, the only One Who is "ghani" (rich), gave them whatever they own, He can take everything away if He wills. Such people adopt a truly crude attitude and mentality, which amounts to associating others with Allah. As a result, they will not realize that everybody other than Allah is poor and helpless, and that Allah can affect any one of His servants with any part of His attributes. Looking at things from such a perspective and acting accordingly leads to forgetting Allah's infinite power and rule, and to associating oneself with Him.

The right attitude is to know that Allah is the true owner of all wealth, to acknowledge that He is the sole governor of all that exists, and to be aware that He can remove the wealth that He gives at any time. One should not look at rich people in terms of whether they are rich or poor, but as servants of Allah to whom He has given wealth. For instance, if such people's families regard them as the true owners of their wealth, if all of their hopes rest on that person so that they forget that Allah is the Lord of all wealth and do not remind them of this reality, then their attitude would be truly misguided. Likewise, the employees of such people should not forget that Allah provides food, drink, and shelter. It would be a grave mistake to forget Allah and to consider one's employer as an independent power capable of many things. The Qur'an reveals the truth of such matters, as follows:

> **Instead of Allah, you worship only idols. You are inventing a lie. Those you worship besides Allah have no power to provide for you. So seek your provision from Allah, and worship Him and give thanks to Him. It is to Him you will be returned.** (Surat al-`Ankabut, 17)

> *"It may well be that my Lord will give me something better than your garden, and send down upon it a fireball from the sky so that morning finds it a shifting heap of dust, or morning finds its water drained into the ground so that you cannot get at it."* (Surat al-Kahf, 40-41)

In these verses, the believing garden owner reminds his proud friend of his helplessness by pointing out that he cannot prevent any disaster sent by Allah, and that showing arrogance in the face of this reality is to be thoughtless.

One of the greatest mistakes of people whose property and wealth make them vain is to forget that these, like all the beauty on Earth, are only temporary. Beauty and youth eventually give way to old age, just as health makes way for illness, incapacity, and weakness.

As all wealth is only temporary, Allah can make a poor person rich and destroy the wealth of a rich person in an instant. People can lose their houses, yachts, cars, or jewelry in floods, earthquakes, or other disasters in a matter of moments. No one can prevent a disaster sent by Allah. Anyone can lose loved ones, die, become disabled, suffer permanent injury, or lose his or her memory and faculties, for: **"No misfortune occurs except with Allah's permission"** (Surat at-Taghabun, 11). Such events cannot be prevented, reversed, or delayed. On such a day, neither wealth nor property will be of any use, for: **"As for those who

Someone who considers his posse(ssions) (e.g., yachts, villas, and oth(er) property) safe forever, realizes h(is) hopelessness after a tornado. All(ah) gives power, wealth, health, and we(ll)being (to) whomev(er) He wills. (He) also lets pe(o)ple grow o(ld) to show the(m) His Sig(ns) and to (re)mind the(m) that just (even) with al(l) the worl(dly) adornmen(ts) they can(not) even cont(rol) their o(wn) bod(ies).

disbelieve, neither their wealth nor their children will ever save them from Allah in any way." (Surah Al `Imran, 10)

Since eveyone experiences only what Allah has ordained, they should submit to and trust in Allah. The garden owner, in his conceit, ignored this truth when he claimed that nothing bad would befall his gardens or their produce until the end of time. He was certain that the river watering his gardens would remain there forever, that no pest would ever attack his produce, and that he would not face drought or similar disasters. He felt that his wealth, intelligence, and effort would be enough to protect his property.

However, Allah can easily turn everything on its head. The river could drain into the ground due to a small-scale tremor. Such a thing can happen in the blink of an eye, rendering the land arid and unproductive. Who, other than Allah, could bring the river back or make this man's field productive once again? Certainly his property and even all of his wealth could not help him here. This is what he earns for his conceit and ungratefulness. Those material things that he valued and claimed ownership over, which caused him to invent lies against Allah and to ascribe partners to Him, will not help him in the Hereafter, for:

Woe to every faultfinding backbiter who has amassed wealth and hoarded it! He thinks that his wealth will make him live forever. No indeed! He will be flung into the Shatterer. And what will convey to you what the Shatterer is? The kindled Fire of Allah reaching right into the heart. It is sealed in above them in towering columns. (Surat al-Humaza, 1-9)

Surat al-Kahf 40-41 also refers to the great gift of Allah willing soothing underground water to rise to the surface. Had this not been so, people would be in great difficulty. But thanks to wells and other means that enable us to reach the clear and mineral-rich underground water, we can benefit from this gift.

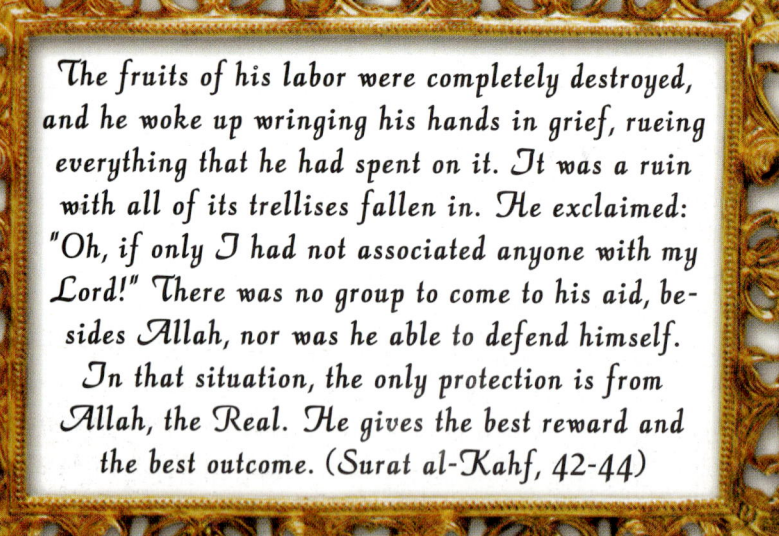

> *The fruits of his labor were completely destroyed, and he woke up wringing his hands in grief, rueing everything that he had spent on it. It was a ruin with all of its trellises fallen in. He exclaimed: "Oh, if only I had not associated anyone with my Lord!" There was no group to come to his aid, besides Allah, nor was he able to defend himself. In that situation, the only protection is from Allah, the Real. He gives the best reward and the best outcome. (Surat al-Kahf, 42-44)*

People who put their faith in others besides Allah, imploring them for mercy and trusting them, will not find what they seek. This is why they feel lost and lonely, especially in moments of trouble. They feel hopeless, confused, and deserted by their false deities in the face of this world's endless chaos and troubles.

Surat al-Isra' 22 proclaims: **"Do not set up any other deity together with Allah lest you become disgraced and forsaken."** Allah left the conceited garden owner stranded by removing all of his property and wealth through an unexpected disaster. In this tragic moment, the garden owner saw the truth and realized what a huge mistake he had made.

This example teaches us a valuable lesson: Those who consider themselves the owners of any power in the land can be made to realize their helplessness instantly by the will of Allah. Such people cannot help either themselves or those near to them. Everything is in Allah's

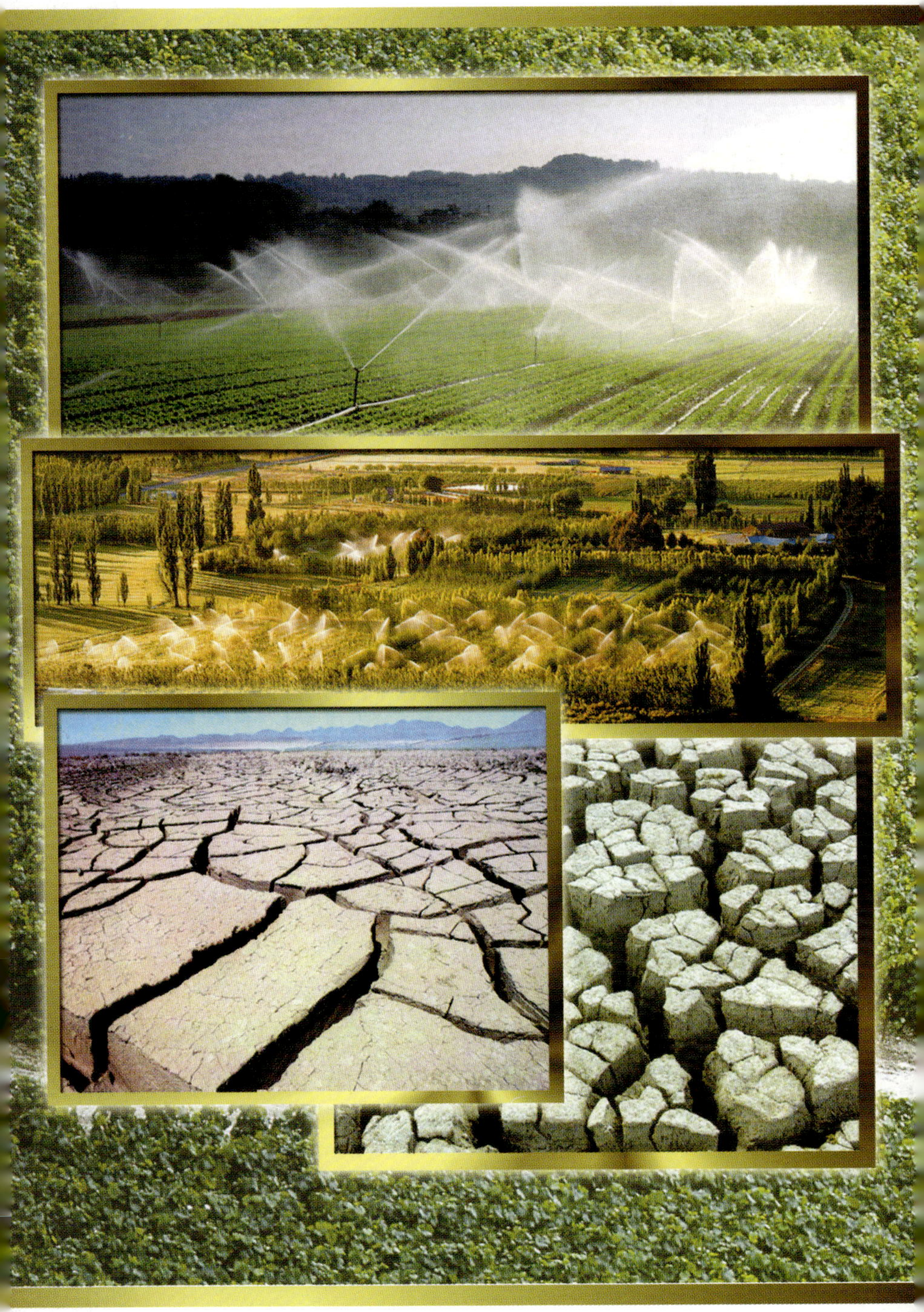

power, and no one else can provide any benefit or cause harm. This reality is related in the following verse:

If Allah touches you with harm, none can remove it but Him. If He touches you with good, He has power over all things. (Surat al-An`am, 17)

Allah is humanity's only friend and protector. All beings besides Allah are only His creation and exist and—continue to exist—because of His will. Allah provides and heals, and brings about both laughter and tears. Every other being is endlessly helpless, poor, and dependent. They have no power and no ability in their own right, and do not have even the power to help themselves. No one other than Allah can be trusted, expected to help, and asked to provide for us.

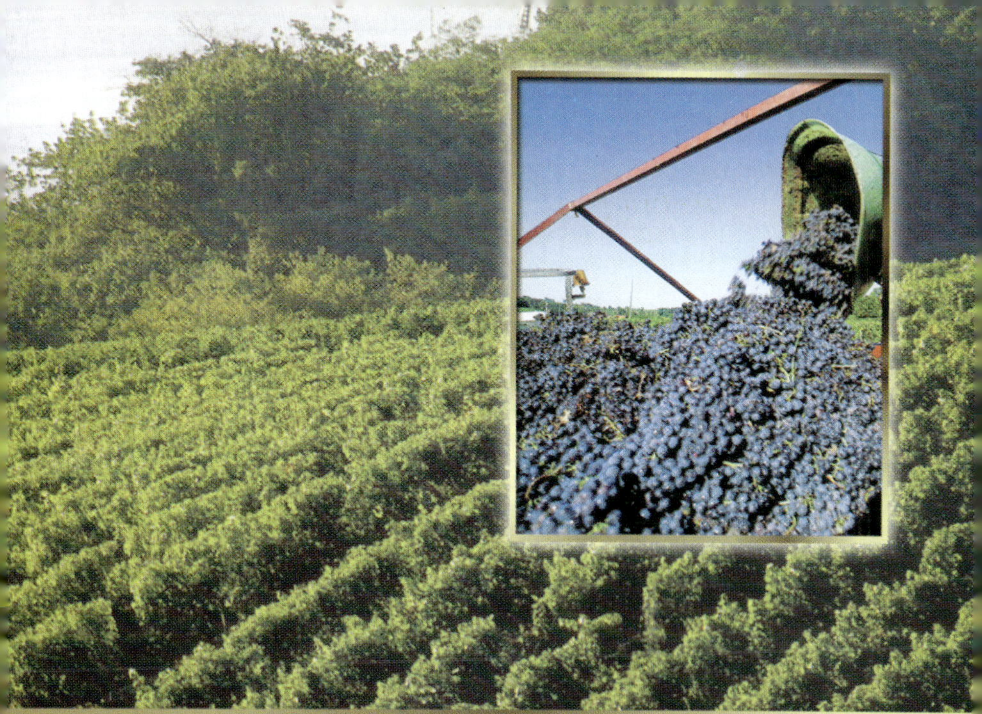

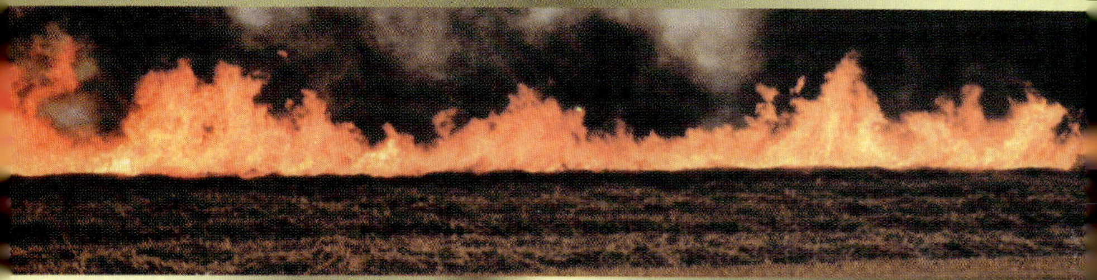

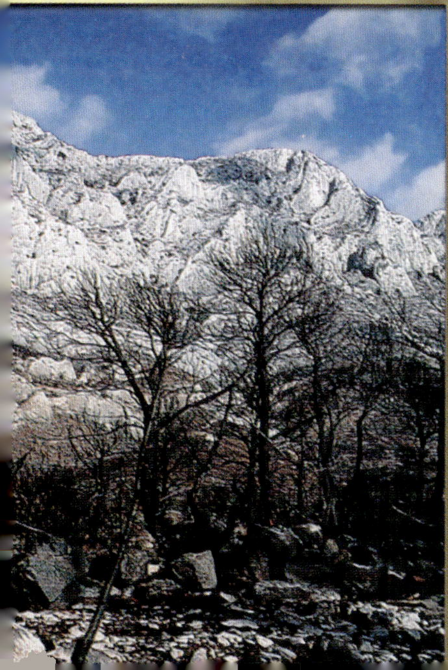

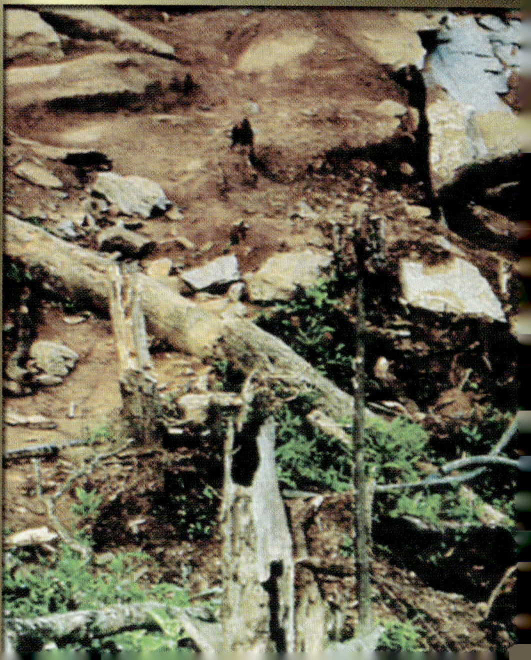

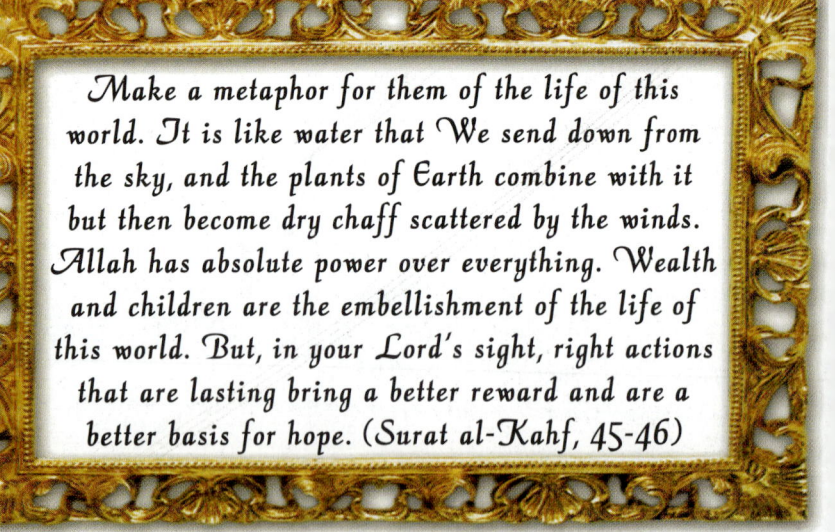

> *Make a metaphor for them of the life of this world. It is like water that We send down from the sky, and the plants of Earth combine with it but then become dry chaff scattered by the winds. Allah has absolute power over everything. Wealth and children are the embellishment of the life of this world. But, in your Lord's sight, right actions that are lasting bring a better reward and are a better basis for hope. (Surat al-Kahf, 45-46)*

This verse mentions lasting right actions, defined as good and beneficial deeds that comply with the Qur'an's morality and are pleasant to Allah. People should do right actions to win His good pleasure and grace, as well as Paradise, for these actions reveal the Muslims' patience and devotion. In sum, it shows that they are serious about their faith.

The intention behind each act is very important. A deed can be a right action only if it is done for Allah's good pleasure. If it is done with any other intention, it is no longer considered a right action and becomes a deed done for the pleasure of others. Allah describes such acts of worship that seek the pleasure of others in the following verses:

So woe to those who establish prayer and are heedless of their prayer, those who show off and deny help to others. (Surat al-Ma`un, 4-7)

The same is true for charity, for some seek Allah's good pleasure while others seek only to impress. The difference between these people is explained, as follows:

O you who believe. Do not nullify your alms by demands for

gratitude or insulting words, like him who spends his wealth, showing off to people and not believing in Allah and the Last Day. His likeness is that of a smooth rock coated with soil, which, when a heavy rain falls on it, is left stripped bare. They have no power over anything they have earned. Allah does not guide unbelieving people. The metaphor of those who spend their wealth, desiring the good pleasure of Allah and firmness for themselves, is that of a garden on a hillside. When a heavy rain falls on it, it doubles its produce; and if a heavy rain does not fall, there is dew. Allah sees what you do. (Surat al-Baqara, 264-265)

Muslims who engage in right action must never forget that they are the ones who benefit from such actions. Allah is exalted and beyond any imperfection, and need. Therefore, He does not need the right actions of Muslims, a fact that is revealed in the Qur'an:

Mankind! You are the poor in need of Allah, whereas Allah is the Rich Beyond Need, the Praiseworthy. If He wills, He can dispense with you and bring about a new creation. That is not difficult for Allah. (Surah Fatir, 15-17)

Our Lord can do anything at anytime and has power over everything, as stated in: "... **Do those who believe not know that if Allah had wanted to He could have guided all mankind?...**" (Surat ar-Ra`d, 31). The Muslims' effort to spread Allah's religion is for their own good. Therefore, those who do right actions benefit only themselves and earn their reward in the Hereafter. According to the Qur'an: **"Whoever strives only strives for himself. Allah is Rich Beyond Need of any being"** (Surat al-`Ankabut, 6).

Another aspect of right actions is their continuity. Some people find it easy enough to do a couple of good deeds a day, to give some charity, or to be selfless in some respect. They could be doing such things habitually or because they do not damage their interests. But what is really important is to do right actions throughout their lives, make an effort to win Allah's good pleasure, act selflessly, and work incessantly to spread His religion. They must continue to do so without ever giving up, even if no one else in their environment is obeying His commands. Thus, they will have proven their determination and the strength of their faith in Allah. As Allah proclaims:

> **Allah augments those who are guided by giving them greater guidance. In your Lord's sight, right actions that are lasting are better both in reward and the end-result. (Surah Maryam, 76)**

The salvation awaiting believers who believe and do right actions throughout their lives is Allah's good pleasure and Paradise. Allah reveals this good news in the following verse:

> **As for those who believe and do right actions—We impose on no self any more than it can bear—they are the Companions of the Garden, remaining in it timelessly, forever. We will strip away any rancor in their hearts. Rivers will flow under them, and they will say: "Praise be to Allah, Who has guided us to this! We would not have been guided had Allah not guided us. The Messengers of our Lord came with the Truth." It will be proclaimed to them: "This is your Garden, which you have inherited for what you did." (Surat al-A`raf, 42-43)**

> *On the Day We make the mountains move and you see Earth laid bare, and We gather them together, not leaving out a single one of them, they will be paraded before your Lord in ranks: "You have come to Us just as We created you at first. Yes indeed! Even though you claimed that We would not fix a time with you."*
> *(Surat al-Kahf, 47-48)*

Just as there is a time fixed for everyone's death, the universe also has a fixed time, known as "the Hour." But only Allah knows when the Hour will occur, as the following verse states: **Truly Allah has knowledge of the Hour, sends down abundant rain, and knows what is in the womb. No self knows what it will earn tomorrow, and no self knows in what land it will die. Allah is All-Knowing, All-Aware. (Surah Luqman, 34)**

Surat al-Kahf relates some of the people's presumptions about when the Hour will come. Allah reveals that the Hour, thought to be far away by people, is approaching: **"Mankind's reckoning has drawn very close to them, yet they heedlessly turn away"** (Surat al-Anbiya', 1).

Most people believe that life on Earth will continue forever, that the Hour will never come, that death is nothingness, and that the Day of Judgment is a myth. While the Hour means an end to Earth, all that it holds, and everything else in the universe, it is not the final "end" rather, it is the beginning of the eternal life in the Hereafter.

Allah created each person from nothing, and Allah will take his or her life at the fixed time in destiny. In His presence, the day, the hour, and even the second, place, and circumstance of every person's death is known. Allah, beyond time and space, encompasses what to human knowledge is an unknown quantity: the time of one's death.

On the Day of Judgment, the believers will not fear, for Allah promises that: **"My servants, you will feel no fear today; you will know no sorrow"** (Surat az-Zukhruf, 68). However, it will be a very difficult day for the unbelievers.

The believers will receive their reward for the care and attention that they paid to winning Allah's good pleasure, to praying and worshipping as commanded, and to heeding Allah as required, in the nicest manner. Allah will not let them feel the panic, remorse, and sorrow felt by the unbelievers. He describes the believers' situation in the Hereafter in the following terms:

> **On the Day you see the male and female believers, with their light streaming out in front of them, and to their right: "Good news for you today of Gardens with rivers flowing under them, remaining in them timelessly, forever. That is the Great Victory." (Surat al-Hadid, 12)**

> *The Book will be set in place, and you will see the evildoers fearful of what is in it. They will exclaim: "Alas for us! What is this Book that does not pass over any action, small or great, without recording it?" They will find there everything that they did, and your Lord will not wrong anyone at all. (Surat al-Kahf, 49)*

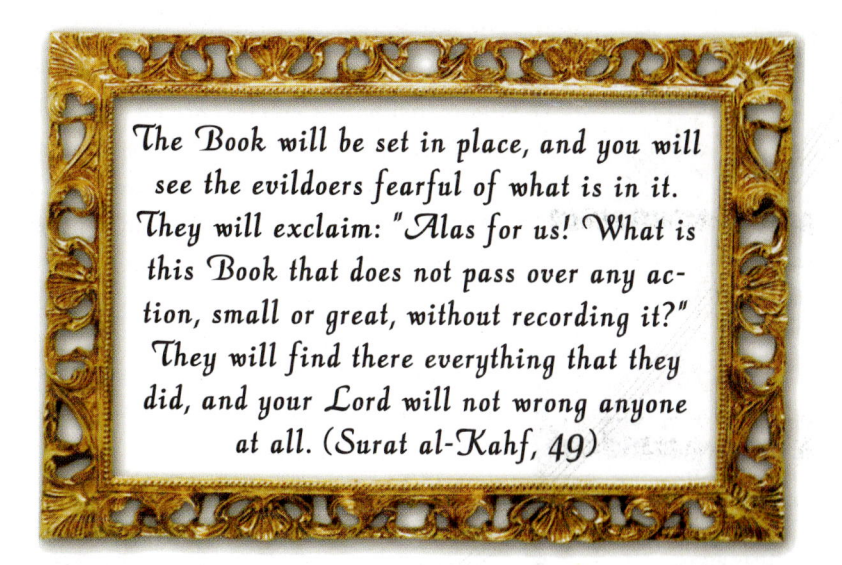

This verse describes the terror that the unbelievers will experience on the Day of Judgment, as well as their surprise that the Book confronts them with everything that they had done on Earth. One reason for their surprise is their ignorance of the fact that Allah controls and encompasses all times and events.

Given that Allah is not bound by such human notions of time as "past," "present," and "future," everything happens in His presence at the same time. Destiny is Allah's knowledge of everything there was, is, and will be, down to the last detail. Our Lord knows all of this, but His way of knowing differs from ours: He creates it all and is therefore in complete control of every moment of people's lives.

On the other hand, people witness the events written in their destiny by Allah, Who preserves them in one moment in His presence, only when is time for them to occur. But most people are unaware of this reality and so misunderstand the true nature of destiny. Some people believe that they can "change" or even "defeat" their own destiny. For example, let's say that you have an accident. Destiny means that all of the related circumstances, your survival, the severity of your injuries, and how long your treatments will last are all written in your destiny. You are still alive because that was your destiny. In other words, you did not "cheat" or "defeat" destiny, for your destiny cannot be changed. If you believe that it can be changed, you are only kidding yourself. It is yet again in their destiny to believe so. Destiny is the science of Allah, Who knows all times as the same moment, Who governs all space and time.

As a result, on the Day of Judgment people will find every one of their actions, words, and intentions brought before them. By the will of our Lord, long-forgotten details will be revealed. People might think that one of their evil or hurtful acts will be forgotten over time, but this is not the case with Allah, for to Him what happens on the Day of Judgment and what happened thousands of years ago exist within the same moment. And so it is a grave mistake to think that one's deeds will remain secret or be forgotten, or that they will never confront them again.

The train's past locations on the way, as well as its present and future locations, are all known and occur in the same moment in Allah's presence.

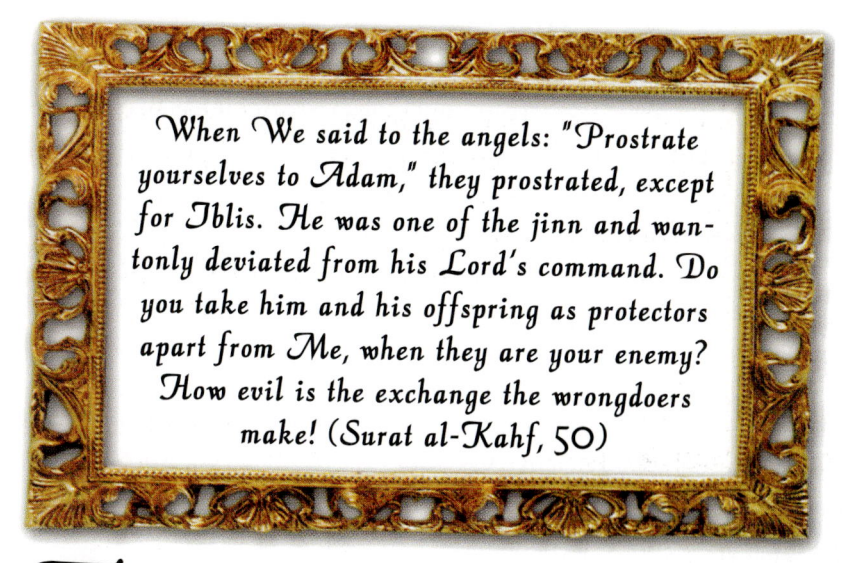

> When We said to the angels: "Prostrate yourselves to Adam," they prostrated, except for Iblis. He was one of the jinn and wantonly deviated from his Lord's command. Do you take him and his offspring as protectors apart from Me, when they are your enemy? How evil is the exchange the wrongdoers make! (Surat al-Kahf, 50)

This verse points out the importance of obedience. Iblis did not prostrate before Adam and thus disobeyed Allah. Therefore, his defining characteristic is disobedience; whereas believers are known for their determined obedience to Allah, his Messengers, and His revelations.

In the lives of people and societies, obedience is very important. In any society, law and order are established by the obedience, respect, and trust that the people give to the state. Many verses command Muslims to obey those in authority, provided that the rulers do not deviate from true religion, and so envisions a society in which people live according the Qur'an's morality and thereby create an environment reflecting obedience and respect.

Religious morality prevents people from acts of violence and terror, because Allah forbids people to cause corruption. Some of these verses are as follows:

Seek the abode of the Hereafter with what Allah has given you, without forgetting your portion of this world. Do good, as Allah has been good to you. Do not seek to cause corruption in the

land. Allah does not love corrupters. (Surat al-Qasas, 77)

... Give full measure and full weight. Do not diminish people's goods. Do not cause corruption in the land after it has been put right. That is better for you, if you are believers. (Surat al-A`raf, 85)

Those people who comprehend and live by religion's morality, therefore, naturally will do their best to refrain from engaging in any type of evil. They will adhere to the Qur'an's morals and acquire thereby contentment and inner peace, tolerance and a measured and non-provocative attitude, and seek to create harmony.

If the Qur'an's social model gains widespread acceptance in society, as opposed to Satan's path, peace and harmony will rule. Those people who oppose the police and other security forces, as well as meet them with anger and trouble, will no longer be able to justify such activities. Those who live according to Islam's morality are helpful and tolerant, side with the security forces, and make things easier for them. Thanks to the existence of such people, anarchy, terror, chaos, and hostility will vanish. The ongoing conflict between people, their arguments and disputes will cease, and all people will be able to go wherever they want, at any time, in complete safety.

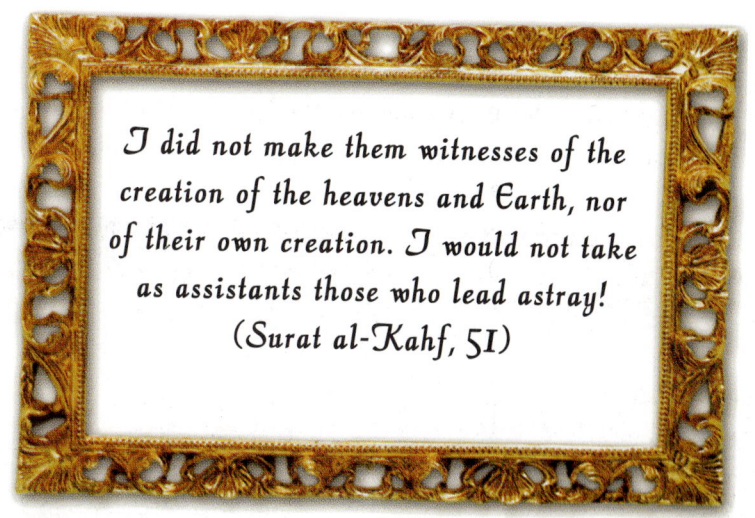

> *I did not make them witnesses of the creation of the heavens and Earth, nor of their own creation. I would not take as assistants those who lead astray!*
> **(Surat al-Kahf, 51)**

This verse indicates that believers should only befriend believers, the obedient, and those who have good character. Being with such people protects the believers from all kinds of danger, prevents them from going astray, and helps them to do right actions. Since the believers are one another's friends and guardians, they will remind each other of Allah's Signs and recommend good morals. Befriending people who lead others astray and provoke rebellion brings nothing but loss and disaster, as the verse below states:

When Satan made their actions appear good to them, saying: "No one will overcome you today, for I am at your side." But when the two parties came in sight of one another, he turned right around on his heels, saying: "I wash my hands of you. I see what you do not see. I fear Allah. Allah is severe in retribution." (Surat al-Anfal, 48)

Do not forget that in this world, Satan appears to people as their friend. But when he comes face to face with Allah's punishment, he deserts those who befriended him. For this reason, the Qur'an always commands believers to choose other believers as friends and protectors, as in:

Your friend is only Allah, His Messenger, and those who believe: those who establish prayer, give alms, and bow [in prayer]. As for those who make Allah their friend, and His Messenger and those who believe: it is the party of Allah who are victorious! (Surat al-Ma'ida, 55-56)

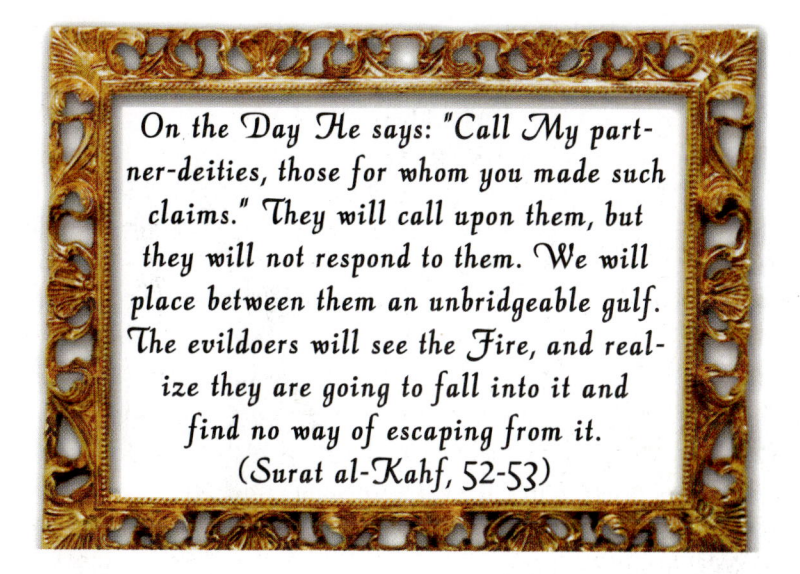

> On the Day He says: "Call My part-ner-deities, those for whom you made such claims." They will call upon them, but they will not respond to them. We will place between them an unbridgeable gulf. The evildoers will see the Fire, and realize they are going to fall into it and find no way of escaping from it.
> (Surat al-Kahf, 52-53)

These verses reveal that those who ascribe partners to Allah will find an unexpected recompense in the Hereafter: Their partners will desert them on that day, and so they will find themselves all alone. Everyone will be accountable only for his or her own actions, and no one will be wronged. The Qur'an says:

> If even a single waft of the punishment were to touch them, they would exclaim: "Alas for us! We were indeed wrongdoers." We will set up the Just Balance on the Day of Rising, and no self will be wronged in any way. Even if it is no more than the weight of a grain of mustard-seed, We will produce it. We are sufficient as a Reckoner. (Surat al-Anbiya', 46-47)

These verses also relate that those who ascribed partners to Allah will search for a "way of escaping," but that a way out will never be found. Their situation is known to Allah. The revelations given in this verse are not known to anyone, the described scene has not been seen by anyone, and the conversations have not been heard by anyone. Thus, these future events are part of the Unseen, which means that they are part of the future, which we cannot know. But in the sight of Allah, Who encompasses all times, these events have already taken place and ended.

Our Lord knows people's excuses, their escape plans, the methods they use, how they will be punished, and how they will suffer for eternity, for He is the One Who created everything. He reveals this to us beforehand so that we can learn from others' mistakes. However, only humanity has a concept of "beforehand." In Allah's presence, "before" and "after" do not exist, for both are in His presence right now. In other words, Allah does not "remember" the past or "wait to know" the future; rather, He "knows" both of them, but His knowing is not like our knowing. Things that are yet to happen are known in Allah's guidance (*hifz*), but this knowledge is not like we learn something. The "after" is right now and also finished now, it has happened and it is finished. Every moment, past, present and future, everything we live exists with Allah as "one moment." Allah encompasses all time and space with his knowledge.

> They will exclaim: "Alas for us! Who has raised us from our resting-place? This is what the All-Merciful promised us. The Messengers were telling the truth."
> (Surah Ya Sin: 52)

Whatever is in our past and future is experienced in Allah's presence as a single moment. We experience the knowledge placed in our memory by Allah as the past, and because the knowledge of the future is not there, we do not know it.

PAST

PRESENT

FUTURE

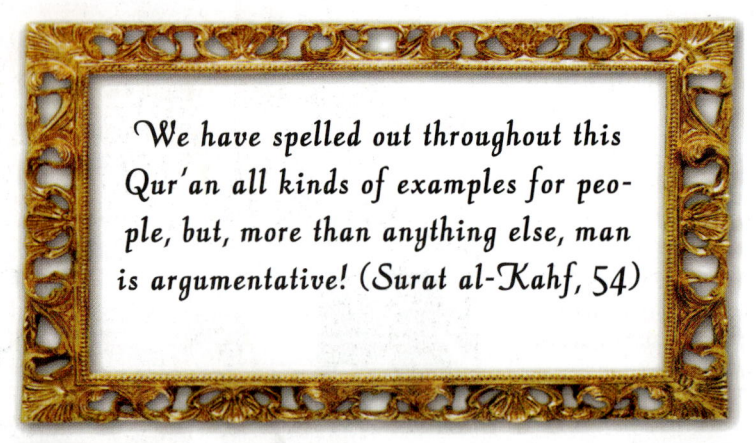

> *We have spelled out throughout this Qur'an all kinds of examples for people, but, more than anything else, man is argumentative! (Surat al-Kahf, 54)*

The Qur'an guides people to faith and separates truth from falsehood It is a gift from Allah, clear and intelligible, a reminder and an admonishment.

The above verse makes clear that the the Qur'an contains many examples and explanations on a variety of subjects to meet the needs of all people while they exist in this world. From morals to everyday matters, from interpersonal relations to commerce, from the signs of creation in the heavens and the Earth to the signs about the future, they are all to be found in the Qur'an. For example, those wishing to live the religious morality are told: "... **We have not omitted anything from the Book...**" (Surat al-An`am, 38). This quality is revealed in the following verses:

> "Am I to desire someone other than Allah as a judge, when it is He Who has sent down the Book to you clarifying everything?" Those to whom We have given the Book know that it has been sent down from your Lord with truth, so on no account be among the doubters. The words of your Lord are perfect in truthfulness and justice. No one can change His words. He is the All-Hearing, the All-Knowing. (Surat al-An`am, 114-115)

> ... We have sent down the Book to you, making all things clear, and as guidance and mercy and good news for the Muslims. (Surat an-Nahl, 89)

An argumentative nature, which Allah discourages, causes disturbance for ourselves and those around us. It is a character defect. The Qur'an advises believers to speak in the nicest possible way.

One of the great benefits of the Qur'an being revealed as such an enlightening book is that people can find in its verses the solutions to their shortcomings and advice on what to do in moments of anger, how to be patient in difficult circumstances, and how to refrain from those qualities (e.g., envy and mocking) that lead away from good character. Furthermore, it informs the believers about the hypocrites, those who associate others with Allah, the unbelievers' character, and how to draw lessons from their situation. Therefore, those who ponder its verses can learn many things about one's self and what is happening around them. As Allah says:

In this way We have sent it down as an Arabic Qur'an, and have diversified therein the warnings so that hopefully they will avoid sin or that it will spur them to remembrance. (Surah Ta Ha, 113)

Surat al-Kahf 54 also points out humanity's argumentative nature. Many people are conceited, consider their views to be superior to those of others, and, because they do not respect their opponents' thoughts, argue and try to win the ensuing battle of words. They do everything in order to convince the others: they get angry, shout, and even become aggressive.

On the other hand, believers respond to such argumentative behavior by judging the matter with the Qur'an and speaking in the nicest manner. They know that this is the only effective way to call others to the righteous path and, with Allah's help, to always be successful. The effect of such behavior is described, as follows:

A good action and a bad action are not the same. Repel the bad with something better and, if there is enmity between you and someone else, he will be like a bosom friend. (Surah Fussilat, 34)

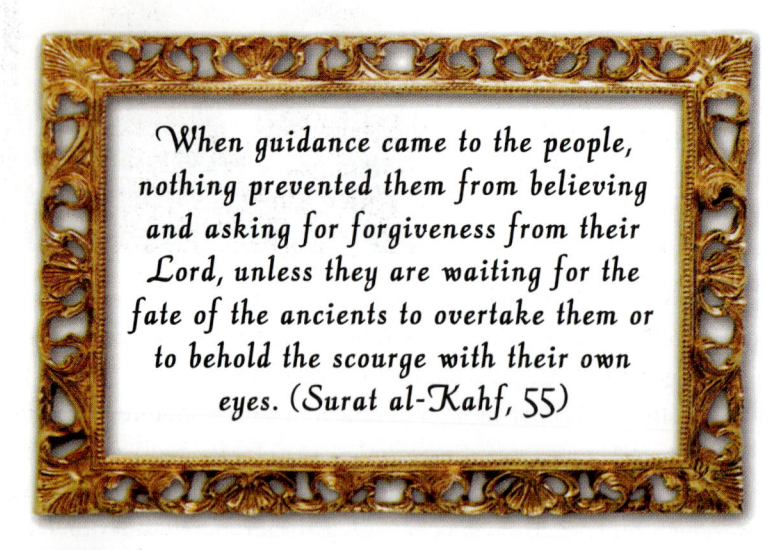

> *When guidance came to the people, nothing prevented them from believing and asking for forgiveness from their Lord, unless they are waiting for the fate of the ancients to overtake them or to behold the scourge with their own eyes. (Surat al-Kahf, 55)*

Here we are presented with the situation of those people who persisted in their unbelief even after being invited to the Qur'an's morality and advised by the Messengers to follow the righteous path. Overcome by their conceit, they would not repent and ask for forgiveness. Rather, they were waiting for Allah to send a disaster. This suggests that they considered it highly unlikely that Allah would send a disaster, that they had little fear, or even no fear, of Allah.

When the Messengers whom Allah had sent to earlier nations invited their people to faith and to live by religion's morality, they encountered similar forms of denial and rejection. Every nation that did not fear Allah persisted in its denial, and thus its people inevitably merited punishment. The Qur'an reveals that Allah's eternal law prescribes punishment for those who persist in their unbelief. Some of these verses are given below:

> **Say to those who do not believe that if they stop, they will be forgiven what is past; but if they return to it, they have the pattern of previous peoples in the past. (Surat al-Anfal, 38)**

Shown by their arrogance in the land and evil plotting. But evil plotting envelops only those who do it. Then do they await anything except the pattern of the former peoples? You will not find any changing in the pattern of Allah. You will not find any alteration in the pattern of Allah. (Surah Fatir, 43)

But when they saw Our violent force, their faith was of no use to them. That is the pattern that Allah has always followed with His servants. Then and there, the unbelievers were lost. (Surah Ghafir, 85)

According to Allah's eternal law, which is absolute and unchanging, all nations that did not accept the Messengers' invitation were destroyed at a time of His determination. Nobody can alter, bring forward, or delay it even by one hour, because our Lord, the Governor of all, determined this in eternity. One verse says:

This is Allah's pattern with those who passed away before. You will not find any alteration in Allah's pattern. (Surat al-Ahzab, 62)

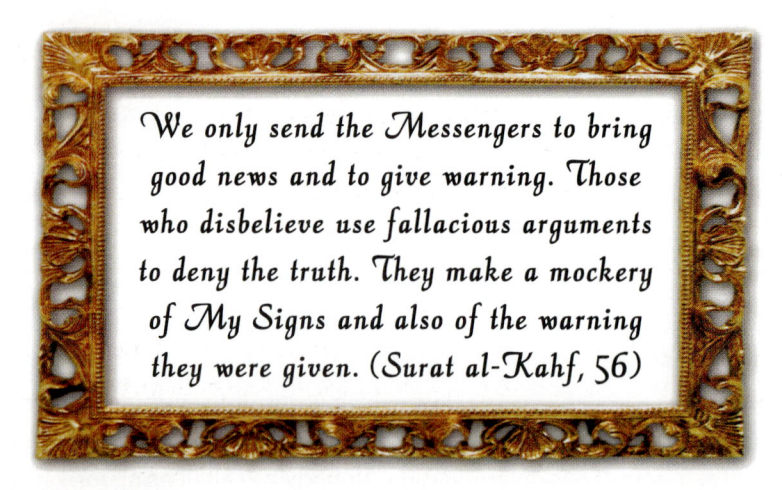

> *We only send the Messengers to bring good news and to give warning. Those who disbelieve use fallacious arguments to deny the truth. They make a mockery of My Signs and also of the warning they were given. (Surat al-Kahf, 56)*

We are informed in the Qur'an that Allah has sent Messengers to every nation to spread His religion and to destroy the entrenched systems of unbelief. They have invited the unbelievers in a variety of ways to believe in Allah and abide by Islam's morals. But throughout history, false beliefs have been deeply rooted in society, and people have vehemently opposed the true religion, defended false beliefs, strenuously promoted irreligion and immorality and flagrantly tried to oppress others. They worked to destroy the positive influence of Allah's Messengers over the people and to prevent the people from abiding by religion's morality.

Societies based upon unbelief tried a variety of methods to prevent the truth: slandering the Messengers to curb their influence and trying to plot against the Prophets, objecting to the Messengers as well as the Books of revelation that they brought, trying to stop people from reading them, and resorting to violence when they deemed it necessary. For instance, the following verse relates the struggle of Nuh's (as) nation to stop him, as follows:

The people of Nuh denied the truth before them and the confederates after them. Every nation planned to seize its Messenger, and used false arguments to rebut the truth. So I seized them, and how

[terrible] was My retribution! (Surah Ghafir, 5)

As Allah says in the above verse, the unbelievers' struggle is an evil one that will end in ultimate loss. Allah has never allowed them to succeed in the past, and will not allow them to do so in the future. At a time of His determination, our Lord will severely punish those who try to lead people astray from the true religion, for He has written this in their destiny. Those who go astray and deny the truth suffer a great loss now and an even greater disaster in the Hereafter, as Allah says:

The kingdom of the heavens and Earth belongs to Allah, and on the Day that the Hour arrives, [on] that Day the liars will be lost. (Surat al-Jathiyya, 27)

Surat al-Kahf 56 also relates that the unbelievers mocked Allah's Signs (i.e. verses), and the approaching punishment in Hell.

One of the greatest reasons for their denial of Allah's verses is their conceit. What they desire most is that no one pronounce Allah's name or take an interest in Islam's morality, because only in such an environment will they be able to continue with their vile character and feel at ease. They think that they can find peace if they deny the evidence for creation or blatantly ignore Allah's power. Such willful ignorance means that even the most clear-cut evidence will never convince them to believe. By denying Allah and religion, they think that they will gain the upper hand and status with the people around them who, like all other living beings, were created by Allah and so are completely dependent upon Him and totally helpless without Him.

Their vanity is founded on the gifts that Allah gave them: intelligence, physical strength, material means, good looks, and whatever else they have. But those people who cannot use their intellect and conscience choose to mock, rather than to be grateful.

The Qur'an states that such people begin to mock Allah's verses the moment they hear them. For instance: **"Each time a sura is sent down, there are some among them who say: 'Which of you has this increased in faith?' As for those who believe, it increases them in faith and they re-**

joice at it (Surat at-Tawba, 124). And yet their mocking does not demoralize or discourage the believers; rather, it only increases their motivation and devotion. In another verse, the unbelievers' lack of understanding and warped attitude toward the verses is described, as follows:

> **Allah is not ashamed to make an example of a mosquito or of an even smaller thing. As for those who believe, they know it is the truth from their Lord. But as for those who do not believe, they say: "What does Allah mean by this example?" He misguides many by it, and guides many by it. But He only misguides the deviators. (Surat al-Baqara, 26)**

As the above verse says, the unbelievers did not understand Allah's purpose behind making an example of the mosquito in one of His verses. Due to their ignorance, they asked "What does Allah mean by this example?" and mocked the verse. But today, science has discovered that the much-maligned mosquito has many miraculous qualities.

Allah pointed at this creature's miraculous qualities 1,400 years ago, and the unbelievers of that time, because they lacked this knowledge, are now exposed as people of small intellect for their mocking words. It is a common practice for unbelievers to mock the acts of worship commanded by Allah, as the verse below reveals:

> **When you call to establish prayer, they make a mockery and a game of it. That is because they are people who do not use their intellect. (Surat al-Ma'ida, 58)**

Allah has revealed many verses on the mocking attitude of those who reject religion, and has advised the believers how to respond to such talk:

> **When you see people engrossed in mocking Our Signs, turn from them until they start to talk of other things… (Surat al-An`am, 68)**

Those who deny Allah's Messengers and religion, as well as those who mock them, meet an end on the Day of Judgment, as described in verse below:

> **That is their repayment—Hell—because they did not believe and mocked My Signs and My Messengers. (Surat al-Kahf, 106)**

> *Who could do greater wrong than someone who is reminded of the Signs of his Lord and then turns away from them, forgetting all that he has done before? We have placed covers on their hearts, preventing them from understanding it, and heaviness in their ears. Though you call them to guidance, they will nonetheless never be guided.*
> *(Surat al-Kahf, 57)*

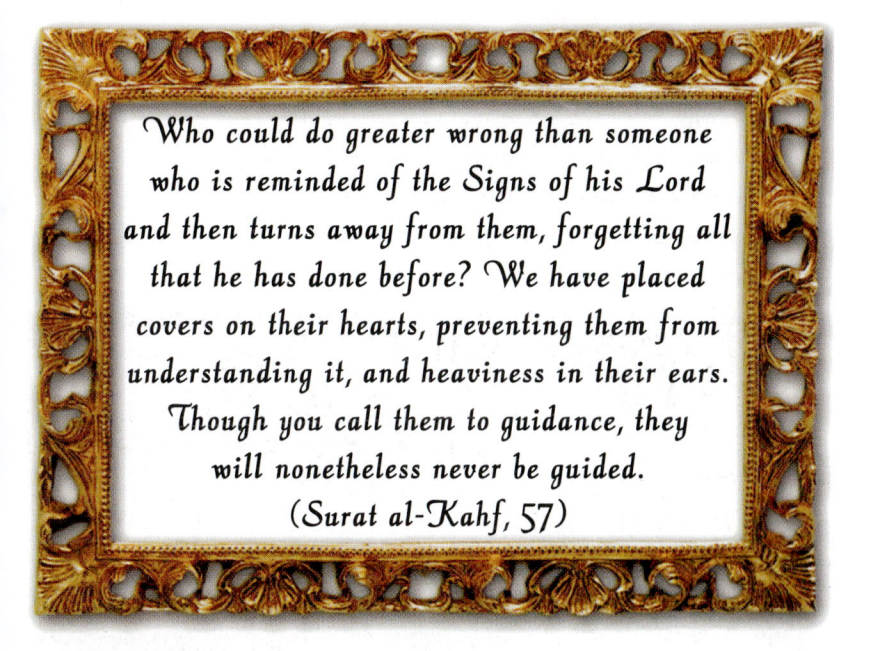

Many people turn away from the verses despite the Messengers' clear invitations and reminders. But as Allah states in this verse, their denial is by His will and command. This state of denial, characterized by their mocking and incomprehension, is determined by their destiny. No matter how much they try to understand, and irrespective of their willpower to do so, they cannot achieve this. They have to live with their destiny.

Only Allah gives faith, and He has written unbelief into their destiny. Therefore, no call or invitation to faith will have an effect on them unless Allah wills it. Allah prevents them from believing by putting a "cover" over their hearts. The verses say:

Some of them listen to you, but We have placed covers on their hearts, preventing them from understanding it, and heaviness in their ears. Though they see every Sign, they still have no faith...
(Surat al-An`am, 25)

Allah has sealed up their hearts and hearing, and over their eyes is a blindfold. They will have a terrible punishment. (Surat al-Baqara, 7)

Allah reveals that these people will "never be guided." With this verse, our Lord reminds us that to change destiny is impossible, and that no matter how hard we try, no one will ever experience anything outside of his or her destiny.

> *Your Lord is the Ever-Forgiving, the Possessor of Mercy. If He had taken them to task for what they have earned, He would have hastened their punishment. Instead, they have a promised appointment and will not find any refuge from it. (Surat al-Kahf, 58)*

This verse reminds us of Allah's infinite mercy and compassion for His servants. Allah, Who is most gracious, lets His endless grace and mercy reflect on everything, without exception. From the air we breathe to the food we eat, from a person's ever-beating heart to the perfect beauty in nature–down to the last detail, everything is a reflection of Allah's grace. All people find life and lead their lives by His grace.

Some of those who appreciate these gifts comprehend creation's purpose and serve Allah, while others are ungrateful and turn away. Allah offers all of Earth's gifts to everyone, so that even the unbelievers, the hypocrites, and those who associate others with Him benefit from the gifts of this life, whether they are open or concealed, from the air they breathe to the water they drink. Allah gives them goods and property, just as He gives the believers, as well as houses to live in and offspring to continue their family lines. He provides them with good foods and gives them health, strength, and beauty.

Allah lets the unbelievers benefit from all of these gifts, for this might enable them to turn to Him, ponder, understand, and become grateful. But this applies only to this worldly life, for in the Hereafter, all gifts belong to the believers, who used them while in this world to get nearer to Allah and win His good pleasure, and who were grateful, for He is the most gracious and has promised Paradise only to the believers. The following verses make this clear:

> **Except for those who repent and believe and act rightly. They will enter Paradise and will not be wronged in any way: Gardens of Eden that the All-Merciful has promised to His servants in the Unseen. His promise is always kept. (Surah Maryam, 60-61)**

Surat al-Kahf 58 also touches upon another subject: There is a fixed time for every nation that will be punished by Allah. In Allah's presence, the exact moment of each person's and each nation's punishment is known, as He reveals in: **"No nation can advance its appointed time, nor can they delay it"** (Surat al-Mu'minun, 43).

The earthquake, flood, tornado, or any other catastrophe that will destroy a nation is known in the destiny determined by Allah, including its timing, severity, duration, and effects. Our Lord, Who encompasses all time, has fixed the time in the destiny of the unbelievers, who deny and do not believe in the Day of Judgment, right down to the day, minute, and second, for:

> **He said: "Go! In this world you will have to say, 'Do not touch me!'" And you have an appointment that you will not fail to keep. Look at your deity to which you devoted so much time. We will burn it up and then scatter it as dust into the sea. (Surah Ta Ha, 97)**

The picture on the right depicts one of the places of worship that was converted into a grain store by the Soviet Union's anti-religious communist regime.

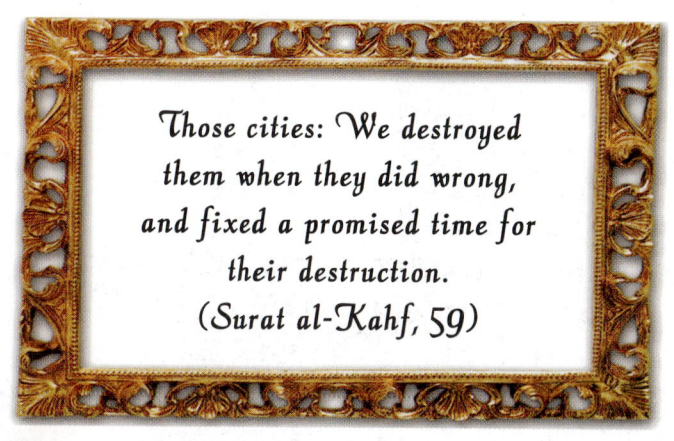

> *Those cities: We destroyed them when they did wrong, and fixed a promised time for their destruction.*
> *(Surat al-Kahf, 59)*

In other words, no nation or country that opposes Allah's law will survive. Every nation that does not respect Allah and religion, that acts contrary to the Qur'an's morals, will be destroyed and wiped off the pages of history.

Many nations have been hostile toward Allah's law and declared war upon Islam's morals. The communist regimes of the last century, which shed so much blood, are only some of the more recent examples. In communist countries, religious institutions were abolished, religious people were oppressed, religious leaders were murdered, and reading the holy Books was forbidden. But none of these regimes lasted. When we look back today, we see that they withdrew from the scenes of history one by one.

SIGNS OF THE END TIMES IN SURAT AL-KAHF

Destroyed places of worship provide one of the most obvious proofs for the war on religion. Above left: A destroyed mosque in Bosnia. On the right: A recently destroyed mosque in Macedonia.

The Qur'an gives many examples of dictators and regimes that made oppression a matter of policy. One of these regimes was that of Pharaoh and his entourage. Pharaoh openly rejected Musa's (as) call to faith and oppressed the believers. As a result, his violent and oppressive regime did not last, for it was wiped out by a great disaster. The verses relate the events surrounding Pharaoh:

> We brought the tribe of Israel across the sea, and Pharaoh and his troops pursued them out of tyranny and enmity. Then, when he was on the point of drowning, he [Pharaoh] said: "I believe that there is no god but Him in Whom the tribe of Israel believe. I am one of the Muslims." "What, now! When previously you rebelled and were one of the corrupters? Today We will preserve your body so that you can be a Sign for people who come after you. Surely, many people are heedless of Our Signs." (Surah Yunus, 90-92)

The Pharaoh to whom Musa (as) was sent was known for his cruelty. He oppressed Musa (as) and his nation and tried to force them to abandon their religion. His destiny, determined in eternity by Allah, provides a lesson for all ouf us. He and his army drowned in the sea by the will of Allah.

The temporary existence of such oppressive and cruel regimes is part of the trial that Allah creates for believers during their worldly life. In one verse Allah addresses Muhammad (saas) with: **"Do not consider Allah to be unaware of what the wrongdoers perpetrate. He is merely deferring them to a Day on which their sight will be transfixed"** (Surah Ibrahim, 42), thereby letting him know that the oppressors will meet their punishment. This truth is also revealed in another verse, as follows:

> We will test you with a certain amount of fear and hunger, and loss of wealth and life and fruits. But give good news to the steadfast: Those who, when disaster strikes them, say: "We belong to Allah, and to Him we will return." (Surat al-Baqara, 155-156)

Surat al-Kahf 59 also states that such nations were punished because of their wrongdoing. Now, we need to analyze just exactly what this term means.

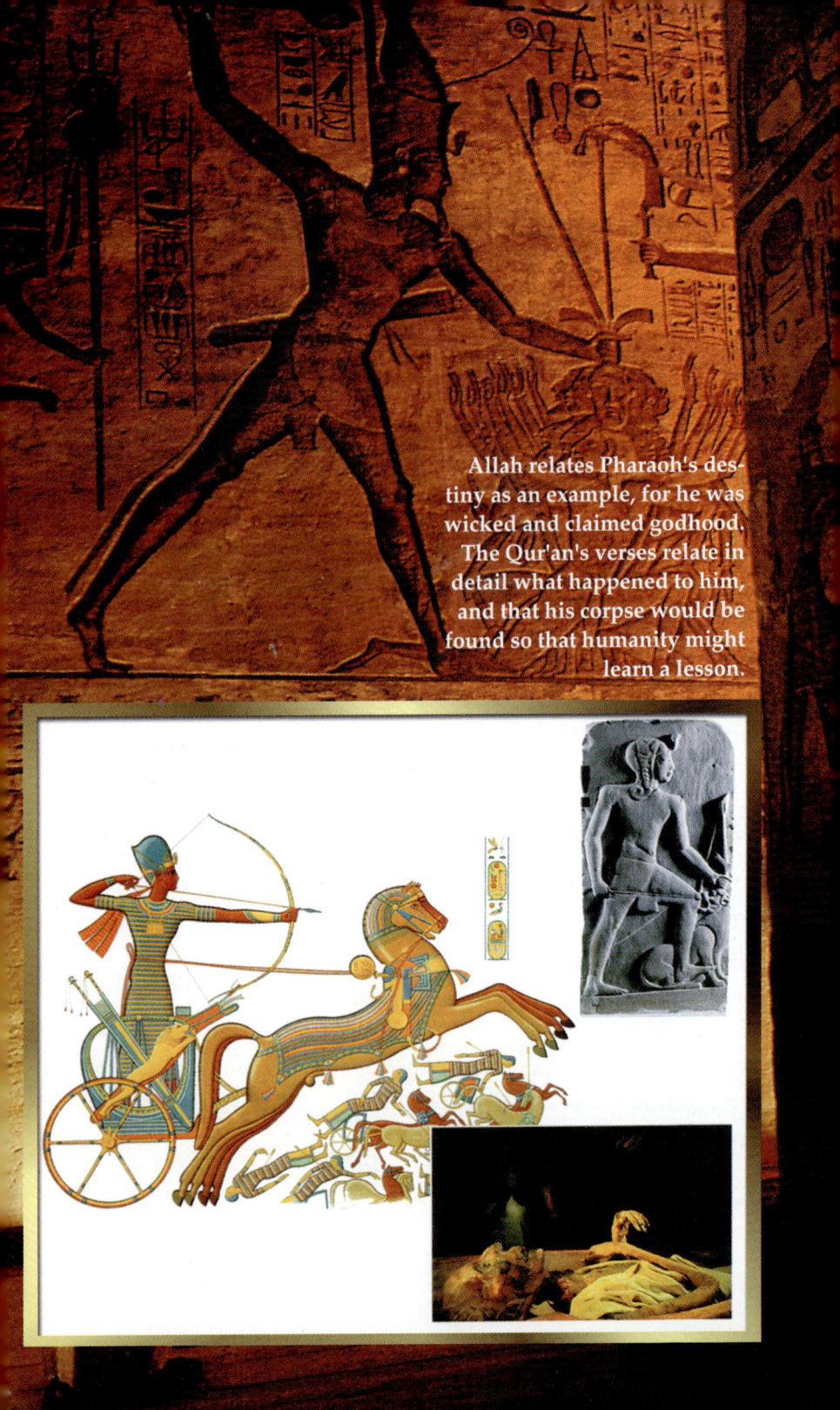

Allah relates Pharaoh's destiny as an example, for he was wicked and claimed godhood. The Qur'an's verses relate in detail what happened to him, and that his corpse would be found so that humanity might learn a lesson.

The Qur'an reveals that the wrongdoers are those who ascribe partners to Allah, who deny His verses, and who reject His Messengers. Allah reveals this reality in: "... **Only wrongdoers deny Our Signs**" (Surat al-Ankabut, 49). Some of the verses on this are:

> Those who do not believe say: "We will never believe in this Qur'an, nor in what came before it." If only you could see when the wrongdoers, standing in the presence of their Lord, cast accusations back and forth at one another!.. (Surah Saba', 31)
>
> After he left, Musa's people adopted a calf made from their ornaments, a form which made a lowing sound. Did they not see that it could not speak to them or guide them to any way? They adopted it, and so they were wrongdoers. (Surat al-A`raf, 148)
>
> How can Allah guide a people who have become unbelievers after having faith? They bore witness that the Messenger was true and that the Clear Signs had come to them. Allah does not guide people who are wrongdoers. (Surah Al `Imran, 86)
>
> When you see people engrossed in mocking Our Signs, turn from them until they start to talk of other things. And if Satan should ever cause you to forget, once you remember, do not stay sitting with the wrongdoers. (Surat al-An`am, 68)

As the above verses reveal, the term "wrongdoers" applies to all those who deny Allah's holy Books; who take deities besides Allah; those who, after witnessing the Messengers to be true, return to denial; and those who mock Allah's verses. Allah reveals many more characteristics of such people in the Qur'an. To sum up, "wrongdoing" is defined as all of the actions done by people and nations who reject His values and do not worship as He commands, who grow arrogant toward Allah and His religion, and who deny the Hereafter and the Day of Judgment.

It must not be forgotten that the Qur'an reveals that all of those people and nations that deny Allah will be punished severely in both this world and the next. Allah says:

As for those who do not believe, I will punish them with a harsh punishment in this world and the Hereafter. They will have no helpers. (Surah Al `Imran, 56)

This verse reveals that every transgressing nation will be punished in both worlds. Surat al-Kahf calls this time a "promised time." When the appointed time comes, all of the wrongdoers' strength and numbers will be destroyed and wiped out of existence, because this is Allah's law.

In addition, the Qur'an says that if a nation is to be destroyed, there will be an appointment between that nation's Messenger and the angels charged with carrying out this destruction. At this meeting, the angels and the Messenger will clarify the time of the catastrophe destined for that nation. The angels' visit to Prophet Lut (as) is an example of this.

Lut (as) invited his people to belief over a long period of time and advised them to reform and abandon their prohibited lifestyles. But his nation had made the denial of Allah's verses and immorality a way of life, and so continued to reject his calls and persist in their denial. Thus, they deserved the decree of punishment, and the angels informed Lut (as) of his people's imminent destruction. Their visit is related in the following verses:

When Our Messengers came to Lut, he was distressed on their account, feeling incapable of protecting them. They said: "Do not fear and do not grieve. We are going to rescue you and your family—except for your wife; she will be one of those who stay behind. We will bring down on the inhabitants of this city a devastating punishment from Heaven because of their deviance." (Surat al-`Ankabut, 33-34)

When the Messengers came to the family of Lut, he [Lut] said: "You are people we do not know." They said: "We have come to you with that about which they had doubts. We have brought you the truth, and we are certainly truthful men. Travel with your family in the dead of night, following behind with them in

front of you. None of you must look back. Go to where you are ordered." (Surat al-Hijr, 61-65)

Thus Allah's angels informed Lut (as) of the catastrophe during their visit and clarified its hour. For Lut's (as) nation, this hour was fixed at dawn:

By your life! They were wandering blindly in their drunkenness! So the Great Blast seized hold of them at the break of day. We turned the place completely upside down, and rained down upon them stones of hard-baked clay. There are certainly Signs in that for the discerning. (Surat al-Hijr, 72-75)

Dead Sea (*Bahr Lut* in Arabic, meaning Sea of Lut) and its vicinity, where Lut (as) and his nation are thought to have lived.

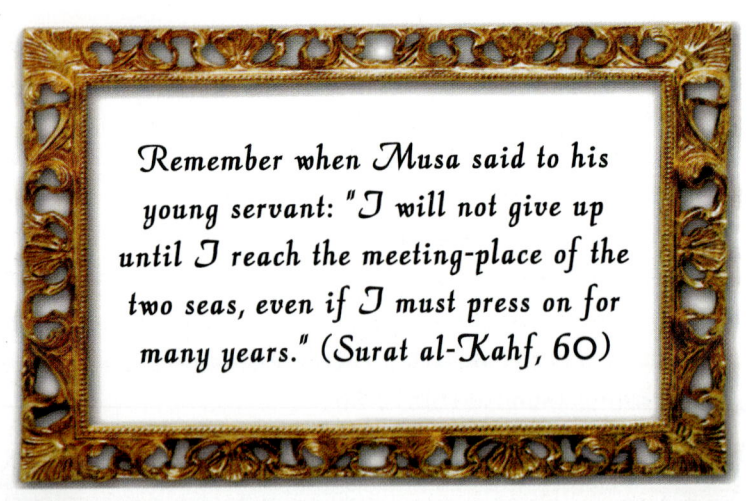

> *Remember when Musa said to his young servant: "I will not give up until I reach the meeting-place of the two seas, even if I must press on for many years." (Surat al-Kahf, 60)*

Here, "young" suggests that when doing something, one should seek the assistance of young people and work with them. Young people should be motivated to use their energy, dynamism, strength, ambition, and excitement for right action for Allah's good pleasure. Some of the verses speak of youth, and the following verse states that only some young people of his nation believed in Musa (as):

No one believed in Musa, except [some] offspring [i.e., youths] among his people, out of fear that Pharaoh and the elders would persecute them. Pharaoh was high and mighty in the land. He was one of the profligate. (Surah Yunus, 83)

Surat al-Kahf 60 refers to the meeting point toward which Musa (as) is traveling. Musa (as) knows that he will meet with someone and that this will take place at the "meeting-place of the two seas." This place could be any place on Earth that fits this description.

The term "even if I must press on for many years" indicates that the meeting place was definitely agreed upon, because Musa (as) intends to go to that particular place and not to any other, even if it takes him many years to reach it, for it cannot take place anywhere else. For this reason, Musa (as) will do his best to get there regardless of how long it will take. And, if need be, he will wait there.

> *But when they reached their meeting-place, they forgot their fish, which quickly burrowed its way into the sea.*
> *(Surat al-Kahf, 61)*

We understand from this verse that Musa (as) and his young servant had planned to eat fish. However, Allah made both of them forget it and allowed it, at this moment of opportunity, to escape into the water.

Now, someone cannot forget or remember something at will. Here, Allah made them forget the fish, for this forgetfulness was written in their destinies. This being the case, irrespective of how hard they try to remember, they cannot do so unless Allah wills it.

There are many reasons behind this forgetting. For example, Musa (as) has been told to come to this particular place to meet an important and blessed person, about whom more is revealed later on. To reach their destined meeting place, Musa (as) and his young servant travel for a long time. However, they need more detailed information about the exact location, because the area described as "where the two seas meet" is quite large. Without this detailed knowledge, they might have trouble finding this person. This is where one of the reasons for the fish's escape becomes apparent: It is a sign, because the fish pinpoints the exact location for this meeting.

In a wider sense, this verse points out the importance of pinpointing the exact location for any meeting. The meeting point in this case of

Musa (as) is a memorable one, defined by an important sign. Generally speaking, a meeting's exact location should be determined and make known in order to prevent difficulties and loss of time, and to make it easier for the people to meet.

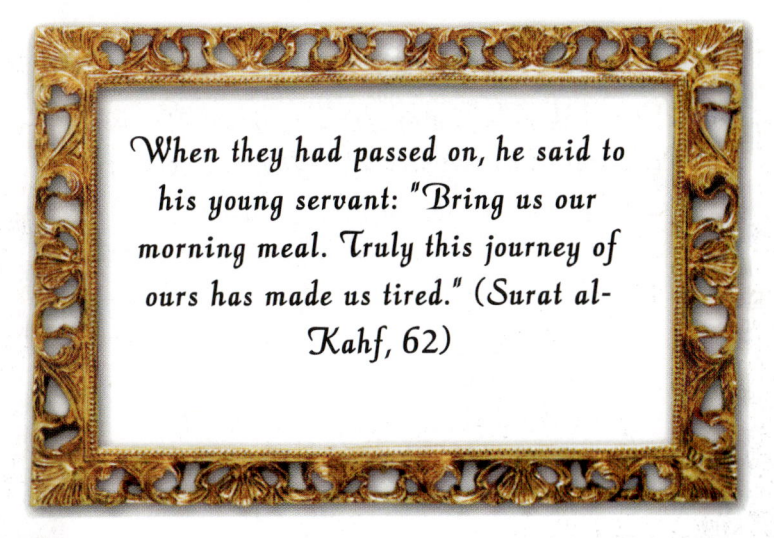

> *When they had passed on, he said to his young servant: "Bring us our morning meal. Truly this journey of ours has made us tired." (Surat al-Kahf, 62)*

This verse reveals that after Musa (as) and his young servant have passed the meeting point, they become tired and hungry. When they want to prepare the meal, they remember the fish and realize that they have left it behind. Allah makes them forget the fish and then, at the appropriate time, remember it, thereby pointing the meeting place out to them.

It is important that Allah chose the fish, for Musa (as) and his assistant would definitely remember it when, following their long journey, they would become tired and hungry and so look for it. As eating when hungry is a necessity for all human beings, it seems that Allah chose the fish to lead them to the meeting point.

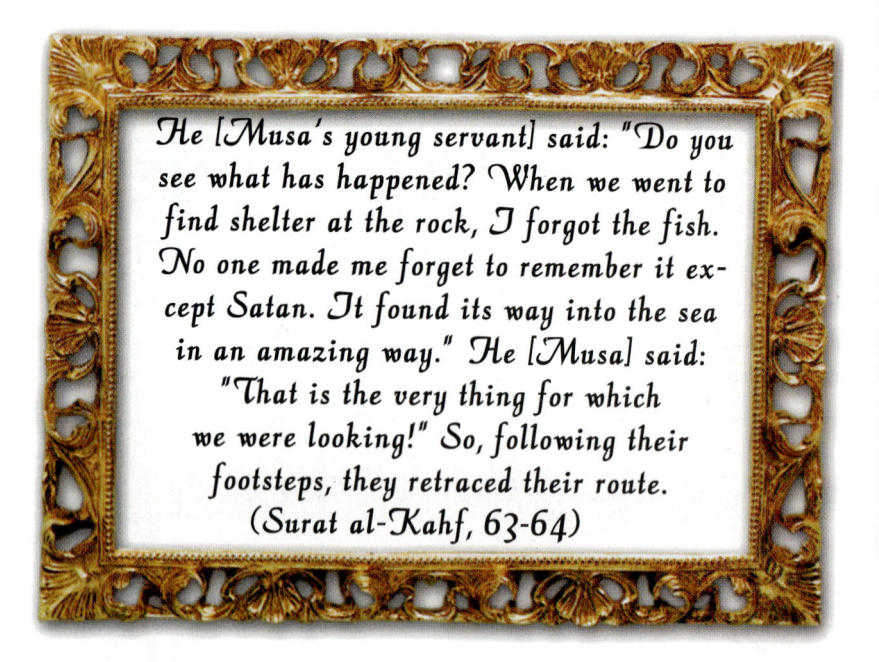

> He [Musa's young servant] said: "Do you see what has happened? When we went to find shelter at the rock, I forgot the fish. No one made me forget to remember it except Satan. It found its way into the sea in an amazing way." He [Musa] said: "That is the very thing for which we were looking!" So, following their footsteps, they retraced their route.
> (Surat al-Kahf, 63-64)

When Musa (as) and his young servant realize that they have left the fish behind, they also remember where they forgot it: a rocky area. This rocky place where the two seas meet is the place where Musa (as) is to meet the blessed person. Thanks to the fish, Musa (as) pinpoints the exact place for this meeting at which, it is supposed, he was to meet Khidhr (as). The fish, having fulfilled its purpose, disappears into the sea.

Also in the verse, Musa's servant states that Satan had made him forget about the fish. Satan's ability to make people forget is also mentioned in other verses, as follows:

> When you see people engrossed in mocking Our Signs, turn from them until they start to talk of other things. And if Satan should ever cause you to forget, once you remember, do not stay sitting with the wrongdoers. (Surat al-An`am, 68)
> He [Yusuf] said to the one of them he knew was saved: "Please

mention me when you are with your Lord," but Satan made him forget to remind his Lord, and so he stayed in prison for several years. (Surah Yusuf, 42)

It must be remembered here that Satan, by himself, has no power. Allah, the sole owner of all power and strength, gave Satan the power to cause

> ... All might belongs to Allah. He is the All-Hearing, the All-Knowing. Yes, indeed! Everyone in the heavens and everyone on Earth belongs to Allah... (Surah Yunus, 65-66)

people to forget. No being can do anything by his or her own willpower. Allah governs all, as the verse **"... There is no creature He does not hold by the forelock..."** (Surah Hud, 56) states, the actions of all living beings, including Satan. Therefore, in reality Allah, not Satan, made Musa (as) and his young servant forget the fish, for it was in their interest to do so and their destiny, determined by Allah, called for it.

In Surat al-Kahf 64, we understand that Musa (as) and his young servant realize that the place where they left the fish was the meeting place, and so "they retraced their route" to that very spot.

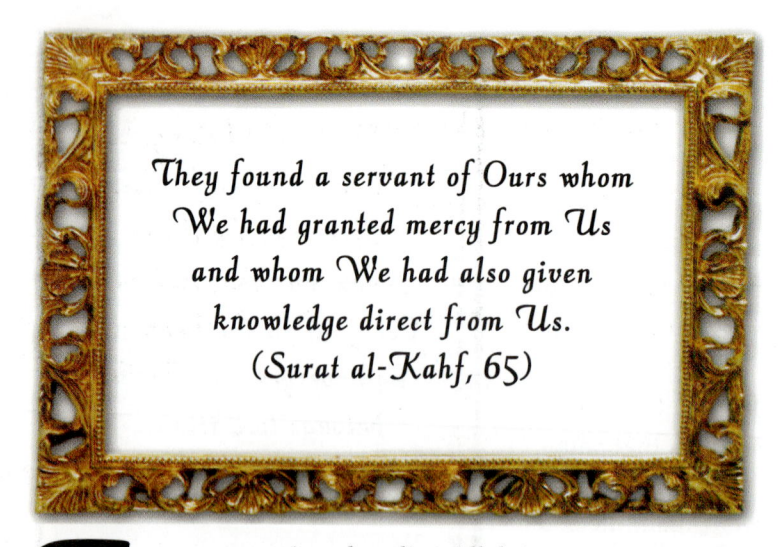

> They found a servant of Ours whom We had granted mercy from Us and whom We had also given knowledge direct from Us.
> (Surat al-Kahf, 65)

As was mentioned earlier, Allah is most compassionate, graceful, and merciful toward His servants. Musa (as) sets out to meet Khidr (as), someone to whom Allah has given mercy. Therefore, Allah's attributes of grace and mercy are reflected on him, which has caused him to receive a superior knowledge from Allah and to become one of His distinguished servants. In the coming parts of the narrative, we will see many examples of his superior sense of mercy.

Here, we are reminded of the concept of compassion in the Qur'an. As Allah states in "**... then to be one of those who believe and urge each other to steadfastness and compassion. Those are the Companions of the Right.**" (Surat al-Balad, 17-18), being compassionate is one of the main characteristics of a believer.

Believers who devote their lives to win Allah's good pleasure do their best to abide by His rules. Their sense of compassion is derived from their genuine faith, for they know that nothing happens unless Allah wills it and that they are dependent upon what He may grant them. This awareness makes them modest. People who are not modest cannot be truly compassionate because they are self-centered and thus value their interests and desires above all else. For this reason, they do not consider other people's needs and therefore, quite naturally, cannot feel compassion and mercy for them. Modest people, on the other hand, who have completely submitted to Allah will feel a deep sense of compassion for all other innocent creatures.

One reason why the believers are so determined to be compassionate is their desire to win Allah's good pleasure. As the verses say, Allah is the most Compassionate of the compassionate, and so the believers strive to live by compassion as much as possible: **"Were it not for Allah's favor to you and His mercy [you would have suffered many difficult situations] for Allah is All-Gentle, Most Merciful"** (Surat an-Nur, 20). Totally dependent upon Allah's grace and compassion, and earnestly seeking His mercy, they are as compassionate as they can be to other believers.

As with everything else, their compassion comes from the Qur'an's guidance. And because of this, they are compassionate only where Allah commands it and with those people whom He has destined to receive that compassion.

Sometimes the love and compassion felt for a fellow believer makes intervention and criticism inevitable, even though this may be hard or difficult to do. However, such actions can become necessary when wrong actions are committed, for the Qur'an commands Muslims to forbid the wrong. This is real compassion, too, for every Muslim can confront fellow Muslims in an attempt to prevent them from engaging in forbidden activities, but they cannot confront the reality of their brothers and sisters going to Hell. This is why Muslims encourage fellow Muslims to abide by the values pleasing to Allah and thus help them to win Paradise. If they did not consider their fellow Muslims' destiny in the Hereafter, and thereby simply observe what wrong acts other Muslims might do, how could they claim to have true compassion?

In: **"A Messenger has come to you from among yourselves. Your suffering is distressing to him; he is deeply concerned for you; he is gentle and merciful to the believers"** (Surat at-Tawba, 128), Allah describes our Prophet's (saas) sense of compassion. And, those who take guidance from this example of morality will be sensitive to one another's destiny in the Hereafter and behave as commanded by Allah.

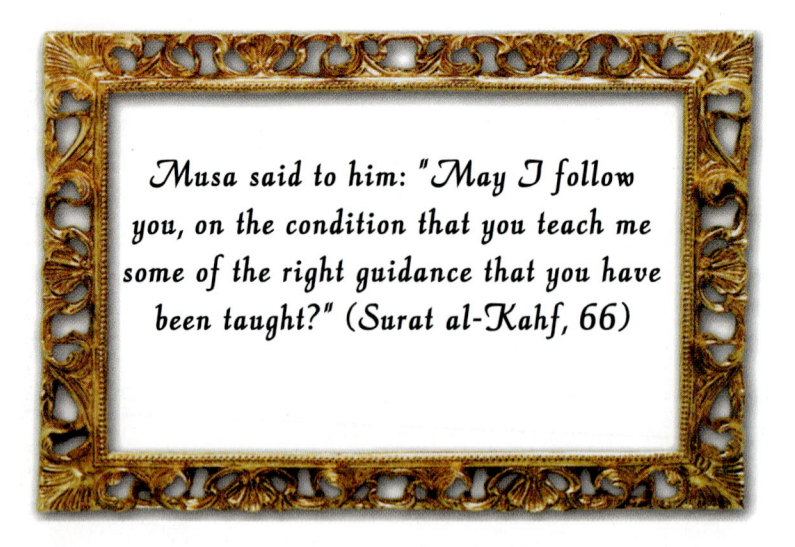

> *Musa said to him: "May I follow you, on the condition that you teach me some of the right guidance that you have been taught?" (Surat al-Kahf, 66)*

From this verse, we can deduce that Musa (as) has already received detailed information, through revelation, about whom he was to meet. He makes a real effort to go to the meeting point despite its distance from his current location, because, even if he encounters hardship while making his way there, he is certain that he will derive a great benefit from meeting with this very special person.

Then, as soon as they meet, Musa (as) recognizes him, as well as his superior character and knowledge, and asks to join him. This shows that he probably already knew that this special person had been taught much superior knowledge (Allah knows best). It is also probable that he received a revelation that this person was on the righteous path and was a guide for it, and that he should join him and learn from him for those very reasons (Allah knows best).

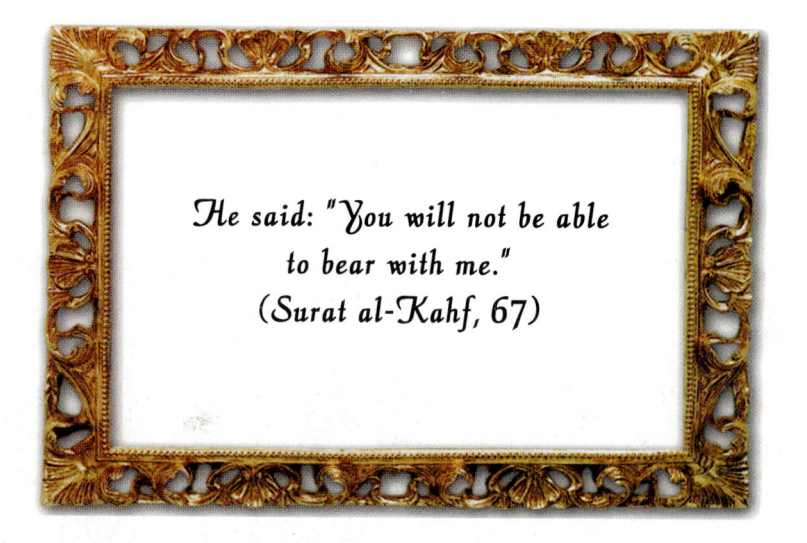

> *He said: "You will not be able to bear with me."*
> *(Surat al-Kahf, 67)*

As we understand from the verses, Khidr (as) also has detailed information about Musa (as). Moreover, it is possible to deduce that Khidr (as) knows things about the future because Allah has informed him of them.

Upon hearing Musa's (as) request, Khidr (as) responds straight away that Musa (as) is not patient enough to travel with him. Why would he say such a thing, before anything happened, before even seeing how Musa (as) would behave? The reason for this is that Khidr (as) knows part of the future (Allah knows best).

Such knowledge indicates that everything happens according to Allah's will, because only He gives such knowledge to his chosen few, and only as much of it as He wills. Thus, Khidr (as) could only reveal such knowledge of the Unseen by Allah's will.

Everything that will happen to Musa (as) is, as stated earlier, already concluded, and every moment thereof is known in Allah's presence, for He has written it in destiny. This is evidence that people will experience only the destiny that Allah has written for them. Another verse also emphasizes that believers must submit to Allah and their destiny, and trust

Him, as follows:

> Say: "I possess no power to harm or help myself, except as Allah wills. Every nation has an appointed time. When their appointed time comes, they cannot delay it a single hour or bring it forward." (Surah Yunus, 49)

> *"How indeed could you bear with patience something you have not encompassed in your knowledge?"*
> (Surat al-Kahf, 68)

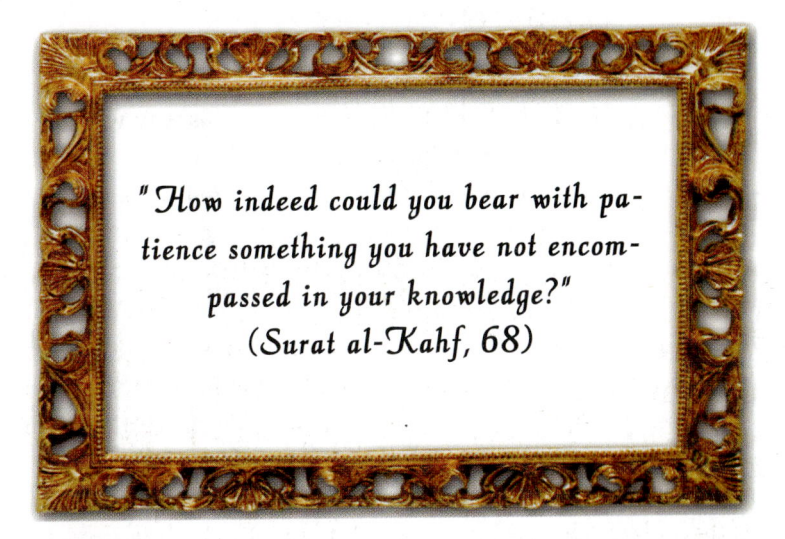

Many troubling, pleasing, and joyful things can happen to people in the course of a day. However, because most people do not think of Allah and the fact that He has already written everything in destiny, they try to explain whatever happens to them as "luck" and "coincidence." However, this prevents them from seeing things in the light of goodness and from drawing beneficial conclusions. For this reason, they become troubled, sad, and unhappy. This is a major difference between the believers and the unbelievers, because the believers are aware that everything is created by Allah's will and for their ultimate good.

Those who have a deep understanding of this reality succeed in being content and seeing the hidden beauty and ultimate good behind everything, irrespective of their position in this world. Allah has created everything that we will ever experience, regardless of whether we consider them good or bad, with a subtle plan and with His endless wisdom and intelligence. He controls all of life, for He is the sole Governor all all that exists. Allah creates everything in a perfect and matchless form, with wisdom and beauty. Therefore, humanity must recognize and appreciate this perfection and try to see the wisdom and goodness in everything knowing that Allah's infinite knowledge creates only the most faultless results. Those who believe in Allah, measure everything with an eye for goodness, and interpret things in this way will always find goodness and beauty both in this world and the next.

Allah's intellect is unlimited; humanity's is limited. Given this reality, people can deal only with the visible side of things and interpret them according to their own understanding. Therefore, they might interpret something that, in reality, is full of goodness and beauty as negative and unfortunate, and vice versa. In such situations, believers need to submit to Allah's infinite knowledge and wisdom and look at things from the perspective of goodness in order to see the truth, because everything that appears to be negative is, for the believers, "a lesson in destiny." Allah says in one verse:

> ... it may be that you hate something when it is good for you, and it may be that you love something when it is bad for you. Allah knows, and you do not know. (Surat al-Baqara, 216)

Believers know that whatever happens to them, even if it appears to be really bad at the time, is created by Allah to try them. As people who submit to Him, they always display good character. On the other hand, those who do not comprehend destiny's reality are hopeless and suffer at every turn.

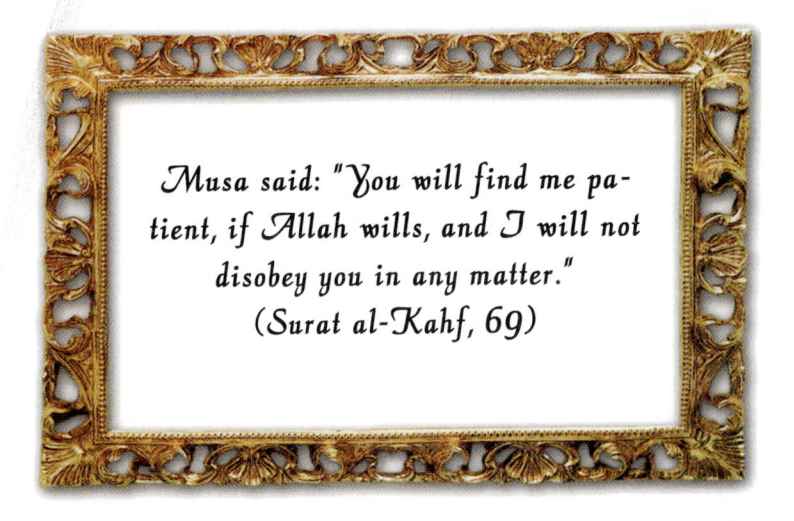

> *Musa said: "You will find me patient, if Allah wills, and I will not disobey you in any matter."*
> *(Surat al-Kahf, 69)*

As we can see in the verse, Musa (as) responds immediately in a Muslim way by saying "In sha' Allah" (if Allah wills). This expression shows the believers' submission to Allah, that they understand how destiny works and are aware that only Allah can grant them success.

As we mentioned in the explanation of Surat al-Kahf 23-24 above, it is Allah's command not to say "I will do this tomorrow," but to say "if Allah wills."

Through this answer, Musa (as) draws our attention to the importance of saying "In sha' Allah" before beginning something, reaching a decision, and planning something for tomorrow, because, ultimately, only Allah bestows success and the necessary capabilities to achieve it. It is essential for Muslims to remember this great truth: Only Allah knows and governs everything that occurs in the universe.

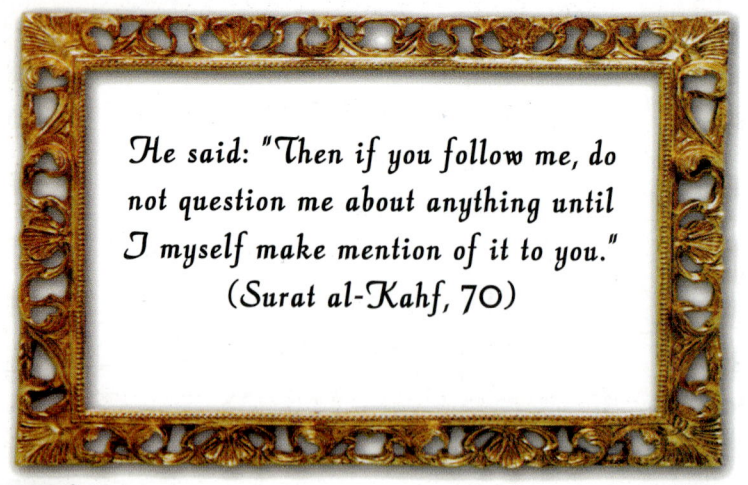

> He said: "Then if you follow me, do not question me about anything until I myself make mention of it to you."
> (Surat al-Kahf, 70)

The narrative of Musa (as) and Khidhr (as) re-emphasizes the importance of obeying the Prophets and Messengers. Believers must pay attention by showing strict respect in their allegiance.

In connection with this, people must see the wisdom and goodness in the actions of the Messenger to whom they have given their allegiance. They must expect goodness in everything that the Messenger does and, if they cannot see the inherent wisdom, must wait patiently and respectfully for its explanation. Believers must not upset the Messenger by asking unnecessary questions or indulging their curiosity.

If the underlying wisdom of the words or actions is not immediately apparent, Muslims must wait respectfully for Allah's Messenger or chosen one to explain it. Those who adopt this perspective will realize immediately that the word or action was appropriate and recognize their mistaken initial response. The verses say that if the person to whom allegiance is given feels the need to explain the wisdom behind the action, decisions, and words, he will do so. For instance, Khidhr (as) says: "**...until I myself make mention of it to you**" thus indicating that he will explain the underlying wisdom at the appropriate time.

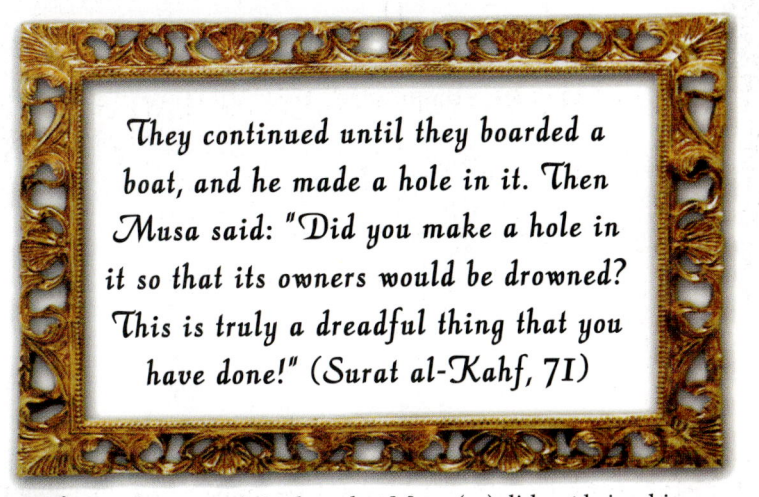

> *They continued until they boarded a boat, and he made a hole in it. Then Musa said: "Did you make a hole in it so that its owners would be drowned? This is truly a dreadful thing that you have done!"* (Surat al-Kahf, 71)

From this verse, it is clear that Musa (as) did not bring his young servant along on this journey. There could be a number of good reasons for this, such as to emphasize the importance of one-to-one education, which is the best form of education. People trying to learn in a crowded environment easily lose their concentration and find it hard to refocus. Even when there are three people, one is easily distracted and finds it hard to concentrate. For this reason, the Qur'an hints at one-to-one education, for such a method makes it easy to concentrate and pay attention. Moreover, such direct communication with the instructor enables the student to learn more efficiently. This is why the benefits of private education, recognized around the world, are important.

Another matter is mentioned: Musa knows Khidhr's (as) value and that he is commanded to do much good.

This situation, like all others, takes place in destiny. Khidhr (as) had said that Musa (as) would become impatient, and thus one part of the knowledge of the future given to him was fulfilled. On the other hand, Musa (as) asks the question because it is written in his destiny. This is called a "zallah" (a slip or error made by a Prophet or Messenger). Such mistakes are part of the Prophets' and Messengers' destinies, because they lead ultimately to goodness and wisdom. By these verses, Allah informs us that such mistakes, whose time and place are known in destiny, can occur.

"... they boarded a boat, and he made a hole in it..."
(Surat al-Kahf, 71)

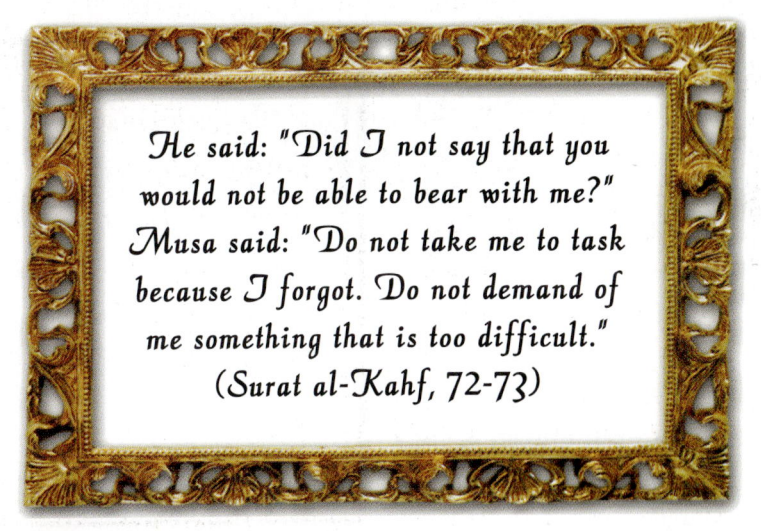

> *He said: "Did I not say that you would not be able to bear with me?" Musa said: "Do not take me to task because I forgot. Do not demand of me something that is too difficult."*
> *(Surat al-Kahf, 72-73)*

Notice the certainty in Khidhr's (as) words when he reveals his knowledge of future events: that Musa (as) will not have the necessary patience to travel with him.

Surat al-Kahf 73 makes it clear that everything happens by Allah's will. People cannot speak or prevent others from speaking by their own will, for only Allah inspires them and gives them speech. Moreover, He can make every being, whether living or nonliving, say whatever He wills them to say. The Qur'an reveals that on the Day of Judgment, Allah will give speech to a person's ears, eyes, and even the skin, as follows:

> When they reach it, their hearing, sight, and skin will testify against them concerning what they did. They will ask their skins: "Why did you testify against us?" and they will reply: "Allah gave us speech, as He has given speech to everything. He created you in the first place, and you will be returned to Him. You did not think to shield yourselves from your hearing, sight, and skin testifying against you, and you thought that Allah would never know much of what you did." (Surah Fussilat, 20-22)

In other verses, our Lord reveals that unless He gives permission, no being can find the power to speak:

> Lord of the heavens and Earth and everything between them, the All-Merciful. They will not have the power to speak to Him. On the Day when the Spirit and the angels stand in ranks, no one will speak, except for him who is authorized by the All-Merciful and says what is right. (Surat an-Naba', 37-38)

> *We have created all things with predestination. Our command is only one word, like the blinking of an eye. (Surat al-Qamar, 49-50)*

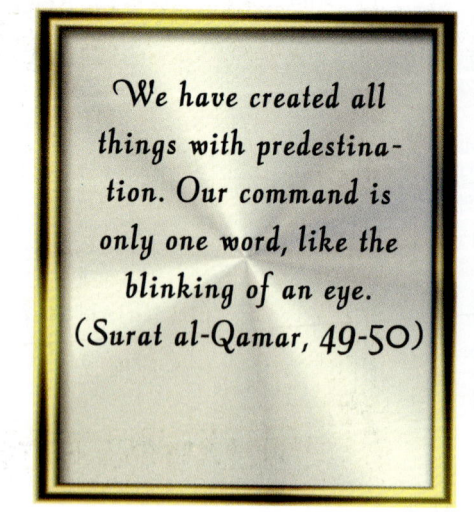

As we mentioned earlier, Allah creates forgetting as well as remembering, and rules over all of our mental activities, be they past, present, or future. It was written in Musa's (as) destiny that he would forget and that he would ask a question that he was not supposed to. No one can gain control over his or her brain and prevent forgetfulness or saying the words that have been written in his or her destiny. Allah makes people forget whatever and whenever He wills them to. He can take away all memory or, if He wills, place within one's memory the knowledge of things not known before. All of these happen by His will.

From Musa's (as) request "do not demand of me something that is too difficult," we understand that he does not want his education to be terminated.

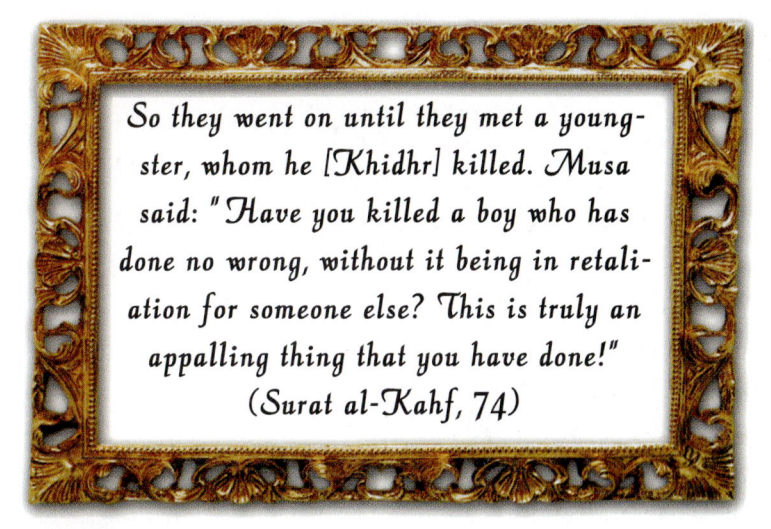

> *So they went on until they met a youngster, whom he [Khidhr] killed. Musa said: "Have you killed a boy who has done no wrong, without it being in retaliation for someone else? This is truly an appalling thing that you have done!"*
> *(Surat al-Kahf, 74)*

Although he promises not to ask questions, Musa (as) cannot overcome his destiny and stop himself from asking these questions. In spite of knowing that Khidhr (as) acts according to Allah's command, knowing that he has deep knowledge, and saying that he is his disciple, Musa (as) reacts to what Khidhr (as) does. Therefore, another "zallah" occurs.

But we must not forget that only Allah gives and takes life. Thus, as revealed in the following verse, no one can kill another person unless Allah wills it, for:

> **You did not kill them; it was Allah Who killed them. And you did not throw, when you threw; it was Allah Who threw, so He might test the believers with this excellent trial from Him. Allah is All-Hearing, All-Knowing. (Surat al-Anfal, 17)**

Khidhr (as) is a true servant of Allah and acts only according to His order and will. Everything he does and says conforms to His will. Besides, no one can know whether or not this life is in retaliation for another, or whether or not the child who gets killed is pure, unless Allah wills it. However, Musa (as) speaks these words because Allah wills him to do so and because it is written in his destiny.

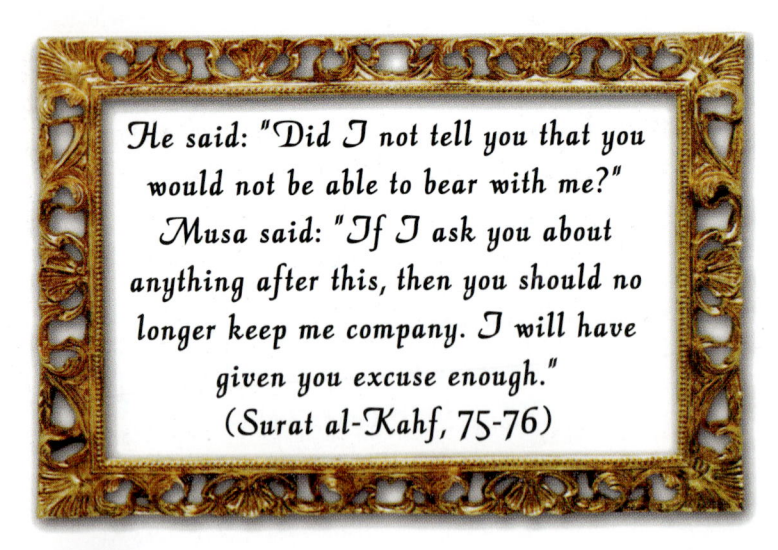

> *He said: "Did I not tell you that you would not be able to bear with me?" Musa said: "If I ask you about anything after this, then you should no longer keep me company. I will have given you excuse enough."*
> *(Surat al-Kahf, 75-76)*

As we also see in this narrative, Allah gives and removes, as He wills, the power to His servants to be patient. This laudable aspect of the believers is mentioned in many verses, along with the fact that only Allah gives patience. For instance, Talut's (as) army asked Allah for patience in war, as follows:

> **When they came out against Jalut and his troops, they said: "Our Lord, pour down steadfastness upon us, make our feet firm, and help us against this unbelieving people." (Surat al-Baqara, 250)**

Surat al-Kahf 76 reveals that Musa (as) is aware of Khidhr's (as) displeasure. In spite of Khidhr's (as) assertions that Musa (as) would become impatient, Musa (as) insists that he would be patient. However, after two failures to keep his promise, he also wants to resolve the situation and so uses a new strategy of persuasion to convince Khidhr (as) not to terminate this process of education and admonition. With this goal in mind, Musa (as) gives him more assurances and guarantees so that he may prolong and continue this education for as long as possible.

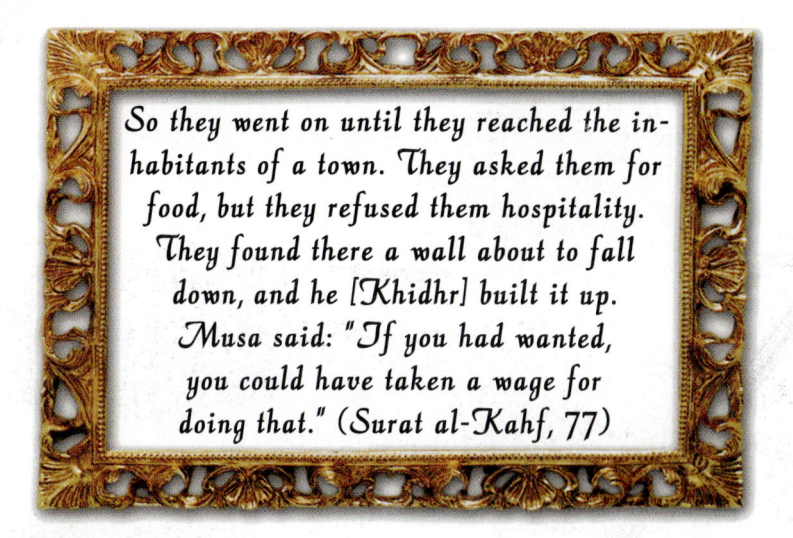

> *So they went on until they reached the inhabitants of a town. They asked them for food, but they refused them hospitality. They found there a wall about to fall down, and he [Khidhr] built it up. Musa said: "If you had wanted, you could have taken a wage for doing that." (Surat al-Kahf, 77)*

Continuing their journey, Musa (as) and Khidhr (as) entered a town. However, given that they were not received favorably or offered food and shelter, we understand that their journey had been a difficult one.

In this verse, Allah could be pointing to the validity of suffering any hardship in the quest for truth and beneficial knowledge. Musa (as) is prepared to suffer any hardship in order to be with Khidhr (as), so that he can benefit from his wisdom and reminders. This is also a reminder for all people, for Muslims should show the same determination and strength of character in similar situations.

The verse also indicates that Khidhr (as) was particularly talented, capable and fast-acting. This can be deduced from the fact that he was able to damage the boat without anyone noticing what he was doing, and also by the quick action he took in building a sturdy wall. Allah indicates his fast decision-taking and experience by saying "They found there a wall about to fall down, and he built it up." Khidhr (as) also displayed great deftness when he made the hole in the boat, since he did so in such a way that the boat was not completely destroyed, but only ren-

SIGNS OF THE END TIMES IN SURAT AL-KAHF

... They found there a wall about to fall down and he built it up...
(Surat al-Kahf, 77)

> Say: "My prayer and my rites, my living and my dying, are for Allah alone, the Lord of all the worlds."
> (Surat al-An`am, 162)

dered unusable. He was thus very familiar with the materials needed to construct a boat and a wall.

Musa (as) now asks his third and last question to Khidhr (as), who already knows, by the wisdom granted to him by Allah, whether or not to seek a wage for his work. Such a practice is not obligatory, because it depends upon the situation and circumstances. As believers do everything for Allah's good pleasure, their labor can be paid work or freely donated work. If it is paid, the money is used to win His good pleasure yet again. It is the person's individual decision whether or not to seek payment in the light of the Prophets' and Messengers' knowledge and Allah's command.

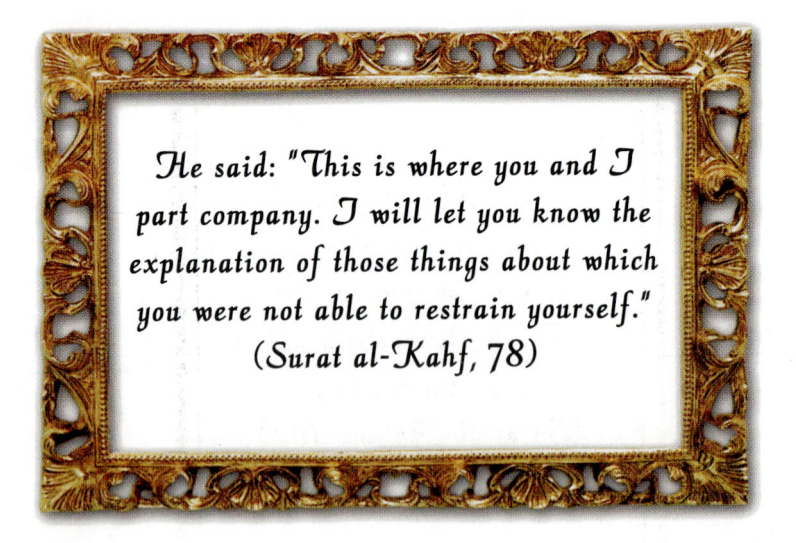

> He said: "This is where you and I part company. I will let you know the explanation of those things about which you were not able to restrain yourself."
> (Surat al-Kahf, 78)

This last question of Musa (as) indicates that it is time for them to part company, for Allah has willed Musa (as) to state this condition when he earlier said: "If I ask you about anything after this, then you should no longer keep me company". Khidhr (as) declares this reason by stating that Musa (as) could not restrain himself due to his not being informed by Allah of the underlying reasons, and that he would now explain. If he had explained these reasons to Musa (as), the latter would have been able to be patient with him. In other words, we should expect ultimate goodness and wisdom in the things that the Prophets or the chosen ones do not explain.

All of the things that Musa (as) and Khidhr (as) experienced on their journey had been written in their destinies and determined by Allah. Nothing could have happened in a different way. The moment of parting, just like the timing and location of their meeting, were all known in Allah's presence, for He had written them in their destinies in the timeless past.

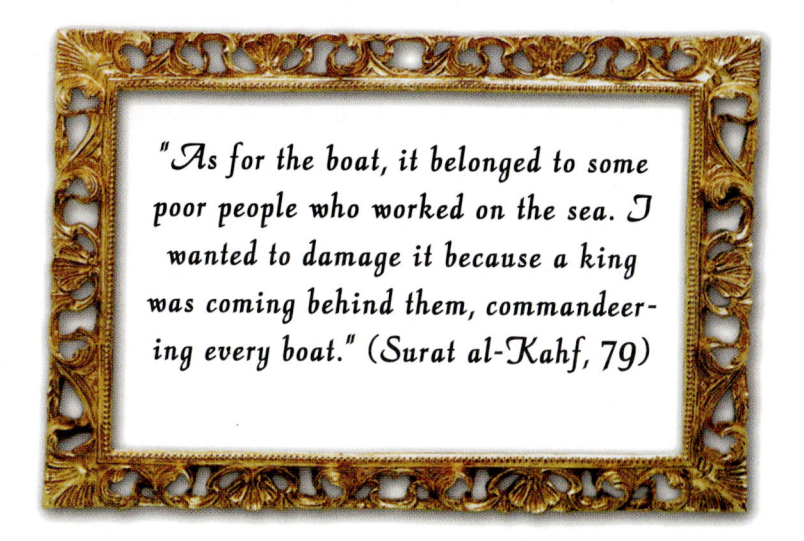

> "As for the boat, it belonged to some poor people who worked on the sea. I wanted to damage it because a king was coming behind them, commandeering every boat." (Surat al-Kahf, 79)

As the verse reveals, now that the time for parting company has come, Khidhr (as) explains his actions. In the first event, he made a hole in the boat for several good reasons.

Before revealing the reasons for Khidhr's (as) actions, it is appropriate to reflect upon his compassionate character. Khidhr (as) aided the destitute, for he wanted to prevent further hardship for them and their suffering from the oppressors' actions. This shows his sympathy for the poor and needy, as well as his compassionate and loving character. Allah's attributes of grace and mercy are focused on him. This is a distinguishing factor between the believers and the unbelievers, for Allah says:

What will convey to you what the steep ascent is? It is freeing a slave or feeding on a day of hunger an orphaned relative or a poor man in the dust; then to be one of those who believe and urge each other to steadfastness and compassion. Those are the Companions of the Right. (Surat al-Balad, 12-18)

Compassion, sympathy for the believers, and love are the most defining characteristics of Allah's Prophets and Messengers. Khidhr (as), a Messenger graced by Allah, is compassionate and loving, just like all

Messengers, and has received, by Allah's will, superior knowledge. For this reason, he wanted to help the needy people by making a hole in the boat so that it would appear useless and not be confiscated by the oppressors.

Khidhr's (as) reason, foresight, wisdom, and sensibility is noticeable immediately, for he damaged it in a way that it could be repaired easily and then used again. Thus the people seeking to confiscate it will see the damage and change their mind about taking it. Once this danger has passed, the boat can be repaired easily and put back into service.

Another noticeable matter is the existence of an oppressive regime ruling over a poor people. It could have been a dictatorship. The leaders of this despotic regime could be confiscating the believers' property without justification, for which reason the believers might have been facing hardship and finding it difficult to escape the situation.

Confiscating the people's property without a just reason was common in despotic feudal and monarchical regimes of the past, and in the fascist and communist regimes of today. These totalitarian regimes took the property of defenseless people and left them destitute and hungry. Thus, this example shows that oppressive regimes have plagued humanity since the beginning of human history.

Children condemned to starve under Stalin's rule.

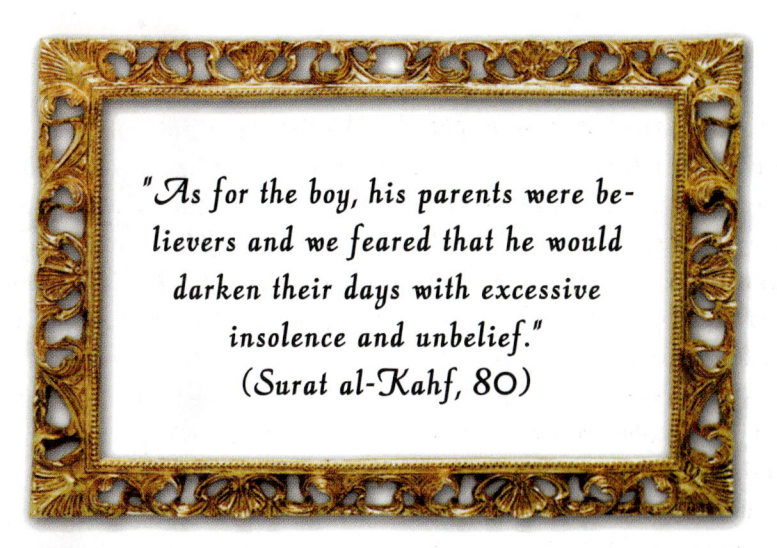

> *"As for the boy, his parents were believers and we feared that he would darken their days with excessive insolence and unbelief."*
> *(Surat al-Kahf, 80)*

The verse reveals that the boy's parents were believers. In other words, in those days true religion existed. When Khidhr (as) took the child's life, it was Allah's will, for He had written the child's time and place of death in his destiny. Allah reminds people of this reality, as follows: **"He created you from clay and then decreed a fixed term, and another fixed term is specified with Him..."** (Surat al-An`am, 2). As the Qur'an also says, angels take the life of every human being:

> **If only you could see when the angels take back those who were unbelievers at their death, beating their faces and their backs [saying]: "Taste the punishment of the Burning!" (Surat al-Anfal, 50)**

However, the angles are just a means, for in reality only Allah takes lives. Ibrahim's (as) wholehearted prayer is given as an example:

> **He Who created me and guides me; He Who gives me food and gives me drink; and when I am ill, it is He Who heals me; He Who will cause my death, then give me life; He Who I sincerely hope will forgive my mistakes on the Day of Reckoning. My**

Lord, give me right judgment and unite me with the righteous. (Surat ash-Shu'ara', 78-83)

Allah willed for Khidhr (as) to take this child's life, but He could have done it through somebody else. The boy could have been killed in an accident, by a heart attack, or by falling and sustaining a deadly head injury. As Allah makes clear: "**... When their specified time arrives, they cannot delay it for a single hour, nor can they bring it forward**" (Surat an-Nahl, 61). In this case, Allah determined that the angels would be the invisible agents and that Khidhr (as) would be the visible agent of this death, whereby Khidhr (as) appeared to be taking the child's life. In reality, Khidhr (as) acts by the revelation he receives from Allah, and certainly does not act against His orders. Also, he cannot act by his own will unless Allah wills so. Allah chose him to be the means for this task.

The same is true for the life that Musa (as) took, as related below:

He entered the city at a time when its inhabitants were unaware, and found two men fighting there—one from his party and the other from his enemy. The one from his party asked for his support against the other from his enemy. So Musa hit him, dealing him a fatal blow. He said: "This is part of Satan's handiwork. He truly is an outright and misleading enemy." He said: "My Lord, I have wronged myself. Forgive me." So He forgave him. He is the Ever-Forgiving, the Most Merciful. (Surat al-Qasas, 15-16)

Musa (as) intervened in a fight to help someone, but unintentionally killed the other person. Here again, he was only the means. Although that man died at Musa's (as) hands, Musa (as) was no more than the visible cause, and the angels were the invisible agents. Allah states in the Qur'an that it is the angels' duty to take lives, although ultimately it is only Allah Who does so.

No matter how much people resist, wherever they look for refuge or wherever they flee, everyone is always proceeding toward his or her death. Allah reminds us that no one can escape death: " **Say, 'Even if you had been inside your homes, those people for whom killing was** decreed would have gone out to their place of death.' So that Allah might test what is in your breasts and purge what is in your hearts. Allah knows the contents of your hearts." (Surah Al 'Imran, 154).

No person is given a choice in this matter, and there is no way to escape it. When the appointed time for death comes, they cannot avoid the angels of death. As the Qur'an states clearly, each person will die at his or her destined time and place:

Say: "Death, from which you are fleeing, will certainly catch up with you. Then you will be returned to the Knower of the Unseen and the Visible, and He will inform you about what you did." (Surat al-Jumu`a, 8)

Wherever you are, death will catch up with you, even if you are in impregnable fortresses… (Surat an-Nisa', 78)

Khidhr (as) kills a child, about whom he has certain knowledge that his destiny is to become an unbeliever. He means to prevent the child from making his family and environment miserable, and drowning in a sea of sin, and thus takes preventive action.

The people who died in this train wreck probably had never pondered the meaning of the word "death" up until that point.

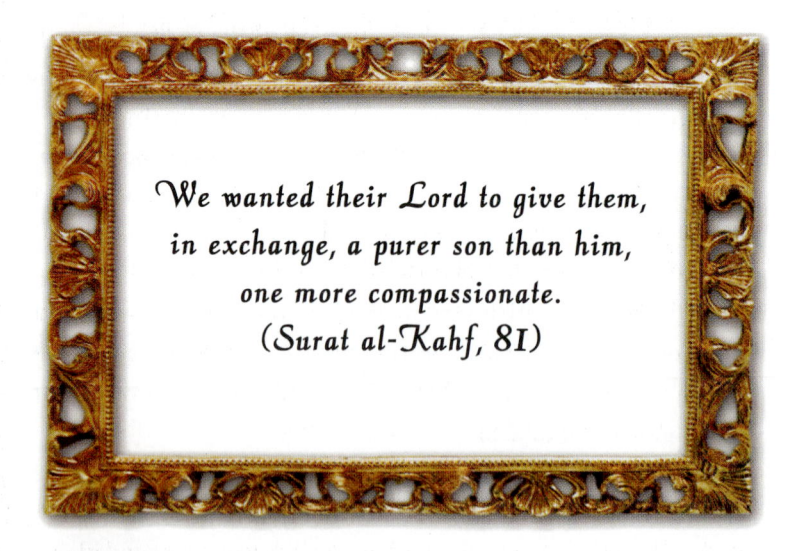

> *We wanted their Lord to give them, in exchange, a purer son than him, one more compassionate.*
> (Surat al-Kahf, 81)

Many people find it hard to see the reason and goodness behind a family member's death, and death in general. However, as with everything else, there is much wisdom and goodness in this. One of these is stated to be "... giving them in exchange a purer son than him, one more compassionate." In this verse, Allah warns those who renounce their faith that He will replace them with more sincere believers:

> **O you who believe. If any of you renounce your religion, Allah will bring forward a people whom He loves and who love Him, humble to the believers, fierce to the unbelievers, who strive in the Way of Allah and do not fear the blame of any censurer. That is the unbounded favor of Allah, which He gives to whoever He wills. Allah is Boundless, All-Knowing. (Surat al-Ma'ida, 54)**
>
> **Your Lord is the Rich Beyond Need, the Possessor of Mercy. If He willed, He could remove you and replace you with anything else He willed, just as He produced you from the descendants of another people. (Surat al-An`am, 133)**

KHIDHR'S (AS) GOOD MORALS

Pondering this account of Khidhr (as) and Musa (as) enables us to realize that every verse contains messages about Khidhr's (as) character, which were explored in detail in the previous pages. Here, we list and summarize them in one place, along with supporting evidence, in order to consider his character traits.

Khidhr (as) instantly obeys all of Allah's orders

His most noticeable characteristic in Surat al-Kahf is his diligence in obeying Allah's order, for he does it immediately upon receiving revelation.

Khidhr's (as) compassion and mercy

His aiding the poor, the orphans, and the vulnerable is the clearest evidence of this.

Khidhr's (as) dedication to the believers and his helpfulness

He helps a believer mother and father because of his dedication to the believers.

Khidhr's (as) intellect, insight, and foresight

His preventive actions and the traps he set for the unbelievers prove his intelligence and foresight.

Khidhr's (as) trust in Allah

He is not affected by any hardship he faces, for he knows that whatever happens does so according to the destiny determined in Allah's presence.

Khidhr's (as) character traits are revealed to us through the verses of the Qur'an. Allah has bestowed His grace upon him, as well as given him wisdom, superior knowledge, and immaculate character. Throughout his time with Musa (as), Khidhr (as) educated him in the best way and advised him through words and deeds. Khidhr (as) set an example for him by displaying his patience, determination, helpfulness and maturity, and taught him to seek the inherent wisdom in all that is experienced.

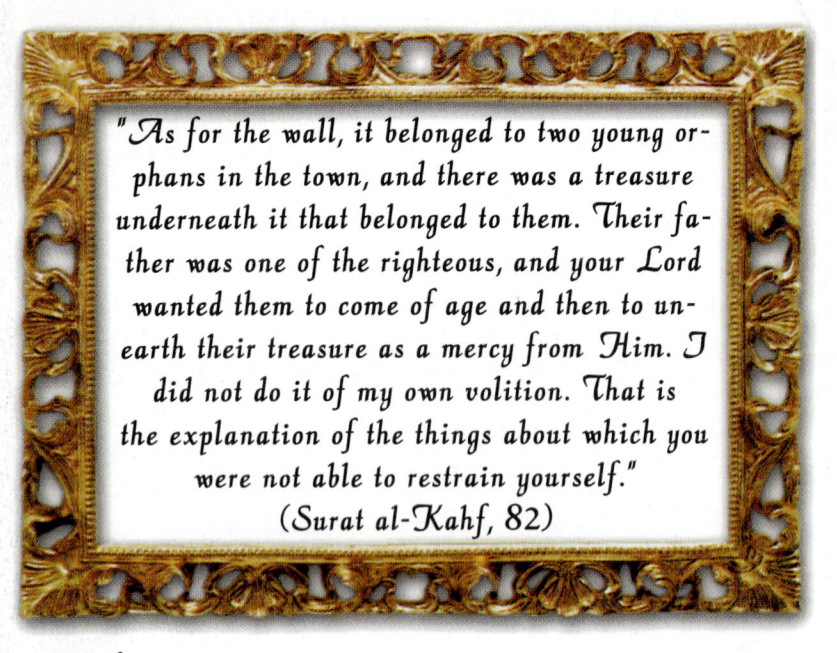

> *"As for the wall, it belonged to two young orphans in the town, and there was a treasure underneath it that belonged to them. Their father was one of the righteous, and your Lord wanted them to come of age and then to unearth their treasure as a mercy from Him. I did not do it of my own volition. That is the explanation of the things about which you were not able to restrain yourself."*
> (Surat al-Kahf, 82)

The last wisdom behind his action, as explained by Khidhr (as), has to do with the orphans' wall. The verse discusses caring for the orphans of faithful parents. As we read elsewhere:

... **They will ask you about the property of orphans. Say: "Managing it in their best interests is best." If you mix your property with theirs, they are your brothers. Allah knows one who plunders from one who improves. If Allah had wanted, He could have been hard on you. Allah is Almighty, All-Wise.** (Surat al-Baqara, 220)

The believers, as pointed out here, take the utmost care to protect the orphans' rights and ensure their moral education, because of their good character and strict adherence to Allah's commands and recommendations. Muslims are generous to orphans: **"Any wealth you give away should go to your parents and relatives, to orphans and the very poor, and travellers. Whatever good you do, Allah knows it"** (Surat al-

Baqara, 215). Even if the Muslims are in need, they give priority to these other people: **"They give food, despite their love for it, to the poor, orphans, and captives"** (Surat al-Insan, 8). Allah warns those who wrong orphans, as follows:

> **People who consume the orphan's property wrongfully consume nothing in their bellies except fire. They will roast in a Searing Blaze. (Surat an-Nisa', 10)**

As the morals of Islam recommend, Khidhr (as) considers the orphans' welfare and invests in their future. If he had not restored the wall, it would have collapsed and revealed the treasure belonging to their father. As a result, they would have lost their treasure to the wrongdoers. Khidhr (as) repairs the wall so that it will last until the children grow up, thus keeping the treasure concealed so that they might benefit from it in the future, as their father had intended.

As we mentioned earlier, Khidhr's (as) compassion and devotion to orphans and the poor reflects Allah's attribute of compassion. By repairing the wall, Khidhr (as) points out the importance of taking precautions to protect the property of children. Khidhr (as) trusts Allah and builds a solid wall that will remain for as long as Allah wills.

Furthermore, the wall's collapse could have caused great injury or damage to passers-by, the surrounding plant and animal life, or be the apparent cause of someone's death. In addition, this verse could be indicating the importance of doing a professional job when restoring damaged walls.

In the verse, Khidhr (as) says: **"I did not do it by my own volition."** In other words, he is aware that Allah does everything within its predetermined destiny, and makes clear thereby, and in the best possible way, that none of his actions are the result of his own decision.

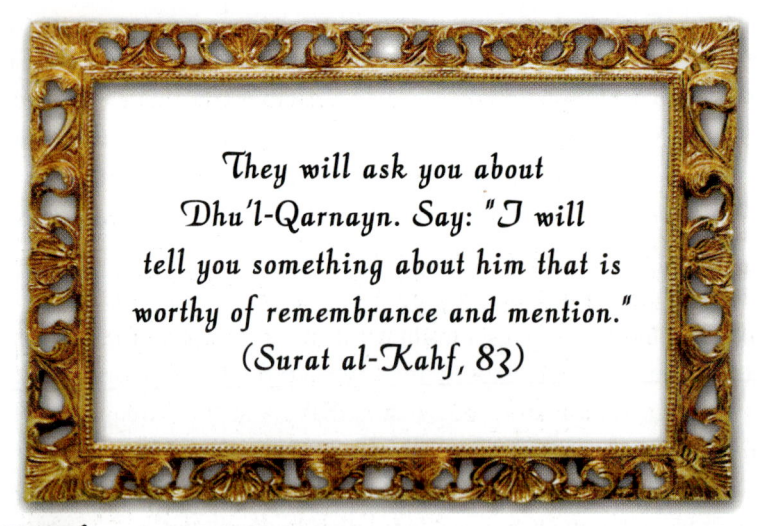

> *They will ask you about Dhu'l-Qarnayn. Say: "I will tell you something about him that is worthy of remembrance and mention."* (Surat al-Kahf, 83)

Throughout history, many scholars have interpreted the narrative of Dhu'l-Qarnayn (as) in many ways. The verse says that it was revealed as a reminder to believers and is connected with the revelations of hidden meanings and reasons.

The Qur'an uses the narrative of Dhu'l-Qarnayn (as) to give more examples of Islamic values for the benefit of the believers, and relates events from which they can learn lessons. Their meanings are so clear and easily understandable that they can be taken literally and reflected upon in order to comprehend and learn. As Allah says:

> **Alif Lam Ra. A Book whose verses are perfected and then presented in detail from One Who is All-Wise, All-Aware. (Surah Hud, 1)**

Believers need to read the Qur'an with a pure heart and the intention to learn, for Allah states in Surat al-Hajj 16 that the verses are "Clear Signs." Other verses on this subject are the following:

> **The month of Ramadan is the one in which the Qur'an was sent down as guidance for mankind, with Clear Signs containing guidance and discrimination… (Surat al-Baqara, 185)**

... A Light has come to you from Allah, and a Clear Book. By it, Allah guides those who follow what pleases Him to the ways of Peace. He will bring them from the darkness to the light by His permission, and guide them to a straight path. (Surat al-Ma'ida, 15-16)

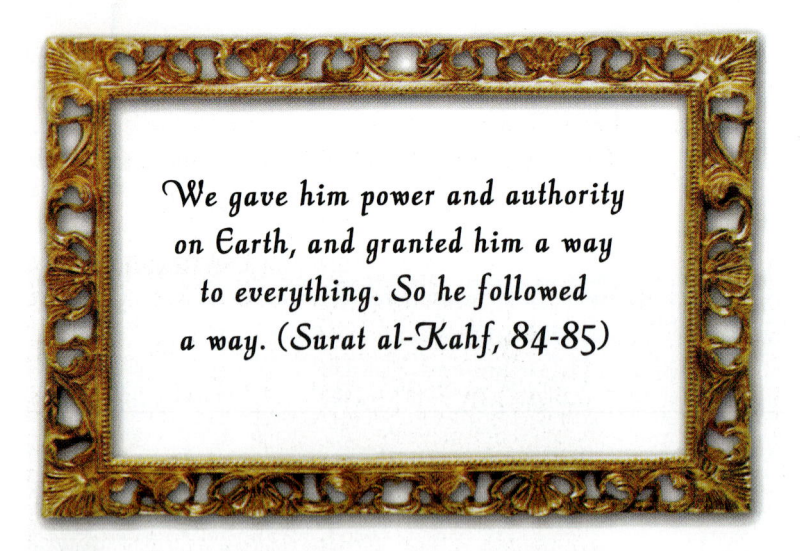

> *We gave him power and authority on Earth, and granted him a way to everything. So he followed a way. (Surat al-Kahf, 84-85)*

This verse mentions power and authority. A nation's government must be powerful in politics, economics, and defense. If the government is weak, the country might come face-to-face with critical situations, especially via foreign powers who try to weaken it further as well as its internal opponents who accelerate their efforts toward the same goal. As a consequence, economic problems, rebellion, and revolts will occur and force the country into chaos. But Dhu'l-Qarnayn's (as) nation is far from this situation, for its government's rule is solid, rational, and strong.

"We granted him a way to everything" suggests that Dhu'l-Qarnayn (as) has been given the ability to solve every problem, which means that he is a very intelligent, sagacious, and perceptive believer. With these Allah-given faculties, he solves all complex issues quickly and removes the obstacles. Allah clears his path and supports him with superior knowledge. As will be seen later on, his qualities are well known and, because of this, his opinion, advice, and help are sought by others.

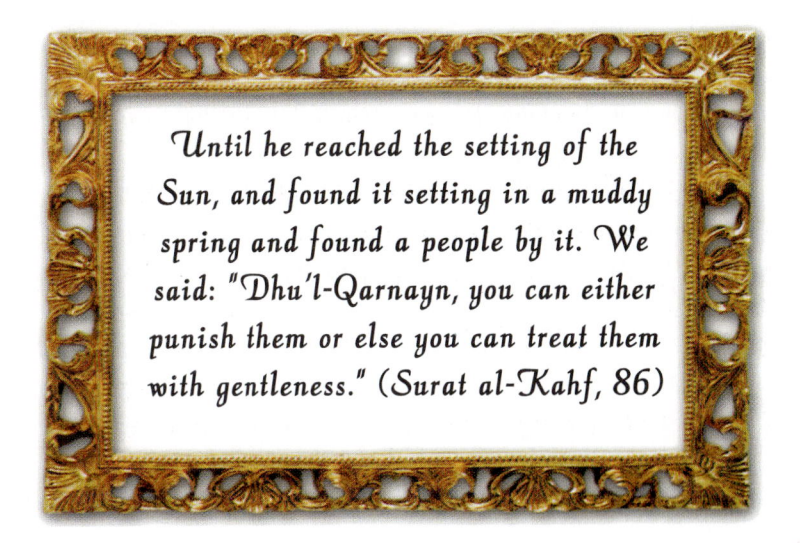

> *Until he reached the setting of the Sun, and found it setting in a muddy spring and found a people by it. We said: "Dhu'l-Qarnayn, you can either punish them or else you can treat them with gentleness." (Surat al-Kahf, 86)*

We understand from the verse that first Dhu'l-Qarnayn (as) heads west, for where the sun sets could be the westernmost place on Earth. If the intended meaning is Europe, this could be Portugal, Spain or the Strait of Gibraltar. If the verse refers to Africa, its westernmost countries are Senegal and Mauritania. (Allah knows best.)

The verse also mentions that this western place is a "muddy spring." In Arabic, this phrase is `aynin hami'ah. `Ayn means "eye, spring, fountain, and source"; hami'ah means "black mud, smudged, and muddy."

Dhu'l-Qarnayn (as) could have been heading for Africa, as Bediuzzaman Said Nursi indicated. According to him:

Firstly, by explaining that Dhu'l-Qarnayn's journey to the west coincided with the intense heat of summer, the area of a swamp, the time of the setting of the sun, and the time of a volcanic eruption, it alludes to many instructive matters, like the complete conquest of Africa… Also the spring is a metaphor. From the distance a large sea appears like a small pool. The likening of a sea appearing beyond *swamps, and mists and vapours rising from it due to the heat, to a muddy spring, together with word `ayn, which in Arabic means both spring, and sun, and eye, is most meaningful and apt according to the mysteries of eloquence...*

Terming the Atlantic Ocean a muddy spring indicates that Dhu'l-Qarnayn saw that huge ocean as a spring due to the distance. But because the Qur'an sees everything from close to, it did not see what Dhu'l-Qarnayn saw, which was a sort of illusion. Indeed, since the Qur'an comes from the heavens and looks to them, it sees the earth sometimes as an arena, sometimes as a palace, sometimes as a cradle, and sometimes as a page. Thus, its calling the vast misty, vaporous Atlantic Ocean a spring shows its great elevatedness. [1]

Someone watching, from a great distance, the sunset on the hori-

... he reached the setting of the Sun and found it setting in a muddy spring... (Surat al-Kahf, 86)

zon, will see this as the Sun dipping into the sea or as descending into the mountain depending behind what it sets. This obviously depends on the person's standpoint and the angle from which this event is being viewed.

Dhu'l-Qarnayn (as), upon reaching this land, meets its inhabitants. Allah tells him how to react to them: If they swear allegiance to him and lead a Muslim way of life, he is to treat them well; if they revolt against Allah's law, do not accept Islam, and do evil, he is to act accordingly.

Dhu'l-Qarnayn's (as) response will be according to the law. Those who do good and behave well will receive the same good treatment; those who choose evil, wickedness, and revolt will be treated appropriately. As only a judge has the authority to determine the appropriate response, we can deduce that Dhu'l-Qarnayn (as), besides being his nation's leader, was also empowered to judge. According to the law of that time, he could choose among imprisonment, arrest, and other forms of punishment.

The expressions in this verse can be interpreted to mean that Dhu'l-Qarnayn's (as) nation has a ruler who serves as the head of state, sole authority, and judge of the legal system. At this point in time, he is that person.

If the wrongdoing person or people revolt, resist, and attack, the nation will defend itself with all its might. The expression "you can punish them" could suggest that the nation can defend itself. While we are considering these means of punishment, Dhu'l-Qarnayn's (as) security and military forces must be mentioned too.

Scholars interpret "spring" in different ways. According to one, Dhu'l-Qarnayn (as), by means of a "cause," made a journey through space and saw the Sun fall into a black hole.[2] Dying suns collapse within and form black holes. This type of star condenses, and the density of their matter increases dramatically. Stars three times the size of our Sun shrink to a diameter of a few kilometers, and their gravitational force increases so much that they swallow up light, sound, and even time. Their gravity pulls in other stars, and each star they swallow increases the gravitational force proportionately.[3]

Since they swallow up anything that comes within their gravitational pull, they are thought of as "black swamps." And, because they do not reflect light, they are called "black holes."

> *He said: "As for those who do wrong, we will punish them. Then they will be returned to their Lord, and He will punish them with a dreadful punishment." (Surat al-Kahf, 87)*

From the expressions used in the verse, we understand that Dhu'l-Qarnayn (as) was a Muslim leader who ruled a Muslim nation. When he spoke, he reminded his people of Allah and the Hereafter. He spoke in a Muslim manner.

Dhu'l-Qarnayn (as) makes it clear that the wrongdoers will be punished according to the law of that time. Allah ordained that he would punish the unbelievers in this life; however, this is only the part of their punishment, for as our Lord states: "**... And the punishment of the Hereafter is much greater, if they only knew**" (Surat al-Qalam, 33).

Everyone who denies Allah's existence and the Hereafter, and who rejects the precepts of the Qur'an, will receive exactly what they deserve in this life as well as in the Hereafter. Many nations throughout history were punished severely in this life, for they rejected the Messengers' invitation to believe. The verses, which reveal the destruction of these nations, also reveal that the punishment of the Hereafter is far worse and should be more feared by people. As Allah says:

So We sent a howling wind against them on disastrous ill-fated days to make them taste the punishment of degradation in this world. The punishment of the Hereafter is even more degrad-

SIGNS OF THE END TIMES IN SURAT AL-KAHF

ing. They will not be helped. **(Surah Fussilat, 16)**

That is how We repay anyone who is profligate and does not believe in the Signs of his Lord. The punishment of the Hereafter is much harsher and longer lasting. **(Surah Ta Ha, 127)**

The punishment awaiting the unbelievers in Hell is described as "dreadful." Various descriptions in the Qur'an inform us that such suffering is far more painful than what we experience in this world. For this reason, people should ponder and fear the punishment in the Hereafter before they worry about their suffering here, for that fear could lead them to repent, turn away from denial, and submit to Allah.

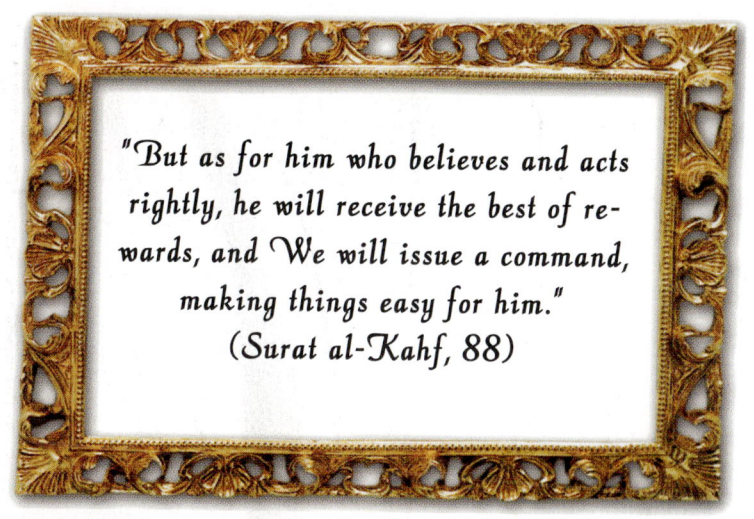

> *"But as for him who believes and acts rightly, he will receive the best of rewards, and We will issue a command, making things easy for him."*
> *(Surat al-Kahf, 88)*

We understand from this verse that Dhu'l-Qarnayn (as) is not just his nation's leader and judge, but also a preaching Muslim calling to faith. It is clear that he educates and rules his people according to Allah's good pleasure.

Dhu'l-Qarnayn (as) immediately calls the people he meets to believe in Allah, devotion, the good deeds prescribed by the Qur'an, and to perform the prayers and acts of worship. He draws their attention, in order to encourage them, to the rewards that they are promised in this world and the next. Every Messenger makes this call to his nation. The Prophets incessantly called the people to guidance, and developed various strategies to stir their consciences.

In addition, the verse indicates that whatever the people's responses may be, the believers are to act with determination and to obey Allah's order to "command the right and forbid the wrong." This is an important responsibility for sincere believers, just as it was for the Prophets, as the following verse points out:

Let there be a community among you who call to the good, enjoin the right, and forbid the wrong. They are the ones who have success. (Surah Al `Imran, 104)

Another important piece of information here is to make things easy for the Muslims and not to complicate matters for them. Things should be made easy, comfortable, and pleasant for good people in their actions, decisions, and everyday affairs. Our Lord reminds the believers of this by saying: "**... Allah desires ease for you; He does not desire difficulty for you...**" (Surat al-Baqara, 185) and: "**We have made the Qur'an easy to remember. But is there any rememberer there?**" (Surat al-Qamar, 17). Therefore, the believers must know that choosing the easier path is a requirement of the Qur'an. In addition, they must not let Allah's promise, **"We will ease you to the Easy Way"** (Surat al-A`la, 8), slip their mind. As Allah says:

> **Strive for Allah with the striving due to Him. He has selected you and not placed any constraint upon you in the religion—the religion of your forefather Ibrahim. He named you Muslims before and also in this, so that the Messenger could be a witness over you and so you could be witnesses over all mankind. So establish prayer, pay the alms, and hold fast to Allah. He is your Protector—the Best Protector, the Best Helper. (Surat al-Hajj, 78)**

> *Anyone who acts rightly, male or female, being a believer, We will give them a good life and recompense them according to the best of what they did. (Surat an-Nahl, 97)*

> *Then he followed a way until he reached the rising of the Sun, and found it rising on a people to whom We had not given any shelter from it. We had encompassed that he had "knowledge comprising essence" near him [or all that he had in knowledge].*
> *(Surat al-Kahf, 89-91)*

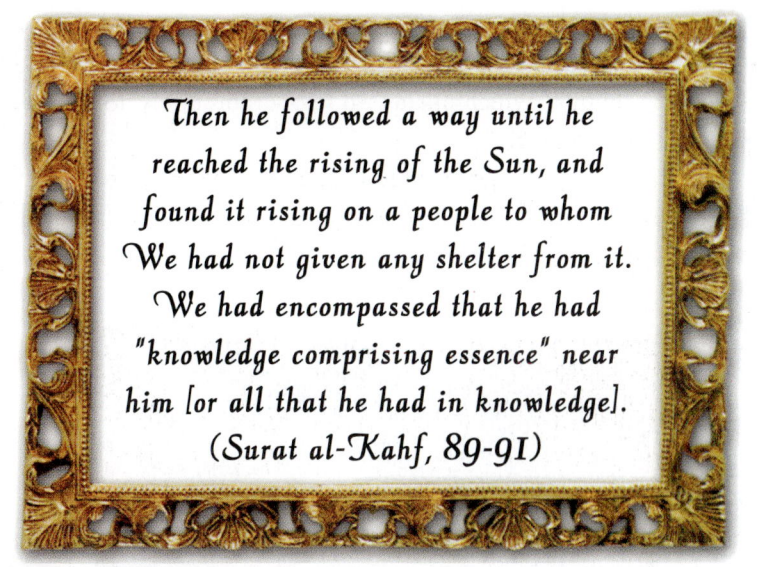

The second time Dhu'l-Qarnayn (as) sets off, he goes east. Applying the verse to a map, he could have gone to Korea, China, or Manchuria (northern China).

The verse mentions "a people to whom We had not given any shelter from the Sun." The Arabic word for shelter is "sitr" (to cover, to hide). It is derived from the root "satara." Thus, in the context of this verse, it means "a cover in the form of cloths or a building."

Therefore, it can be assumed that these people did not live in houses but rather in the open, wide land. They had no forms of shelter or devices like umbrellas. They may have been nomadic, or a people who worked at night and spent the days in underground shelters. Or, they might have been a people who had no clothes or civilization. Omer Nasuhi Bilmen interprets the verse in this way:

> *"Dhu'l-Qarnayn, in this journey, came to the land of the rising sun (where the sun is born). For these people there was no protection from the rays of the sun like a piece of cloth, a building, or a mountain. These people were either entering the sea or an underground cavity when the sun rose and came out to do their work when the sun set."*[4]

Surat al-Kahf 91 speaks of Dhu'l-Qarnayn's (as) knowledge of the essence of things. The Arabic word for "knowledge comprising the essence" is "khubr," which means "to know thoroughly, to be fully acquainted with the truth."

This knowledge is a special knowledge that Allah gives only to His chosen few. As Surat al-Kahf 68 indicates above, Khidhr (as) also was graced with this special knowledge.

... he reached the rising of the Sun...
(Surat al-Kahf, 90)

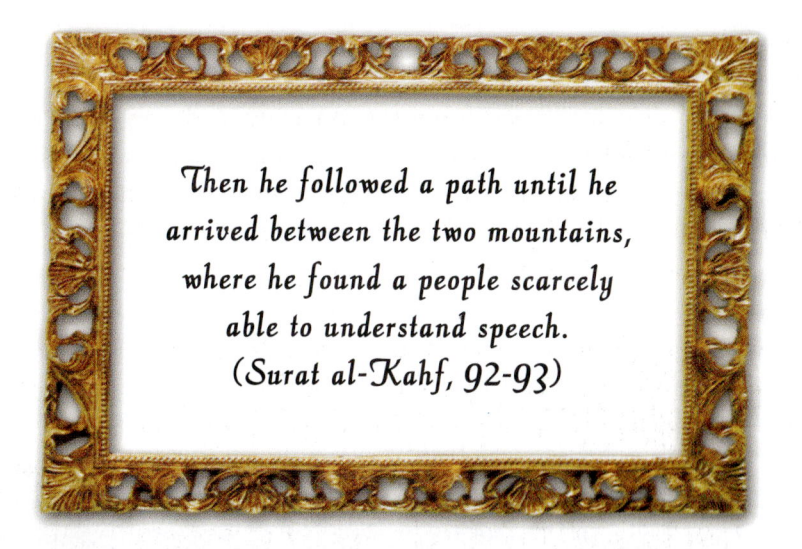

> *Then he followed a path until he arrived between the two mountains, where he found a people scarcely able to understand speech.*
> *(Surat al-Kahf, 92-93)*

The third time Dhu'l-Qarnayn sets off on his journey, he reaches an area between the East and the West. This could be an area in the Himalayas. Bediuzzaman Said Nursi indicates these areas too, and reminds us that "... *The Great Wall of China covers a distance of several days' journeying and was built to halt the incursions against the oppressed peoples of India and China of the savage tribes... These tribes several times threw the world of humanity into chaos, and pouring out from behind the Himalayas wrought destruction from East to West. A long wall was built between two mountains close to the Himalayan mountains which for a long time prevented the frequent assaults of those savage peoples...*"[5] As Bediuzzaman says, the two mountains could be mountain chains.

The verse also indicates that the people he encountered were scarcely able to understand what was said to them. Perhaps the expression "scarcely able to understand speech" indicates that they spoke a very different or unusual language.

Dhu'l-Qarnayn (as), however, is able to communicate with them, either through being able to speak their language because of his special knowledge or because a member of his party knows that particular language. This verse could be indicating that he had a special group of people with him who were trained in such matters.

We also can understand from the verses that wherever Dhu'l-Qarnayn (as) goes, he comes across people who are destitute and miserable, needy and weak. Those in the East cannot even protect themselves from the Sun. The people between the mountains are ignorant and primitive in terms of culture and technology, and also cannot defend themselves from external enemies. Thus, they face the threat of anarchy. The most important reason for them to seek Dhu'l-Qarnayn's (as) help could be their existing poverty, ignorance, and state of chaos. These are important factors for our understanding of the situation at that time.

... when he had made it level between the two high mountainsides, he said: "Blow!"...
(Surat al-Kahf, 96)

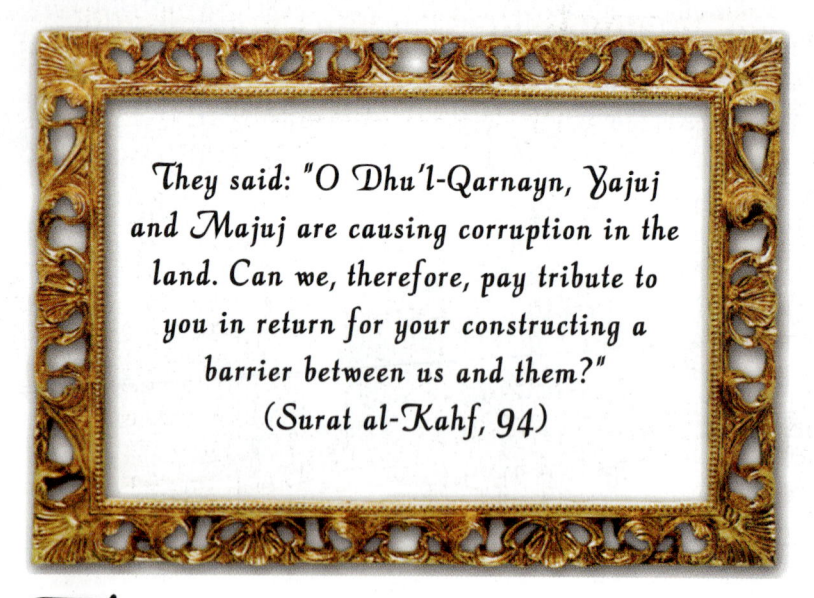

> They said: "O Dhu'l-Qarnayn, Yajuj and Majuj are causing corruption in the land. Can we, therefore, pay tribute to you in return for your constructing a barrier between us and them?"
> (Surat al-Kahf, 94)

Through the words "Yajuj" and "Majuj," thought to have been introduced into Arabic from another language, we learn of a people who are causing corruption in the land. Interpretations by scholars indicate that these people are one or more nations who were oppressing, abusing, and ill-treating the people of that area.

Due to this corruption, the people in trouble seek Dhu'l-Qarnayn's (as) help and offer to pay him a tax in return. From this, we understand that he does not represent a single person; rather, he rules a nation and commands an army, just like Prophet Sulayman (as).

From the previous verses, we understand that he had a team of linguists with him. However, this verse also indicates that he must have had teams of construction experts and civil engineers as well. From the people's request, we can deduce that Dhu'l-Qarnayn (as) is interested in, and knowledgeable about, construction and civil engineering. He might even have been renowned for his expertise in these fields and helping other nations when they ask for it. All of these factors demonstrate the size and power of his nation.

Dhu'l-Qarnayn (as) is also known as someone who prevents corruption and wickedness. For this reason, nations that are in trouble, experiencing difficulties or internal chaos, or facing external pressure ask for his help. It could be that he brings law and order to the region, that neighboring nations ask for his help because they trust his military power and his ability to end corruption, and because he heads a very powerful nation. The fact that one nation requests the help of another, and even offers to pay a fee in return, shows that it cannot resolve the troubling situation on its own and that the nation from which help is sought can. In other words, the helping nation is powerful and well established.

That Dhu'l-Qarnayn (as) is well respected and effective in the East and the West could indicate that he rules a nation possessing extensive power. Therefore, he is a leader, aware of his responsibility to bring peace, justice, and security not only to his own nation, but also to every

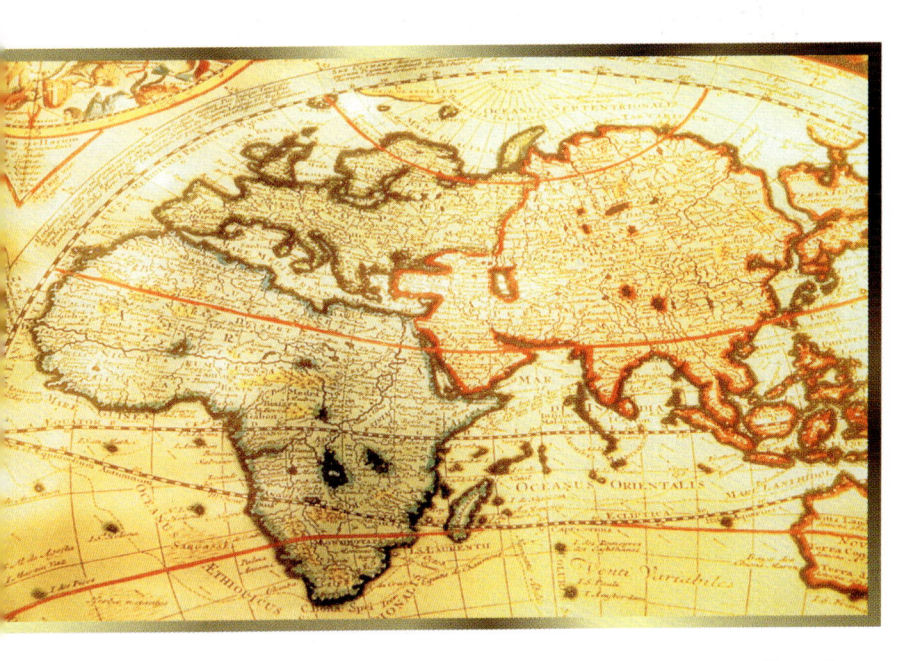

We can deduce from this narrative that Dhu'l-Qarnayn (as) was a Muslim ruler who controlled many lands.

part of the region. With this verse, Allah indicates that it is every Muslim's responsibility to work for justice, peace, and security. Every country should take an interest, within its means, in the problems facing the world and help those nations that are in financial and other need.

The narrative of Dhu'l-Qarnayn (as) indicates that in the End Times, just as it was during his own time, the values of Islam will rule the world.

Allah reveals this good news to the believers, as follows:

Allah has promised those of you who believe and do right actions that He will make them successors in the land, just as He made those before them successors, and will firmly establish for them their religion with which He is pleased, and give them, in place of their fear, security. "They worship Me, not associating anything with Me." Any who do not believe after that, such people are deviators. (Surat an-Nur, 55)

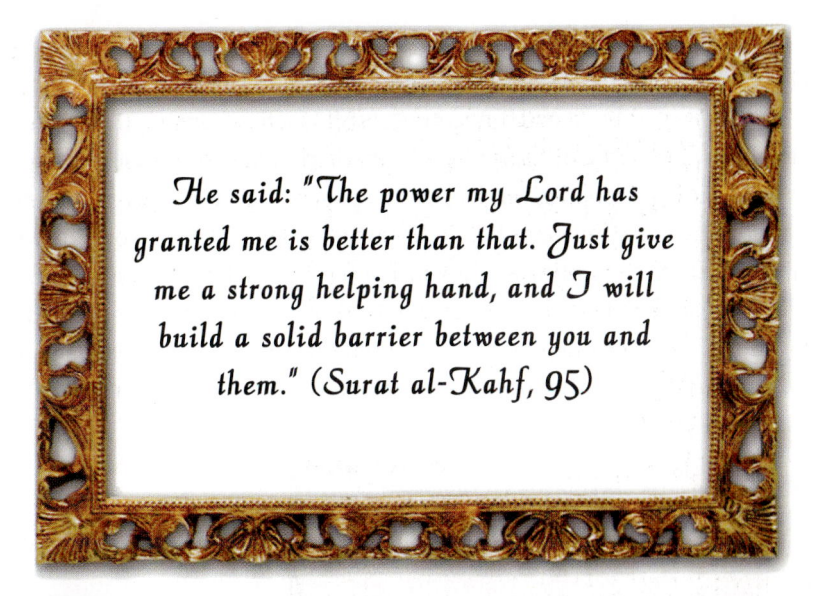

> He said: "The power my Lord has granted me is better than that. Just give me a strong helping hand, and I will build a solid barrier between you and them." (Surat al-Kahf, 95)

This verse again indicates the solidity of Dhu'l-Qarnayn's (as) power. His nation is not so weak as to collapse easily. On the contrary, it is exceedingly strong, assures its own people as well as other needy nations, and does not cause anxiety in people with its methods of rule and practices. It appears to be invulnerable, with Allah's will, for this verse indicates that no internal or external opposition, pressure, or force could ever affect it, and that his rule is so solid that no conflict, outbreak of dissent, or revolt could rock it.

Dhu'l-Qarnayn (as) does not accept any recompense in return for his help. The Qur'an gives other examples about this character of the Prophets. For instance, Prophet Sulayman (as) rejected the gifts sent to him:

> "I [the queen of Saba] will send them a gift, and then wait and see what the messengers bring back." When it reached Sulayman, he said: "Would you give me wealth when what Allah has given me is better than what He has given you? No, rather it is you who delight in your gift." (Surat an-Naml, 35-36)

There could be several reasons why Sulayman (as) and Dhu'l-Qarnayn (as) rejected offers of material returns. Perhaps accepting such a reward would have had a negative result, such as causing those who gave it to lose some of their respect, obedience, and submission to the one to whom they had given it. This is a psychological frame of mind in people. The verse indicates that in these cases, it is better to avoid such a situation by not accepting any reward or fee. No doubt, such an attitude will increase the love and allegiance of those who have been helped. Besides, Dhu'l-Qarnayn (as), just like Sulayman (as), is the leader of a rich nation that does not need to expect a return for its assistance.

Balqis was the queen of Saba, a powerful nation at that time. The Qur'an informs us that Sulayman (as) refused to accept her gifts. The picture on the right portrays the convoy carrying these gifts to Sulayman (as).

Nevertheless, Dhu'l-Qarnayn (as) requests the people's support in terms of labor. Thus, he seems to have preferred to give jobs and a degree of responsibility to the local population. In this way, he teaches them art and science and helps them to advance in culture and technology. He also makes use of unemployed people, saves his own nation's wealth, and makes his new employees useful by giving them roles in their nation's defense. No doubt, such a relationship based on justice, respect, and fairness will strengthen mutual trust and win the people's support.

Such a practice has many positive aspects, among them the people's education and the increase in skilled labor, an escape from laziness and stagnation, and the chance to experience the high spirits of achieving success by their own efforts. This practice also increases the nation's self-confidence, for those who work to improve their own nation will hardly cause trouble or be inclined to revolt and rebel. As a result, the people will easily be ruled during this period of assistance. Besides, people work better and more efficiently with their own people and enjoy serving their nation. Of course, in things done for Allah's good pleasure, this is unimportant. However, we cannot expect everybody to be diligent in this matter or that they all seek Allah's good pleasure. With this in mind, everyone's rights must be guaranteed, regardless of the level or lack of devotion to Allah. Here we see how clever Dhu'l-Qarnayn's policy is.

According to this verse, Dhu'l-Qarnayn (as) builds a solid barrier, which prevents crossing and is an example of solid architecture and high technology. It is crucially important that every building, especially bridges, be constructed solidly so that they can withstand such natural disasters as earthquakes, floods, and rain, as well as military attacks.

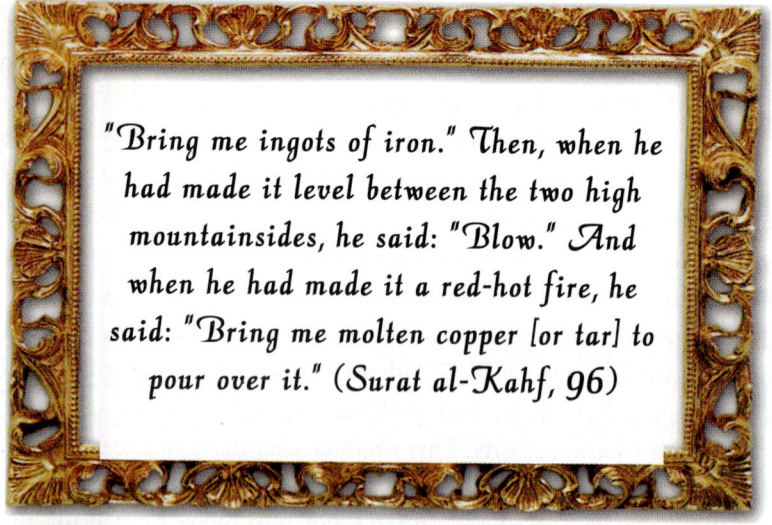

> *"Bring me ingots of iron."* Then, when he had made it level between the two high mountainsides, he said: *"Blow."* And when he had made it a red-hot fire, he said: *"Bring me molten copper [or tar] to pour over it."* (Surat al-Kahf, 96)

Based upon this verse, this barrier might have been a concrete structure. This type of construction is used today in almost all types of buildings and huge dams.

The verse also states that Dhu'l-Qarnayn (as) used iron and molten copper—or tar according to some interpreters—in this structure. Iron, the strongest building material, is an essential component of bridges and dams, for it increases the structure's rigidity. In its absence, the slightest damage or tremor would cause it to collapse.

It is possible that Dhu'l-Qarnayn (as) used blocks of iron and mortar to build a huge barrier. It is possible that he may have joined the blocks of iron end to end by pouring mortar over them and built a strong concrete structure. (Allah knows best).

The Arabic word *qitr* translated as "molten copper" also means tar.[6] Tar, which is used to protect iron from moisture and seawater, is a protective coating obtained by the destructive distillation of pine wood or coal. Dhu'l-Qarnayn (as) could have poured tar over this structure to prevent the iron from being subjected to oxidation and rust. Similar insulation materials are usually found in modern concrete structures.

Dhu'l-Qarnayn could have combined the tar-coated iron with a mortar mixed of gravel, chalk, sand, and water in order to increase its strength. Normally, mortar mixed with sand and chalk can be perforated quite easily. However, it becomes indestructible when supported by iron. Such a structure would be a preventive measure, and no force applied to it could destroy or damage it, let alone break through it, under the conditions existing at that time, unless Allah willed it.

tar

It is possible that the wall built by Dhu'l-Qarnayn (as) was constructed by employing similar techniques that are used today to construct dams. As the pictures show, iron-concrete structures are so solid that they cannot be destroyed or overcome unless special technology is used against them. In the picture below, we see the wall's internal iron structure that prevents its collapse.

> *They were, therefore, unable to climb over it; nor were they able to make a breach in it. He said: "This is a mercy from my Lord. But when my Lord's promise comes about, He will crush it flat. The promise of my Lord is surely true."*
> (Surat al-Kahf, 97-98)

The first verse reveals that this barrier is impregnable. This suggests that it was a quite high structure, and the fact that it could not be breached proves that it is structurally sound. All of these facts could be indicating that it was built by using a concrete-iron construction method similar to what we see all around us today.

According to verse 98, the first thing that Dhu'l-Qarnayn (as) remembers after completing this project is Allah's attributes of mercy and grace. Knowing that no one could build such a barrier unless Allah wills it, he remembers immediately that our Lord was the real builder and seeks to prevent the people from considering it to be their own achievement.

Surat al-Kahf 98 also reveals that this wall will remain until the Day of Judgment. The word "promise" stands for that day, as will be seen in the subsequent verse. In other words, it will be protected until then.

The wall's exact location may or may not be found within time, for this knowledge rests with Allah. The important thing is that it will not be destroyed until the Day of Judgment, for on that day everything will be destroyed. Many verses reveal that mountains will move and noth-

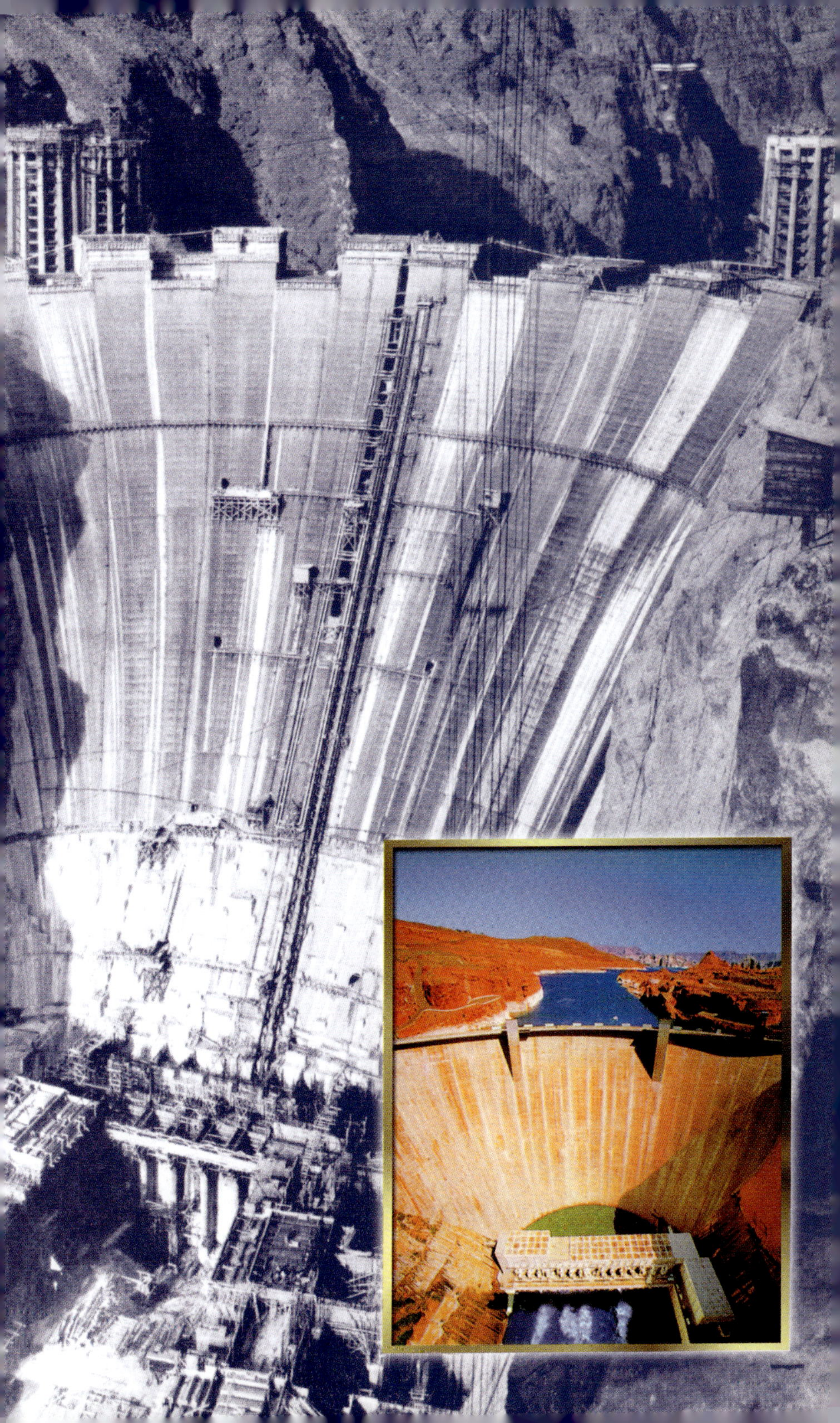

ing will remain on Earth's surface. Some of these are given below:

> On the Day We make the mountains move and you see Earth laid bare… (Surat al-Kahf, 47)
>
> When Earth is flattened out, disgorges what is inside it, and empties out, harkening to its Lord as it is bound to do! (Surat al-Inshiqaq, 3-5)
>
> They will ask you about the mountains. Say: "My Lord will scatter them as dust. He will leave them as a barren, level plain upon which you will see no dip or gradient." (Surah Ta Ha, 105-107)

ANOTHER POSSIBILITY ABOUT THE DHU'L-QARNAYN NARRATIVE

Another possibility is that this narrative conveys events that will happen in the future.

In Allah's presence, all time is one. Future, past, and present are experienced all at once. In some verses, the events of the Day of Judgment, Hell and Paradise are related as if they have already taken place. The following verses are an example of this:

The Trumpet is blown, and all who are in the heavens and all who are on Earth swoon away, save him whom Allah wills. Then it is blown a second time, and behold them standing waiting! And Earth shone with the light of her Lord, the Book is set up, the Prophets and the witnesses are brought, and it is judged between them with truth. They are not wronged. (Surat az-Zumar: 68-69)

The events related in this verse are told as if they have already taken place, even though to us they will happen in the future. Therefore it is possible that the Dhu'l-Qarnayn (as) narrative is from the future, related to us in the past tense. Surat al-Kahf 84 says: that **"[We] granted him a way to everything."** This might indicate that Dhu'l-Qarnayn (as) will rule the world in the future.

In today's world, a powerful leader or nation must have both communication technology and conventional power. As the leader cannot inspect all of them personally, we can assume that he will stay in a central capital city and control the other areas through satellites and other means of communication. As verse 95 proclaims: He said: **"The power my Lord has granted me is better than that,"** Dhu'l-Qarnayn's (as) power is probably well-established. If we look at the narrative from this perspective, we realize that each verse could be conveying a different message. For example, Dhu'l-Qarnayn (as) went first to the West, then

SIGNS OF THE END TIMES IN SURAT AL-KAHF

to the East, and then back again. These verses might be implying that he communicates with different areas by changing channels broadcasting from satellites. The verses speak constantly of "finding." Dhu'l-Qarnayn (as) "found" a people by the "spring" and a people in the East who did not understand. These acts of "finding" happen by searching, and thus could be a finding based upon looking up satellite channels.

Satellite technology allows us to take detailed pictures of the ground. Spy satellites, in particular, can "watch" every country closely. Here are two pictures taken by the Ikonos satellite. On the left is the Washington Monument, and on the right is Venice.

The verses say that the people of the East had no shelter from the sun. If we consider this information in the light of communication technology, there are two possible messages here. Dhu'l-Qarnayn (as) could be watching or gathering intelligence via satellites about these areas (Allah knows best). Or they could be implying infrared technology, which is used in many different areas today. For example, infrared cameras are used in medicine, criminal pathology, meteorology, criminology, intelligence, industry, and other fields. Such cameras also can observe the human body in great detail.

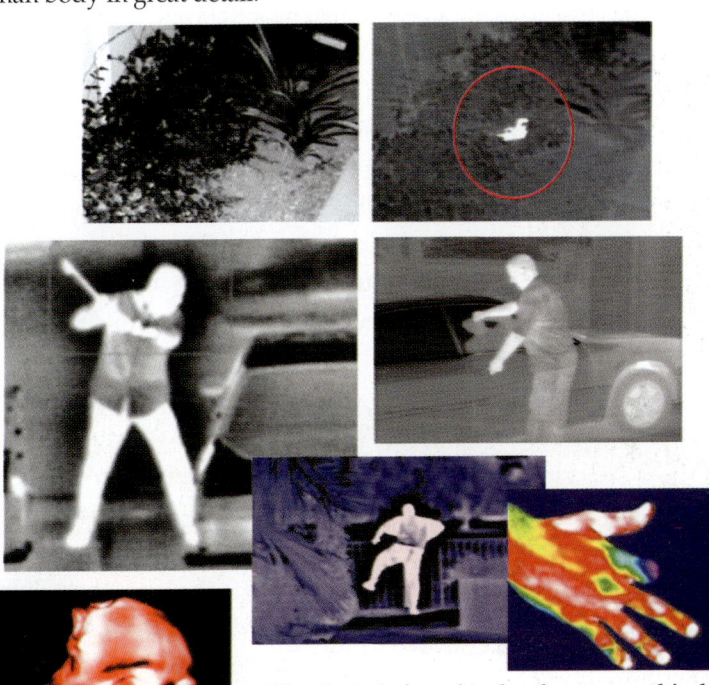

Thanks to infrared technology, every kind of criminal tool can be detected easily at the crime scene, and crimes committed in the dark can be seen in detail. Important advances also have been made in diagnosing illnesses.

If Dhu'l-Qarnayn (as) is addressing a nation, he could be doing so via satellite and TV broadcasts. This would enable him to learn of the people's needs and complaints, regardless of where they lived, and then rule the areas under his control accordingly.

The Yajuj and Majuj corruption could be a classic act of terror or anarchy, or even be committed by means of broadcasting. For example, they could be disrupting other broadcasts in order to broadcast their corrupted ideas. Dhu'l-Qarnayn (as) could have prevented this broadcast and thus the corruption For instance, he could have used the copper and iron mentioned in the verse to create an electromagnetic field and disrupt the radio and TV broadcasts. Transformers, which are made by winding copper wire around an iron core, are one of the sources of electromagnetic fields. A powerful electromagnetic field can disrupt radio and TV broadcasts.

Another possibility is that a huge communal satellite dish is implied. The reason for it being so big could have been to overcome Yajuj and Majuj's global disruptive system. The surfaces of these dishes are usually made of the cheaper and lighter aluminum, which is not the ideal material for performance. Copper is a much better conductor, and might have been preferred for this reason. However, covering such a huge dish with copper sheets is not rational. On the other hand, copper-plating the dish with molten copper would give it the smoothest surface and deliver the highest possible performance.

The wall or barrier created by counter-broadcasts or by creating a magnetic field could be termed an "invisible barrier." Some scholars read the word *saddayn* in verse 93 as *suddayn*, and *sadd* in the following verse as *sudd*. In the first case, the meaning would be a "visible barrier"; in the second, it means an "invisible barrier" (Allah knows best).

"They were, therefore, unable to climb over it, nor were they able to make a breach in it," as stated in verse 97, might be referring to this, because Yajuj and Majuj attempt to overcome or breach the transmitter's broadcast. Significantly, the current expression used for pirate stations that broadcast by interfering with another broadcast is "breaching transmission."

Considering the expression "scarcely able to understand speech" in this light might mean that this satellite broadcast is sometimes not understood by some people. When the broadcast is disrupted, the people cannot understand; but when the normal broadcast is restored, they begin to understand (Allah knows best).

The expression **"a muddy spring"** (verse 86) is also interesting, because seeing the sunset on the TV screen is just like the sun setting in a spring. The colors on the screen change as the sun sets in the distance over the sea, and this appears grayer on the screen. Thus, for someone viewing this, it will appear as if setting in a muddy spring. The `aynin hami'ah* expression, made up of `ayn (spring) and *hami'ah* (muddy) could be implying this unclear view.

Also, his contact with the East and the West could indicate that he is in touch with the various parts of the globe. While the sun rises over one part, it sets on the other.

SIGNS OF THE END TIMES IN SURAT AL-KAHF

> *We will abandon them, that Day, to pound against each other in surging waves. The Trumpet will be blown, and We will gather them all together. That Day We will display Hell in its totality to the unbelievers.*
> *(Surat al-Kahf, 99-100)*

The Qur'an reveals that the entire universe, including humanity, animals, plants, stars—in short, everything that has been created—will die. In the Qur'an, this day is described as **"the Day mankind will stand before the Lord of all the worlds"** (Surat al-Mutaffifin, 6).

The Hour is a day of terror. Those who did not believe before will, for the first time, feel Allah's sheer power and might ... and very strongly at that. For the unbelievers, this is a day of great suffering, terror, remorse, pain, and surprise. Everyone witnessing this day will experience an indescribable fear that is far worse than all of the fears experienced in this world.

The Hour begins with the sounding of the trumpet, which is the sign for the beginning of Earth's and the universe's end. There is no way back anymore, for this is the sound of the end of everyone's worldly life and the beginning of the real life, the life of the Hereafter. This is the sound that starts the unbelievers' fear, terror, misery, and panic, which will be everlasting. The Qur'an reveals what kind of day this will be for the unbelievers, as follows:

For when the Trumpet is blown, that Day will be a difficult day, not easy for the unbelivers. (Surat al-Muddaththir, 8-10)

Surat al-Kahf states that these people will surge against one another like great waves on the Day of Judgment. They will be as if drunk on fear, and will go back and forth like surging waves. Their fear will cause them to lose all control and awareness of what they do or where they go.

The greater the people's insensitivity and ignorance of this day, the greater will be their terror on that day. This sense of fear and terror will remain with them from the moment they die and last throughout eternity. The Qur'an reveals that this fear will cause children's hair to turn gray, as follows:

How will you safeguard yourselves, if you do not believe, against a Day that will turn children grey, by which Heaven will be split apart? His promise will be fulfilled. (Surat al-Muzammil, 17-18)

Those who thought that Allah was unaware of their actions will realize that they were His helpless servants and that He had given them time until the Day of Judgment. He did so because this is Allah's promise, as revealed in: "**... He is merely deferring them to a Day on which their sight will be transfixed**" (Surah Ibrahim, 42). Other verses also describe this day:

The Crashing Blow! What is the Crashing Blow? What will convey to you what the Crashing Blow is? It is the Day when mankind will be like scattered moths, and the mountains like tufts of colored wool. (Surat al-Qari`a, 1-5)

The verses of Surat al-Hajj reveal that people will be like those who have lost their minds:

Mankind, heed your Lord! The quaking of the Hour is a terrible thing. On the day that they see it, every nursing woman will be oblivious of the baby at her breast, every pregnant woman will abort the contents of her womb, and you will think that people are drunk when they are not drunk; it is just that the punish-

ment of Allah is so severe. (Surat al-Hajj, 1-2)

Some verses which relate the helplessness of the people on that day are the following:

And the Moon is eclipsed, and the Sun and Moon are fused together. On that Day, man will say: "Where can I run?" No indeed! There will be no safe place. That Day, the only resting place will be your Lord. (Surat al-Qiyama, 8-12)

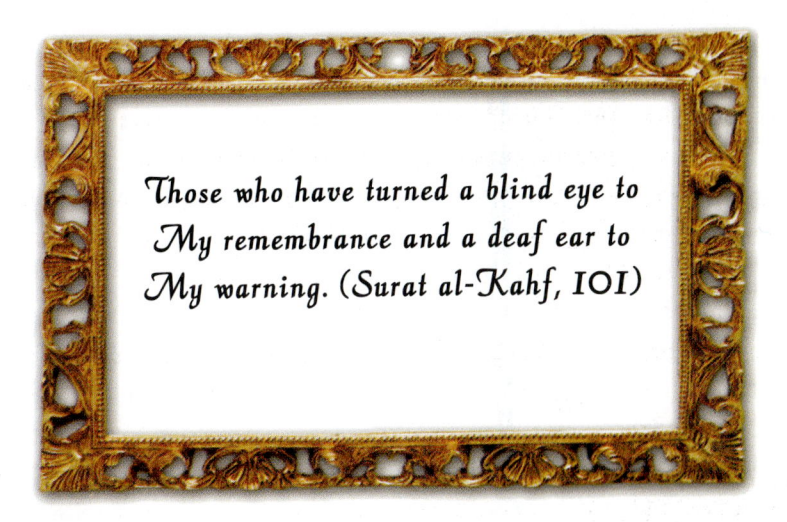

> *Those who have turned a blind eye to My remembrance and a deaf ear to My warning. (Surat al-Kahf, 101)*

This verse emphasizes the unbelievers' heedlessness about Allah's remembrance. In another verse, He states: "**… Yet they turn away from the remembrance of their Lord**" (Surat al-Anbiya', 42). They deny Allah's verses, ignore the signs of creation in every detail of the universe, and refuse to listen to the Qur'an, which Allah revealed as guidance to faith. Many verses clearly state the importance of remembering Allah and that the alternative is heedlessness:

Remember your Lord in yourself humbly and fearfully, without loudness of voice, morning and evening. Do not be one of the unaware. (Surat al-A`raf, 205)

People are responsible for seeking Allah's good pleasure in everything they do, and for abiding by His commands and recommendations. The importance of remembrance is mentioned in the following verse:

Recite what has been revealed to you of the Book, and establish prayer. Prayer precludes indecency and wrongdoing. And remembrance of Allah is greater still. Allah knows what you do. (Surat al-`Ankabut, 45)

About the believers, Allah says: "O you who believe, do not let your wealth or children divert you from the remembrance of Allah. Whoever does that is lost" (Surat al-Munafiqun, 9). In other words, remembrance is more important than anything else. He also says: "Remember the Name of your Lord, and devote yourself to Him completely" (Surat al-Muzammil, 8). The Muslims' determination in remembrance is revealed in the following verse:

> [The believers are] not distracted by trade or commerce from the remembrance of Allah, establishing prayer, and giving alms; fearing a day when all hearts and eyes will be in turmoil. (Surat an-Nur, 37)

Surat al-Kahf 101 also maintains that the unbelievers cannot bear to hear the Qur'an being recited. They would like to see everyone else turn their backs on the Qur'an, because someone who listens to it might follow the voice of his or her conscience, side with the righteous, and begin to practice truth and advise others to do same. For this reason, the unbelievers develop various means of rejecting the calls to faith, one of which is related in: "Those who do not belive say: 'Do not listen to this Qur'an. Drown it out, so that hopefully you will gain the upper hand'" (Surah Fussilat, 26).

As the above verse reveals, the unbelievers try to drown out the Qur'an's voice, change the subject, or prevent its recitation. If all of this fails, they resort to violence and intimidation, and apply all kinds of pressure to silence the believers. The only reason for them to do so is their fear of being influenced by the truth, that their consciences might be touched and cause them to realize how mistaken they are. Their fear is visible in their facial expressions, behavior, and panic when they hear the Qur'an being recited or the truth of creation being told. Surah Ya Sin reveals that the unbelievers will not listen to the voice of truth, although adhering to the Qur'an's values is their only route to salvation:

> They are told: "Heed what is before you and behind you, so that hopefully you will have mercy shown to you." Not one of your

Lord's Signs comes to them without their turning away from it. (Surah Ya Sin, 45-46)

However, those who shut their ears to the Qur'an must know that they will feel great remorse on the Day of Judgment, a day on which they will seek only for death to finish them off. The Qur'an says:

But as for him who is given his Book in his left hand, he will say: "If only I had not been given my Book and had not known about my Reckoning! If only death had really been the end! My wealth has been of no use to me. My power has vanished." (Surat al-Haqqa, 25-29)

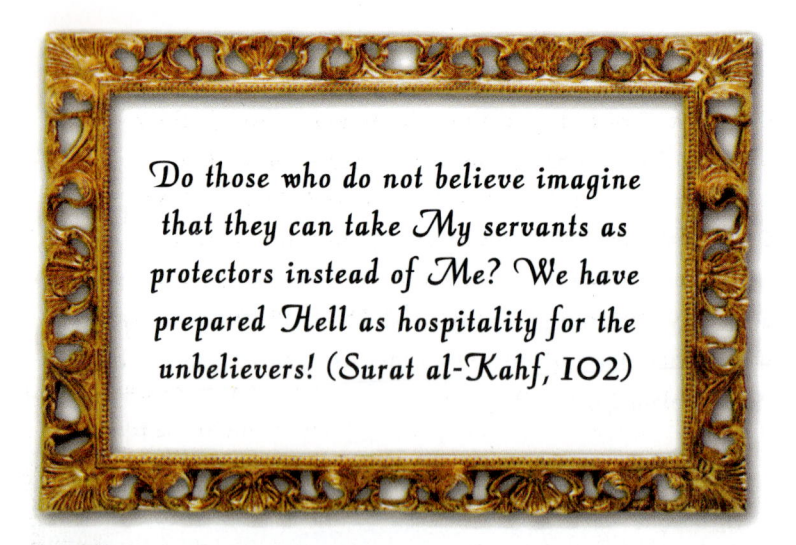

> *Do those who do not believe imagine that they can take My servants as protectors instead of Me? We have prepared Hell as hospitality for the unbelievers! (Surat al-Kahf, 102)*

In other words, some people forget Allah and take others instead of Him as friends and protectors. They believe, mistakenly, that when they need some help, their protectors will help them and take care of their troubles. It is a great mistake to hope for salvation and assistance from people, because no one can help anyone else unless Allah wills it, for everything that exists is part of His creation. They came into being only because Allah wills it, and continue to exist only by His will. Only Allah clears away hardship and brings about ease, provides health and nourishment, and causes laughter as well as tears. In short, every other being is infinitely helpless, poor, and dependent. They have no power or means, and even lack the power to help themselves. Therefore, people should have faith in, expect help from, and seek any other thing only from Allah, for there is no other deity or being who can do anything for them.

This being so, to seek help from others or taking them as protectors; forgetting about Allah and not trusting in Him but in causes, means, and people; and considering Allah's creations as independent powers, forces, or influences constitutes a blatant association (*shirk*). The Qur'an reveals this serious mistake in the following terms:

> They have taken deities besides Allah, so that perhaps they may be helped. They cannot help them, even though they are an army mobilized in their support. (Surah Ya Sin, 74-75)

In Hell, the ultimate place of punishment, Allah's attributes of *Al-Qahhar* (the Crusher, the Subduer), *Al-Jabbar* (the Irresistible), and *Al-Muntaqim* (the Avenger) will be reflected in eternity. Surat al-Kahf 102 indicates that this eternal suffering is prepared as hospitality for the unbelievers.

After accounting for their deeds in Allah's presence, the unbelievers will receive their books from the left. At this moment, these people will truly realize that they will be driven to eternal suffering in Hell. There is no way out for them. Each of the companions of Hell will be accompanied by two angels: a driver and a witness. The following verses provide more information on this subject:

> The Trumpet will be blown. That is the Day of the Threat. Every self will come together with a driver and a witness. [It will be said]: "You were heedless of this, so We have stripped you of your covering and today your sight is sharp." His inseparable comrade [the angel] will say: "This is what I have ready for you." [Allah will say:] "Hurl into Hell every obdurate unbeliever, impeder of good, and doubt-causing aggressor who set up another deity together with Allah. Hurl him into the terrible punishment." (Surah Qaf, 20-26)

This is how the unbelievers will be taken to that scary place. They will be flung into Hell group by group and will hear the terrifying gasping sound of Hell's fire from afar (Surat al-Mulk, 7-8).

The verses reveal that from the very moment of their resurrection, they will be feeling what is expecting them. Their heads will be bowed from degradation and shame. In abject disgrace, friendless, and helpless, they will lose their conceit. Due to their shame, they will watch from the corner of their eyes without looking up. Our Lord says in one verse:

> You will see them as they are exposed to it, abject in their abasement, glancing around them furtively. Those who believe will say: "Truly the losers are those who lose themselves and their families on the Day of Rising." The wrongdoers are in an everlasting punishment. (Surat ash-Shura, 45)

In addition, the deniers will be received at Hell's gates in the following manner:

> Those who do not believe will be driven to Hell in companies. When they arrive there and its gates are opened, its custodians will say to them: "Did Messengers from yourselves not come to you, reciting your Lord's Signs to you and warning you of the meeting on this Day of yours?" They will say: "Indeed they did, but the decree of punishment is justly carried out against the unbelievers." They will be told: "Enter the gates of Hell and stay there timelessly, forever. How evil is the abode of the arrogant!" (Surat az-Zumar, 71-72)

The gates of Hell will be closed behind them. The suffering they face is described as a **"severe punishment"** (Surah Al `Imran, 4), a **"painful punishment"** (Surah Al `Imran, 21), and a **"terrible punishment"** (Surah Al `Imran, 176). Nothing on Earth can compare with it, as the following veses reveal:

> That Day no one will punish as He punishes, and no one will shackle as He shackles. (Surat al-Fajr, 25-26)

The people destined for Hell will be cast into its fire, which is a **"raging blaze"** (Surat al-Ma`arij, 15), **"a raging fire"** (Surat al-Layl, 14), and **"a searing blaze"** (Surat al-Furqan, 11) Another verse says:

> But as for him whose balance is light, his motherland is Hawiya. And what will convey to you what that is? A raging fire! (Surat al-Qari`a, 8-11)

The fire is only one of the physical and psychological sufferings waiting for the unbelievers in Hell. Suffering comes from every side, as the

Qur'an says. In addition, they are not given the chance to defend themselves and are engulfed by all of this suffering. They cannot find a way to deflect the pain coming to them, and it will continue to come to them forever.

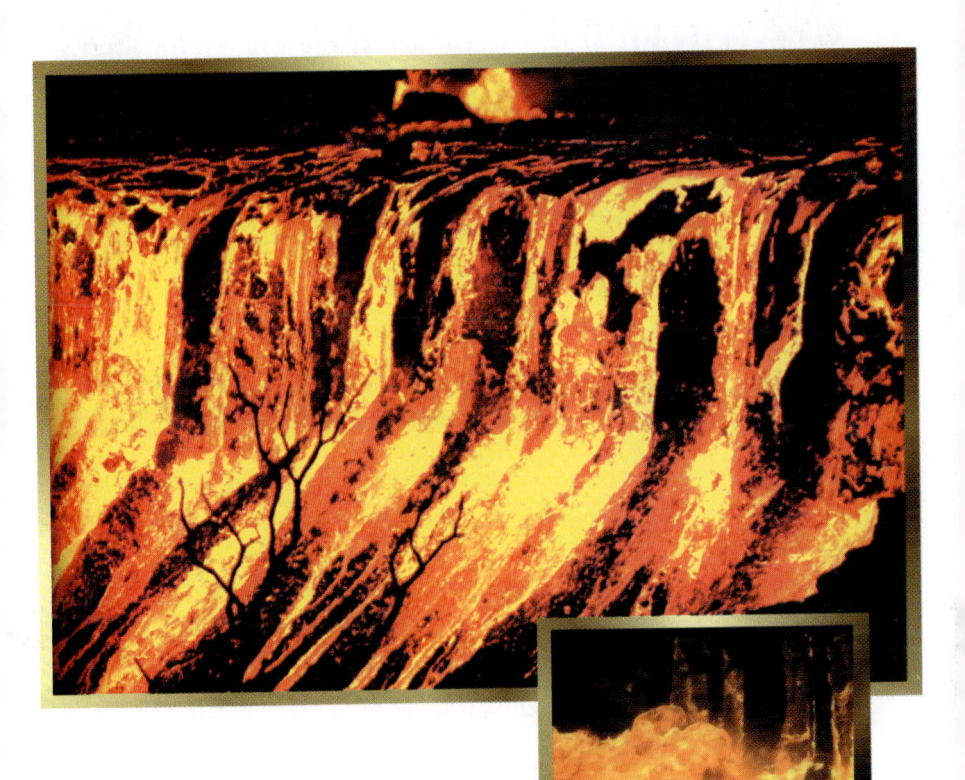

... Those who are too proud to worship Me will enter Hell abject.
(Surah Ghafir, 60)

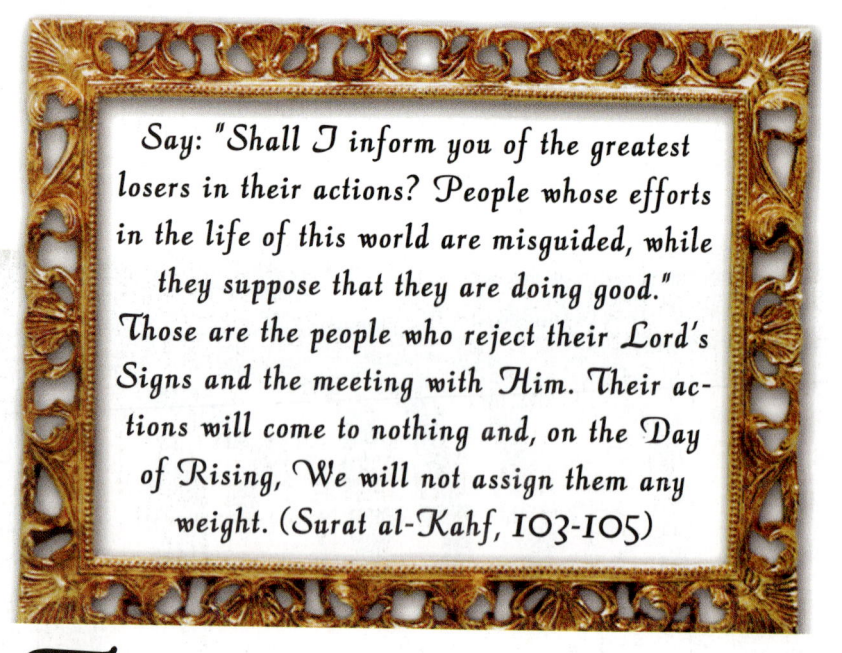

> Say: "Shall I inform you of the greatest losers in their actions? People whose efforts in the life of this world are misguided, while they suppose that they are doing good." Those are the people who reject their Lord's Signs and the meeting with Him. Their actions will come to nothing and, on the Day of Rising, We will not assign them any weight. (Surat al-Kahf, 103-105)

These verses speak of people who worked hard in their worldly lives, achieved financial success, had a career, and made works of art or scientific discoveries. But all this is wasted in the Hereafter, because they denied Allah's existence and revelation.

Irrespective of how great their achievements or how important their inventions, if they deny the Qur'an's revelations they will be at a loss in the Hereafter. Their situation is explained in the following verses:

But as for anyone who rejects faith, his actions will come to nothing and in the Hereafter he will be among the losers. (Surat al-Ma'ida, 5)

As for those who denied Our Signs and the encounter of the Hereafter, their actions will come to nothing. Will they be repaid except for what they did? (Surat al-A`raf, 147)

Like those before you who had greater strength than you and

more wealth and children. They enjoyed their portion; so enjoy your portion as those before you enjoyed theirs. You have plunged into defamation as they plunged into it. The actions of such people come to nothing in this world or the Hereafter. They are the lost. (Surat at-Tawba, 69)

The verses reveal that while the unbelievers's efforts are being wasted, the believers will be rewarded in the most pleasant way for every good deed that they do. As the following verse states, none of their efforts will be wasted:

Their Lord responds to them: "I will not let the deeds of anyone among you go to waste, male or female—you are both the same in that respect. Those who emigrated, were driven from their homes, suffered harm in My Way, and fought and were killed, I will erase their bad actions and admit them into Gardens with rivers flowing under them, as a reward from Allah. The best of all rewards is with Allah." (Surah Al `Imran, 195)

> Those who repent, those who worship, those who praise, those who fast, those who bow, those who prostrate, those who command the right, those who forbid the wrong, those who preserve the limits of Allah: give good news to the believers.
> (Surat at-Tawba, 112)

> *That is their repayment—Hell—because they did not believe and mocked My Signs and My Messengers.*
> *(Surat al-Kahf, 106)*

This verse reveals that the unbelievers will suffer in Hell because they mocked Allah's Signs and His Messengers. Mockery is an often-used method to prevent the Qur'an from being heard. This character deficiency, which the unbelievers recommend to each other, is revealed by the following verses:

Not one of their Lord's Signs comes to them without their turning away from it. They deny the truth each time it comes to them, but news of what they were mocking will certainly reach them. (Surat al-An`am, 4-5)

In addition, another verse says:

But when he [Musa] came to them with Our Signs, they merely laughed at them. (Surat az-Zukhruf, 47)

The main reason for this mockery is that these people do not want to hear what is being said, because they fear that their consciences might stir, that they might begin to consider the Hereafter's existence or their responsibilities related to this life and death. Intending to mock Allah's religion, sent to us through His Messengers, they draw caricatures, write sarcastic articles, and hope to have fun by doing so. Through such means, they try to forget about the realities revealed by the Qur'an.

Mockery is the ignorant strategy of weak people who are trying to cover up their inferiority complexes, for they have no evidence to support their arguments against the truth. Those people who mock what is right will be able to do only for a while, as revealed in: **"But Allah is mocking them, and drawing them on, as they wander blindly in their excessive insolence"** (Surat al-Baqara, 15). They will meet with what they mocked, and **"… what they used to mock at will engulf them"** (Surat az-Zumar, 48). Allah also clarifies what will happen to those who mock the Qur'an in the face of Hell's fire:

No wonder you are surprised as they laugh with scorn! When they are reminded, they do not pay heed. When they see a Sign, they only laugh with scorn. They say: "This is just downright magic. When we are dead and turned to dust and bones, will we then be raised up again alive? And our earlier ancestors as well?" Say: "Yes, and you will be in a despicable state." There will be but one Great Blast, and then their eyes will open. They will exclaim: "Alas for us! This is the Day of Reckoning!" This is the Day of Decision that you used to deny. (Surat as-Saffat, 12-21)

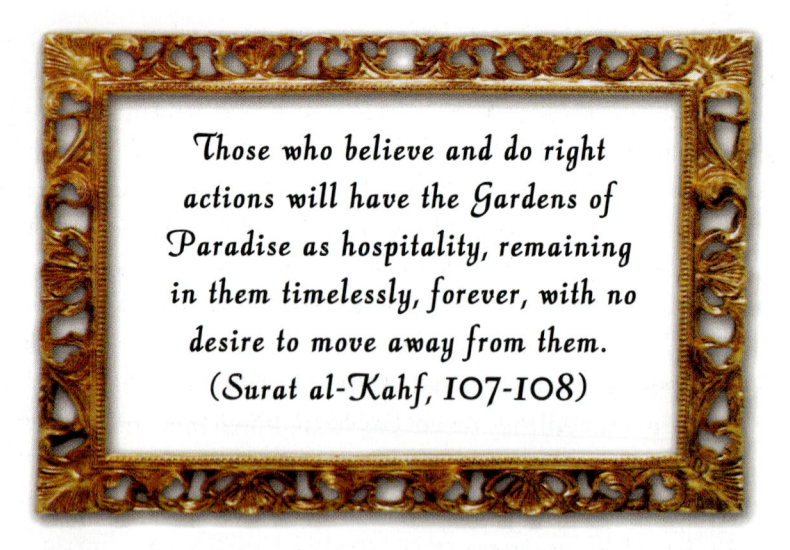

> *Those who believe and do right actions will have the Gardens of Paradise as hospitality, remaining in them timelessly, forever, with no desire to move away from them. (Surat al-Kahf, 107-108)*

On the Day of Judgment, sincere believers will receive their accounts, which contain all of their actions in life, from the right side. The Qur'an uses this expression for those people, destined for Paradise, who will have an easy trial. Other verses say this as well, among them:

> **As for him who is given his Book in his right hand, he will be given an easy reckoning and return to his family joyfully. (Surat al-Inshiqaq, 7-9)**

Once their trial is over, the believers experience great joy, for they have found salvation. As the following verse says:

> **Enter them [Gardens and Springs] in peace, in complete security! (Surat al-Hijr, 46)**

A believer who is told to enter Paradise will say:

> **If my people only knew how my Lord has forgiven me and placed me among the honored ones! (Surah Ya Sin, 26-27)**

In another verse, the believers are told:

> **…This is the Day when the sincerity of the sincere will benefit them. They will have Gardens with rivers flowing under**

them... (Surat al-Ma'ida, 119)

Countless gifts are awaiting the believers in Paradise, for:

They will enter Gardens of Eden in which they will be adorned with gold bracelets and pearls, and where their clothing will be of silk. They will say: "Praise be to Allah, Who has removed all sadness from us. Truly our Lord is Ever-Forgiving, Ever-Thankful: He Who has lodged us, out of His favor, in the Abode of Permanence, where no weariness or fatigue affects us." (Surah Fatir, 33-35)

The blessings of Paradise are indescribable. As the verses reveal, in Paradise our five senses will experience the greatest pleasures and joys. But the greatest gift of all in Paradise is Allah's good pleasure. Real happiness is the peace and happiness of having won Allah's good pleasure, of being pleased with everything that He has given, and of being grateful for it all. Allah says of the people in Paradise:

... **Allah is pleased with them, and they are pleased with Him. That is the Great Victory. (Surat al-Ma'ida, 119)**

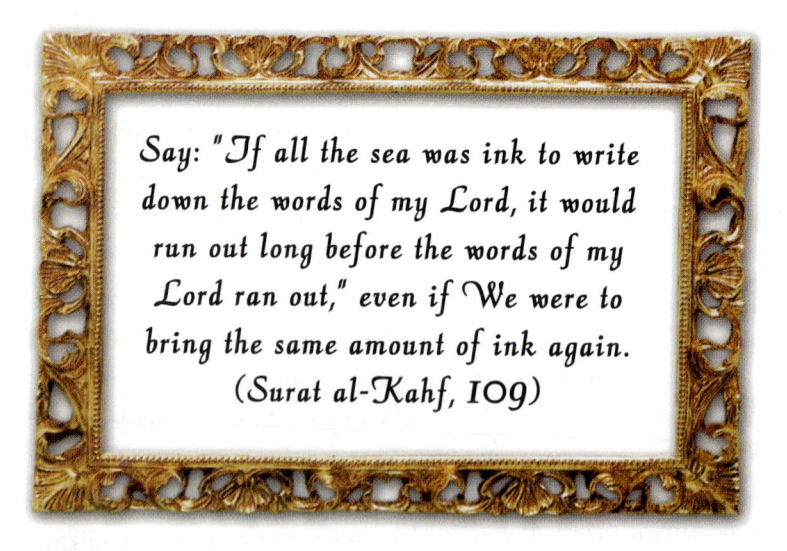

> Say: "If all the sea was ink to write down the words of my Lord, it would run out long before the words of my Lord ran out," even if We were to bring the same amount of ink again.
> (Surat al-Kahf, 109)

In this verse, Allah's infinite wisdom is described through an example. Allah has the knowledge of the heavens and Earth, of every being in between, of every law of nature and science, and of anything happening at anytime and anywhere, because He created it all.

Allah's knowledge has no boundaries. He knows simultaneously the identity of every person who lives and who has ever lived, when every single leaf falls from each tree, the state of every star among billions of stars in billions of galaxies, and of all the things that we could never finish writing about in these pages. He knows everything that happens on Earth, as well as everything happening in the universe and in the genetic code of every one of the billions of people, animals, and plants, simultaneously and regardless of when they lived. Allah, Who controls every point in space, also controls everything within and without of every human being. Allah has revealed this infinite knowledge in many verses, among them the following:

Do you not see that everyone in the heavens and Earth glorifies Allah, as do the birds with their outspread wings? Each one

knows its prayer and glorification. Allah knows what they do. (Surat an-Nur, 41)

See how they wrap themselves around, trying to conceal their feelings from Him! No, indeed! When they wrap their garments around themselves, He knows what they keep secret and what they make public. He knows what their hearts contain. (Surah Hud, 5)

... He knows what is before them and what is behind them, but they cannot grasp any of His knowledge, save what He wills. His Footstool encompasses the heavens and Earth, and their preservation does not tire Him. He is the Most High, the Magnificent. (Surat al-Baqara, 255)

He is Allah in the heavens and in Earth. He knows what you keep secret and what you make public, and He knows what you earn. (Surat al-An`am, 3)

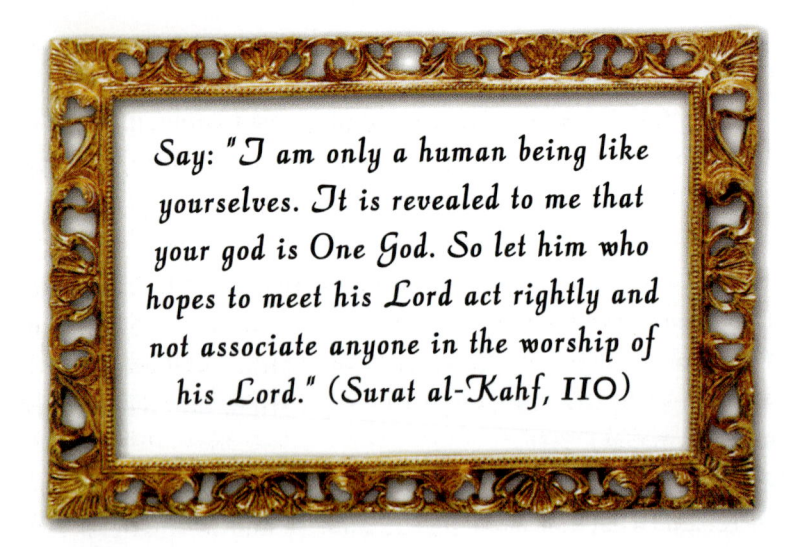

> Say: "I am only a human being like yourselves. It is revealed to me that your god is One God. So let him who hopes to meet his Lord act rightly and not associate anyone in the worship of his Lord." (Surat al-Kahf, 110)

Messengers have been sent to every nation, past and present, to call them to Allah's righteous path. Messengers are blessed people who explain Allah's existence and unity to their people, invite them to His religion, inform them of what Allah expects of them and what they should and should not do, and warn them about the punishment of Hell and, at the same time, give them the good news of Paradise.

The Messengers' lives are full of valuable lessons for those believers who understand and remember. Believers should not distinguish between the Messengers, whose noble attitude, behavior, and superior character are examples to emulate, and should take their advice and warnings seriously.

The calls to faith made by Allah's Messengers are, as revealed in the Qur'an, alike. Each of them invited people to believe in Allah and to abide by true revelation, not to transgress, and not to disobey His commands. For this reason, the believers should not prefer one Messenger over the other, should believe in what has been sent down to each Messenger, and answer their calls conscientiously. The verse proclaims:

> Say: "We believe in Allah and what has been sent down to us; what was sent down to Ibrahim, Isma`il, Ishaq, Ya`qub, and the Tribes; what Musa and `Isa were given; and what all the Prophets were given by their Lord. We do not differentiate between any of them. We are Muslims submitted to Him." (Surat al-Baqara, 136)

All Prophets called people to the true faith and the right path. Their calls were valid for both their own nations and for us. The basic concepts of faith and morals to which they called, as well as their superior characters, are a source of guidance for every generation, including ours. The Qur'an reveals, from many perspectives, the truths to which they called and their exemplary moral qualities. Allah commands the believers to follow the Prophets' righteous path.

> They are the ones to whom We gave the Book, Judgment, and Prophethood. If these people reject it, We have already entrusted it to a people who did not. They are the ones Allah has guided, so be guided by their guidance. Say: "I do not ask you for any wage for it. It is simply a reminder to all beings." (Surat al-An`am, 89-90)

For this reason, believers must read the accounts about the Messengers in the Qur'an carefully, accept their advice, and follow the righteous path diligently.

THE SIGNS IN SURAT AL-KAHF FOR THE END TIMES

Throughout this book on Surat al-Kahf, we have pointed out many of its signs addressing the End Times. The numerical (*abjad*) values of some of the verses fall close to our own era, such as:

> We fortified their hearts... (Surat al-Kahf, 14)
> Islamic era: 1400; Christian era: 1979

> He said: "The power my Lord has granted me is better than that..." (Surat al-Kahf, 95)
> Islamic era: 1409; Christian era: 1988 (without shaddah)

> We gave him power and authority on Earth... (Surat al-Kahf, 84)
> Islamic era: 1440; Christian era: 2019 (with shaddah)

A sign pointing at the beginning of the fifteenth Islamic century and the end of the twentieth and the beginning of the twenty-first Christian century is the number 1980, which is obtained by multiplying Surat al-Kahf's number of verses with its numerical order in the Qur'an.

> Surat al-Kahf, surah number 18 in the Qur'an, has 110 verses. Thus, 18x110=1980

Bediuzzaman Said Nursi also often indicated that this time was the beginning of the End Times. He says, for example:

> Thus, unfair people who do not know this truth say: "Why did the Companions of the Prophet with their vigilant hearts and keen sight, who had been taught all the details of the hereafter, suppose a fact that would occur one thousand four hundred years later to be close to their century, as though their ideas had deviated a thousand years from the truth?"[7]

Bediuzzaman, by saying "1400 years after" the Prophet's Companions, indicated the years around 1980 as the End Times. Here it is important to note that he said 1400, not 1373, 1378, and not 1398. In other words, the fifteenth Islamic century.

Conclusion

Throughout this book, we examined the revelation of wisdom, remembrance, and lessons contained in Surat al-Kahf. We explained the inherent wisdom in its verses, as our Lord commands in: **"Remember Allah's blessing to you, and the Book and Wisdom He has sent down to you to admonish you"** (Surat al-Baqara, 231).

Every Muslim is responsible for trying to understand and live by the wisdom revealed in the verses and for telling people about them, as Allah says:

There is instruction in their stories for people of intelligence. This is not a narration that has been invented, but a confirmation of all that came before, a clarification of everything, and a guidance and a mercy for people who believe. (Surah Yusuf, 111)

For every person seeking guidance and wisdom, the book you are holding in your hands contains very important reflections on devotion, obedience, submission to destiny, this worldly and temporary life, Allah's being beyond time and space, His servants who are blessed by special knowledge, the end awaiting those who grow arrogant toward Allah's revelation, and the blissful future waiting those who believe.

Surat al-Kahf also contains very good news for the believers: the approaching glorious period of the End Times. If Surat al-Kahf is viewed from this perspective, it points at the different phases (the beginning, development, and conclusion) of Islam during the End Times, which culminates in the rule of Islam and concludes with the arrival of

Prophet `Isa (as).

As we understand from many verses, victory and dominion are promised to believers of depth and wisdom. This is the last phase, and an era in which the revelations of Surat an-Nur will come true by Allah's will, as follows:

Allah has promised those of you who believe and do right actions that He will make them successors in the land, just as He made those before them successors, and will firmly establish for them their religion with which He is pleased, and give them, in place of their fear, security. "They worship Me, not associating anything with Me." Any who do not believe after that, such people are deviators. (Surat an-Nur, 55)

The Deception of Evolution

Darwinism, in other words the theory of evolution, was put forward with the aim of denying the fact of creation, but is in truth nothing but failed, unscientific nonsense. This theory, which claims that life emerged by chance from inanimate matter, was invalidated by the scientific evidence of clear "design" in the universe and in living things. In this way, science confirmed the fact that Allah created the universe and the living things in it. The propaganda carried out today in order to keep the theory of evolution alive is based solely on the distortion of the scientific facts, biased interpretation, and lies and falsehoods disguised as science.

Yet this propaganda cannot conceal the truth. The fact that the theory of evolution is the greatest deception in the history of science has been expressed more and more in the scientific world over the last 20-30 years. Research carried out after the 1980s in particular has revealed that the claims of Darwinism are totally unfounded, something that has been stated by a large number of scientists. In the United States in particular, many scientists from such different fields as biology, biochemistry and paleontology recognize the invalidity of Darwinism and employ the concept of intelligent design to account for the origin of life. This "intelligent design" is a scientific expression of the fact that Allah created all living things.

We have examined the collapse of the theory of evolution and the proofs of creation in great scientific detail in many of our works, and are still continuing to do so. Given the enormous importance of this subject, it will be of great benefit to summarize it here.

The Scientific Collapse of Darwinism

Although this doctrine goes back as far as ancient Greece, the theory of evolution was advanced extensively in the nineteenth century. The most important development that made it the top topic of the world of science was Charles Darwin's *The Origin of Species*, published in 1859. In this book, he denied that Allah created different living species on Earth separately, for he claimed that all living beings had a common ancestor and had diversified over time through small changes. Darwin's theory was not based on any concrete scientific finding; as he also accepted, it was just an "assumption." Moreover, as Darwin confessed in the long chapter of his book titled "Difficulties of the Theory," the theory failed in the face of many critical questions.

Darwin invested all of his hopes in new scientific discoveries, which he expected to solve these difficulties. However, contrary to his expectations, scientific findings expanded the dimensions of these difficulties. The defeat of Darwinism in the face of science can be reviewed under three basic topics:

Charles Darwin

1) The theory cannot explain

how life originated on Earth.

2) No scientific finding shows that the "evolutionary mechanisms" proposed by the theory have any evolutionary power at all.

3) The fossil record proves the exact opposite of what the theory suggests.

In this section, we will examine these three basic points in general outlines:

The First Insurmountable Step: The Origin of Life

The theory of evolution posits that all living species evolved from a single living cell that emerged on the primitive Earth 3.8 billion years ago. How a single cell could generate millions of complex living species and, if such an evolution really occurred, why traces of it cannot be observed in the fossil record are some of the questions that the theory cannot answer. However, first and foremost, we need to ask: How did this "first cell" originate?

Since the theory of evolution denies creation and any kind of supernatural intervention, it maintains that the "first cell" originated coincidentally within the laws of nature, without any design, plan or arrangement. According to the theory, inanimate matter must have produced a living cell as a result of coincidences. Such a claim, however, is inconsistent with the most unassailable rules of biology.

"Life Comes from Life"

In his book, Darwin never referred to the origin of life. The primitive understanding of science in his time rested on the assumption that living beings had a very simple structure. Since medieval times, spontaneous generation, which asserts that non-living materials came together to form living organisms, had been widely accepted. It was commonly believed that insects came into being from food leftovers, and mice from wheat. Interesting experiments were conducted to prove this theory. Some wheat was placed on a dirty piece of cloth, and it was believed that mice would originate from it after a while.

Similarly, maggots developing in rotting meat was assumed to be evidence of spontaneous generation. However, it was later understood that worms did not

Louis Pasteur destroyed the belief that life could be created from inanimate substances.

appear on meat spontaneously, but were carried there by flies in the form of larvae, invisible to the naked eye.

Even when Darwin wrote *The Origin of Species*, the belief that bacteria could come into existence from non-living matter was widely accepted in the world of science.

However, five years after the publication of Darwin's book, Louis Pasteur announced his results after long studies and experiments, that disproved spontaneous generation, a cornerstone of Darwin's theory. In his triumphal lecture at the Sorbonne in 1864, Pasteur said: *"Never will the doctrine of spontaneous generation recover from the mortal blow struck by this simple experiment."*[8]

For a long time, advocates of the theory of evolution resisted these findings. However, as the development of science unraveled the complex structure of the cell of a living being, the idea that life could come into being coincidentally faced an even greater impasse.

Inconclusive Efforts in the Twentieth Century

The first evolutionist who took up the subject of the origin of life in the twentieth century was the renowned Russian biologist Alexander Oparin. With various theses he advanced in the 1930s, he tried to prove that a living cell could originate by coincidence. These studies, however, were doomed to failure, and Oparin had to make the following confession:

Alexander Oparin

> *Unfortunately, however, the problem of the origin of the cell is perhaps the most obscure point in the whole study of the evolution of organisms.*[9]

Evolutionist followers of Oparin tried to carry out experiments to solve this problem. The best known experiment was carried out by the American chemist Stanley Miller in 1953. Combining the gases he alleged to have existed in the primordial Earth's atmosphere in an experiment set-up, and adding energy to the mixture, Miller synthesized several organic molecules (amino acids) present in the structure of proteins.

Barely a few years had passed before it was revealed that this experiment, which was then presented as an important step in the name of evolution, was invalid, for the atmosphere used in the experiment was very different from the real Earth conditions.[10]

After a long silence, Miller confessed that the atmosphere medium he used was unrealistic.[11]

All the evolutionists' efforts throughout the twentieth century to explain the origin of life ended in failure. The geochemist Jeffrey Bada, from the San Diego Scripps Institute accepts this fact in an article published in *Earth* magazine in 1998:

> *Today as we leave the twentieth century, we still face the biggest unsolved problem that we had when we entered the twentieth century: How did life originate on Earth?*[12]

The Complex Structure of Life

The primary reason why the theory of evolution ended up in such a great impasse regarding the origin of life is that even those living organisms deemed to be the simplest have incredibly complex structures. The cell of a living thing is more complex than all of our man-made technological products. Today, even in the most developed laboratories of the world, a living cell cannot be produced by bringing organic chemicals together.

The conditions required for the formation of a cell are too great in quantity to be explained away by coincidences. The probability of proteins, the building blocks of a cell, being synthesized coincidentally, is 1

All information about living beings is stored in the DNA molecule. This incredibly efficient information storage method alone is a clear evidence that life did not come into being by chance, but has been purposely designed, or, better to say, marvellously created.

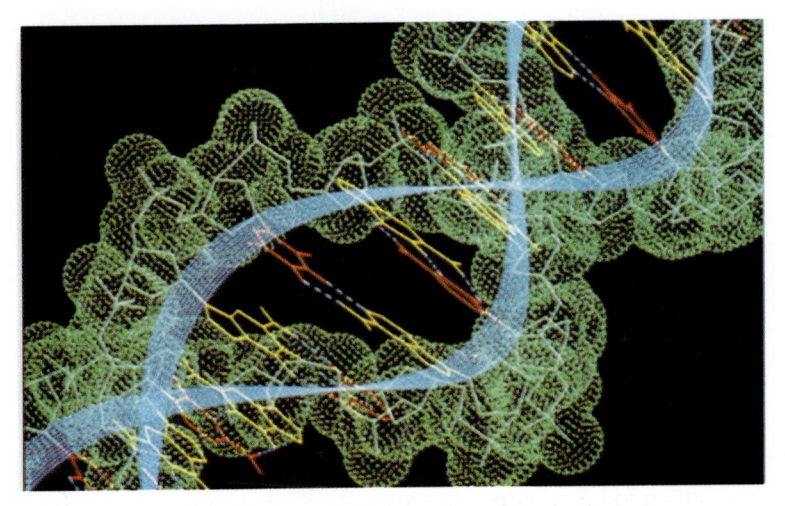

One of the evolutionists' gravest deceptions is the way they imagine that life could have emerged spontaneously on what they refer to as the primitive Earth, represented in the picture above. They tried to prove these claims with such studies as the Miller experiment. Yet they again suffered defeat in the face of the scientific facts; The results obtained in the 1970s proved that the atmosphere on what they describe as the primitive Earth was totally unsuited to life.

in 10^{950} for an average protein made up of 500 amino acids. In mathematics, a probability smaller than 1 over 10^{50} is considered to be impossible in practical terms.

The DNA molecule, which is located in the nucleus of a cell and which stores genetic information, is an incredible databank. If the information coded in DNA were written down, it would make a giant library consisting of an estimated 900 volumes of encyclopedias consisting of 500 pages each.

A very interesting dilemma emerges at this point: DNA can replicate itself only with the help of some specialized proteins (enzymes). However, the synthesis of these enzymes can be realized only by the information coded in DNA. As they both depend on each other, they have to exist at the same time for replication. This brings the scenario that life originated by itself to a deadlock. Prof. Leslie Orgel, an evolutionist of epute from the University of San Diego, California, confesses this fact in the September 1994 issue of the *Scientific American* magazine:

> It is extremely improbable that proteins and nucleic acids, both of which are structurally complex, arose spontaneously in the same place at the same time. Yet it also seems impossible to have one without the other. And so, at first glance, one might have to conclude that life could never, in fact, have originated by chemical means.[13]

No doubt, if it is impossible for life to have originated from natural causes, then it has to be accepted that life was "created" in a supernatural way. This fact explicitly invalidates the theory of evolution, whose main purpose is to deny creation.

Imaginary Mechanisms of Evolution

The second important point that negates Darwin's theory is that both concepts put forward by the theory as "evolutionary mechanisms" were understood to have, in reality, no evolutionary power.

Darwin based his evolution allegation entirely on the mechanism of "natural selection." The importance he placed on this mechanism was evident in the name of his book: *The Origin of Species, By Means of Natural Selection…*

Natural selection holds that those living things that are stronger and more suited to the natural conditions of their habitats will survive in the struggle for life. For example, in a deer herd under the threat of attack by wild animals, those that can run faster will survive. Therefore, the deer herd will be comprised of faster and stronger individuals. However, unquestionably, this mechanism will not cause deer to evolve and transform themselves into another living species, for instance, horses.

Therefore, the mechanism of natural selection has no evolutionary power. Darwin was also aware of this fact and had to state this in his book *The Origin of Species*:

Natural selection can do nothing until favourable individual differences or variations occur.[14]

Lamarck's Impact

So, how could these "favorable variations" occur? Darwin tried to answer this question from the standpoint of the primitive understanding of science at that time. According to the French biologist Chevalier de Lamarck (1744-1829), who lived before Darwin, living creatures passed on the traits they acquired during their lifetime to the next generation. He asserted that these traits, which accumulated from one generation to another, caused new species to be formed. For instance, he claimed that giraffes evolved from antelopes; as they struggled to eat the leaves of high trees, their necks were extended from generation to generation.

French biologist Lamarck

Darwin also gave similar examples. In his book *The Origin of Species*, for instance, he said that some bears going into water to find food transformed themselves into whales over time.[15]

However, the laws of inheritance discovered by Gregor Mendel (1822-84) and verified by the science of genetics, which flourished in the twentieth century, utterly demolished the legend that acquired traits were passed on to subsequent generations. Thus, natural selection fell out of favor as an evolutionary mechanism.

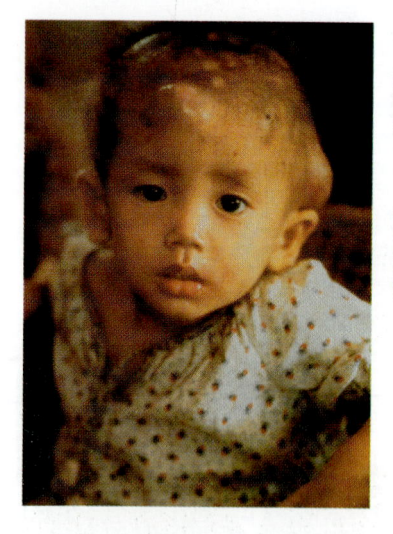

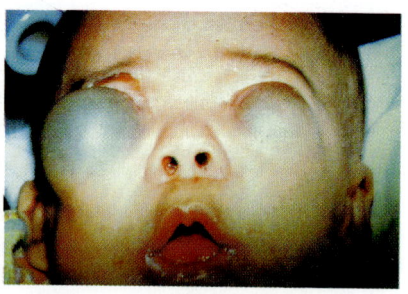

Accidental mutations develop into defects in humans as well as other living beings. The Chernobyl disaster is an eye-opener for the effects of mutations.

Neo-Darwinism and Mutations

In order to find a solution, Darwinists advanced the "Modern Synthetic Theory," or as it is more commonly known, Neo-Darwinism, at the end of the 1930's. Neo-Darwinism added mutations, which are distortions formed in the genes of living beings due to such external factors as radiation or replication errors, as the "cause of favorable variations" in addition to natural mutation.

Today, the model that stands for evolution in the world is Neo-Darwinism. The theory maintains that millions of living beings formed as a result of a process whereby numerous complex organs of these organisms (e.g., ears, eyes, lungs, and wings) underwent "mutations," that is, genetic disorders. Yet, there is an outright scientific fact that totally undermines this theory: Mutations do not cause living beings to develop; on the contrary, they are always harmful.

The reason for this is very simple: DNA has a very complex structure, and random effects can only harm it. The American geneticist B.G. Ranganathan explains this as follows:

First, genuine mutations are very rare in nature. Secondly, most mutations are harmful since they are random, rather than orderly

antennae
eye
leg
mouth

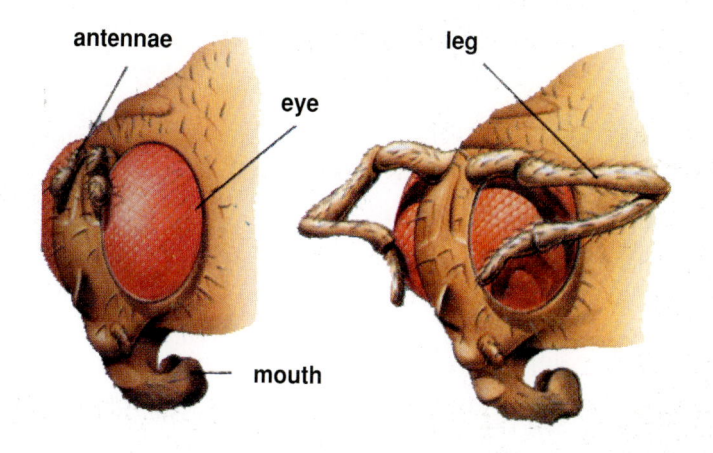

Since the beginning of the twentieth century, evolutionary biologists have sought examples of useful mutations by creating mutant flies. But these efforts have always resulted in sick and deformed creatures. The top picture shows the head of a normal fruit fly, and the picture on the right shows the head of fruit fly with legs coming out of it, the result of mutation.

changes in the structure of genes; any random change in a highly ordered system will be for the worse, not for the better. For example, if an earthquake were to shake a highly ordered structure such as a building, there would be a random change in the framework of the building which, in all probability, would not be an improvement.[16]

Not surprisingly, no mutation example, which is useful, that is, which is observed to develop the genetic code, has been observed so far. All mutations have proved to be harmful. It was understood that mutation, which is presented as an "evolutionary mechanism," is actually a genetic occurrence that harms living things, and leaves them disabled. (The most common effect of mutation on human beings is cancer.) Of course, a destructive mechanism cannot be an "evolutionary mechanism." Natural selection, on the other hand, "can do nothing by itself," as Darwin also accepted. This fact shows us that there is no "evolutionary mechanism" in nature. Since no evolutionary mechanism exists, no such any imaginary process called "evolution" could have taken place.

The Fossil Record: No Sign of Intermediate Forms

The clearest evidence that the scenario suggested by the theory of evolution did not take place is the fossil record.

The theory of evolution claims that living species gradually evolved from one another. The fossil record, however, explicitly falsifies this claim. For example, in the Cambrian Period, some 550 million years ago, tens of totally distinct living species emerged suddenly. These living beings depicted in the above picture have very complex structures. This fact, referred to as the "Cambrian Explosion" in scientific literature is plain evidence of creation.

The 150-200-million-year-old fossil dragonfly (Jurassic-Recent age) is no different from specimens living today.

According to this theory, every living species has sprung from a predecessor. A previously existing species turned into something else over time and all species have come into being in this way. In other words, this transformation proceeds gradually over millions of years.

Had this been the case, numerous intermediary species should have existed and lived within this long transformation period.

For instance, some half-fish/half-reptiles should have lived in the past which had acquired some reptilian traits in addition to the fish traits they already had. Or there should have existed some reptile-birds, which acquired some bird traits in addition to the reptilian traits they already had. Since these would be in a transitional phase, they should be disabled, defective, crippled living beings. Evolutionists refer to these imaginary creatures, which they believe to have lived in the past, as "transitional forms."

If such animals ever really existed, there should be millions and even billions of them in number and variety. More importantly, the remains of these strange creatures should be present in the fossil record. In *The Origin of Species*, Darwin explained:

> If my theory be true, numberless intermediate varieties, linking most closely all of the species of the same group together must assuredly

have existed.... Consequently, evidence of their former existence could be found only amongst fossil remains.[17]

Darwin's Hopes Shattered

However, although evolutionists have been making strenuous efforts to find fossils since the middle of the nineteenth century all over the world, no transitional forms have yet been uncovered. All of the fossils, contrary to the evolutionists' expectations, show that life appeared on Earth all of a sudden and fully-formed.

One famous British paleontologist, Derek V. Ager, admits this fact, even though he is an evolutionist:

The point emerges that if we examine the fossil record in detail, whether at the level of orders or of species, we find – over and over again – not gradual evolution, but the sudden explosion of one group at the expense of another.[19]

This means that in the fossil record, all living species suddenly emerge as fully formed, without any intermediate forms in between. This is just the opposite of Darwin's assumptions. Also, this is very strong evidence that all living things are created. The only explanation of a living species emerging suddenly and complete in every detail without any evolutionary ancestor is that it was created. This fact is admitted also by the widely known evolutionist biologist Douglas Futuyma:

Creation and evolution, between them, exhaust the possible explanations for the origin of living things. Organisms either appeared on the earth fully developed or they did not. If they did not, they must have developed from pre-existing species by some process of modification. If they did appear in a fully developed state, they must indeed have been created by some omnipotent intelligence.[18]

Fossils show that living beings emerged fully developed and in a perfect state on the earth. That means that "the origin of species," contrary to Darwin's supposition, is not evolution, but creation.

The Tale of Human Evolution

The subject most often brought up by advocates of the theory of evolution is the subject of the origin of man. The Darwinist claim holds that modern man evolved from ape-like creatures. During this alleged evolutionary process, which is supposed to have started 4-5 million years ago, some "transitional forms" between modern man and his ancestors are supposed to have existed. According to this completely imaginary scenario, four basic "categories" are listed:

1. *Australopithecus*
2. *Homo habilis*
3. *Homo erectus*
4. *Homo sapiens*

Evolutionist newspapers and magazines often print pictures of primitive man. The only available source for these pictures is the imagination of the artist. Evolutionary theory has been so dented by scientific data that today we see less and less of it in the serious press.

Evolutionists call man's so-called first ape-like ancestors *Australopithecus*, which means "South African ape." These living beings are actually nothing but an old ape species that has become extinct. Extensive research done on various *Australopithecus* specimens by two world famous anatomists from England and the USA, namely, Lord Solly Zuckerman and Prof. Charles Oxnard, shows that these apes belonged to an ordinary ape species that became extinct and bore no resemblance to humans.[20]

Evolutionists classify the next stage of human evolution as "*homo*," that is "man." According to their claim, the living beings in the *Homo* series are more developed than *Australopithecus*. Evolutionists devise a fanciful evolution scheme by arranging different fossils of these creatures in a particular order. This scheme is imaginary because it has never been proved that there is an evolutionary relation between these different classes. Ernst Mayr, one of the twentieth century's most important evolutionists, contends in his book *One Long Argument* that "particularly historical [puzzles] such as the origin of life or of *Homo sapiens*, are extremely difficult and may even resist a final, satisfying explanation."[21]

By outlining the link chain as *Australopithecus* > *Homo habilis* > *Homo erectus* > *Homo sapiens*, evolutionists imply that each of these species is one another's ancestor. However, recent findings of paleoanthropologists have revealed that *Australopithecus*, *Homo habilis*, and *Homo erectus* lived at different parts of the world at the same time.[22]

Moreover, a certain segment of humans classified as *Homo erectus* have lived up until very modern times. *Homo sapiens neandarthalensis* and *Homo sapiens sapiens* (modern man) co-existed in the same region.[23]

This situation apparently indicates the invalidity of the claim that they are ancestors of one another. A paleontologist from Harvard University, Stephen Jay Gould, explains this deadlock of the theory of evolution, although he is an evolutionist himself:

> What has become of our ladder if there are three coexisting lineages of hominids (A. africanus, the robust australopithecines, and H. habilis), none clearly derived from another? Moreover, none of the three display any evolutionary trends during their tenure on earth.[24]

Put briefly, the scenario of human evolution, which is "upheld" with the help of various drawings of some "half ape, half human" creatures appearing in the media and course books, that is, frankly, by means of propaganda, is nothing but a tale with no scientific foundation.

Lord Solly Zuckerman, one of the most famous and respected scientists in the U.K., who carried out research on this subject for years and studied *Australopithecus* fossils for 15 years, finally concluded, despite being an evolutionist himself, that there is, in fact, no such family tree branching out from ape-like creatures to man.

Zuckerman also made an interesting "spectrum of science" ranging from those he considered scientific to those he considered unscientific. According to Zuckerman's spectrum, the most "scientific"—that is, depending on concrete data—fields of science are chemistry and physics. After them come the biological sciences and then the social sciences. At the far end of the spectrum, which is the part considered to be most "unscientific," are "extra-sensory perception"—concepts such as telepathy and sixth sense—and finally "human evolution." Zuckerman explains his reasoning:

We then move right off the register of objective truth into those fields of presumed biological science, like extrasensory perception or the interpretation of man's fossil history, where to the faithful [evolutionist] anything is possible – and where the ardent believer [in evolution] is sometimes able to believe several contradictory things at the same time.[25]

The tale of human evolution boils down to nothing but the prejudiced interpretations of some fossils unearthed by certain people, who blindly adhere to their theory.

Darwinian Formula!

Besides all the technical evidence we have dealt with so far, let us now for once, examine what kind of a superstition the evolutionists have with an example so simple as to be understood even by children:

Evolutionary theory asserts that life is formed by chance. According to this claim, lifeless and unconscious atoms came together to form the cell and then they somehow formed other living things, including man. Let us think about that. When we bring together the elements that are the building-blocks of life such as carbon, phosphorus, nitrogen and potassium, only a heap is formed. No matter what treatments it undergoes, this atomic heap cannot form even a single living being. If you like, let us formulate an "experiment" on this subject and let us examine on the behalf of evolutionists what they really claim without pronouncing loudly under the name "Darwinian formula":

Let evolutionists put plenty of materials present in the composition of living beings such as phosphorus, nitrogen, carbon, oxygen, iron, and magnesium into big barrels. Moreover, let them add in these barrels any material that does not exist under normal conditions, but they think as necessary. Let them add in this mixture as many amino acids—which have no possibility of forming under natural conditions—and as many proteins—a single one of which has a formation probability of 10^{-950}—as they like. Let them expose these mixtures to as much heat and moisture as they like. Let them stir these with whatever technologically developed device they like. Let them put the foremost scientists beside these barrels. Let these experts wait in turn beside these barrels for billions, and even trillions of years. Let them be free to use all kinds of conditions they believe to be necessary for a human's formation. No matter what they do, they cannot produce from these barrels a human, say a professor that examines his cell structure under the electron microscope. They cannot produce giraffes, lions, bees, canaries, horses, dolphins, roses, orchids, lilies, carnations, bananas, oranges, apples, dates, tomatoes, melons, watermelons, figs, olives, grapes, peaches, peafowls, pheasants, multicolored butterflies, or millions of other living beings such as these. Indeed, they could not obtain even a single cell of any one of them.

Briefly, unconscious atoms cannot form the cell by coming together. They cannot take a new decision and divide this cell into two, then take other decisions and create the professors who first invent the electron microscope and then examine their own cell structure under that microscope. Matter is an unconscious, lifeless heap, and it comes to life with Allah's superior creation.

Evolutionary theory, which claims the opposite, is a total fallacy

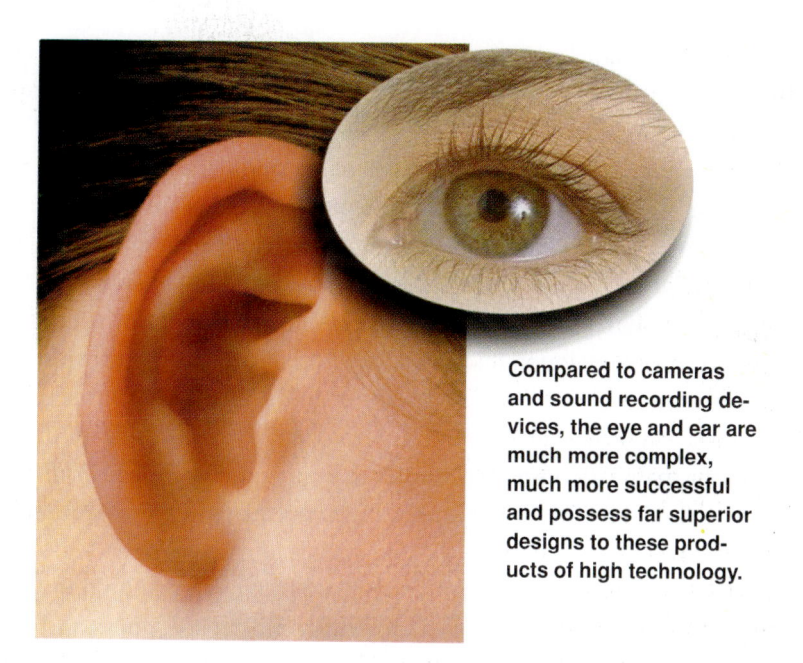

Compared to cameras and sound recording devices, the eye and ear are much more complex, much more successful and possess far superior designs to these products of high technology.

completely contrary to reason. Thinking even a little bit on the claims of tevolutionists discloses this reality, just as in the above example.

Technology in the Eye and the Ear

Another subject that remains unanswered by evolutionary theory is the excellent quality of perception in the eye and the ear.

Before passing on to the subject of the eye, let us briefly answer the question of how we see. Light rays coming from an object fall oppositely on the eye's retina. Here, these light rays are transmitted into electric signals by cells and reach a tiny spot at the back of the brain, the "center of vision." These electric signals are perceived in this center as an image after a series of processes. With this technical background, let us do some thinking.

The brain is insulated from light. That means that its inside is completely dark, and that no light reaches the place where it is located. Thus, the "center of vision" is never touched by light and may even be the darkest place you have ever known. However, you observe a luminous, bright world in this pitch darkness.

The image formed in the eye is so sharp and distinct that even the technology of the twentieth century has not been able to attain it. For instance, look at the book you are reading, your hands with which you are holding it, and then lift your head and look around you. Have you ever seen such a sharp and distinct image as this one at any other place? Even the most developed television screen produced by the greatest television producer in the world cannot provide such a sharp image for you. This is a three-dimensional, colored, and extremely sharp image. For more than 100 years, thousands of engineers have been trying to achieve this sharpness. Factories, huge premises were established, much research has been done, plans and designs have been made for this purpose. Again, look at a TV screen and the book you hold in your hands. You will see that there is a big difference in sharpness and distinction. Moreover, the TV screen shows you a two-dimensional image, whereas with your eyes, you watch a three-dimensional perspective with depth.

For many years, tens of thousands of engineers have tried to make a three-dimensional TV and achieve the vision quality of the eye. Yes, they have made a three-dimensional television system, but it is not possible to watch it without putting on special 3-D glasses; moreover, it is only an artificial three-dimension. The background is more blurred, the foreground appears like a paper setting. Never has it been possible to produce a sharp and distinct vision like that of the eye. In both the camera and the television, there is a loss of image quality.

Evolutionists claim that the mechanism producing this sharp and distinct image has been formed by chance. Now, if somebody told you that the television in your room was formed as a result of chance, that all of its atoms just happened to come together and make up this device that produces an image, what would you think? How can atoms do what thousands of people cannot?

If a device producing a more primitive image than the eye could not have been formed by chance, then it is very evident that the eye and the image seen by the eye could not have been formed by chance. The same situation applies to the ear. The outer ear picks up the available sounds by the auricle and directs them to the middle ear, the middle ear transmits the sound vibrations by intensifying them, and the inner ear sends these vibrations to the brain by translating them into electric signals. Just as with the eye, the act of hearing finalizes in the center of hearing in the brain.

The situation in the eye is also true for the ear. That is, the brain is insulated from sound just as it is from light. It does not let any sound in. Therefore, no matter how noisy is the outside, the inside of the brain is completely silent. Nevertheless, the sharpest sounds are perceived in the brain. In your completely silent brain, you listen to symphonies, and hear all of the noises in a crowded place. However, were the sound level in your brain was measured by a precise device at that moment, complete silence would be found to be prevailing there.

As is the case with imagery, decades of effort have been spent in trying to generate and reproduce sound that is faithful to the original. The results of these efforts are sound recorders, high-fidelity systems, and systems for sensing sound. Despite all of this technology and the thousands of engineers and experts who have been working on this endeavor, no sound has yet been obtained that has the same sharpness and clarity as the sound perceived by the ear. Think of the highest-quality hi-fi systems produced by the largest company in the music industry. Even in these devices, when sound is recorded some of it is lost; or when you turn on a hi-fi you always hear a hissing sound before the music starts. However, the sounds that are the products of the human body's technology are extremely sharp and clear. A human ear never perceives a sound accompanied by a hissing sound or with atmospherics as does a hi-fi; rather, it perceives sound exactly as it is, sharp and clear. This is the way it has been since the creation of man.

So far, no man-made visual or recording apparatus has been as sensitive and successful in perceiving sensory data as are the eye and the ear. However, as far as seeing and hearing are concerned, a far greater truth lies beyond all this.

To Whom Does the Consciousness That Sees and Hears within the Brain Belong?

Who watches an alluring world in the brain, listens to symphonies and the twittering of birds, and smells the rose?

The stimulations coming from a person's eyes, ears, and nose travel to the brain as electro-chemical nerve impulses. In biology, physiology, and biochemistry books, you can find many details about how this image forms in the brain. However, you will never come across the most important fact: Who perceives these electro-chemical nerve impulses as images, sounds, odors, and sensory events in the brain? There is a consciousness in the brain that perceives all this without feeling any need for an eye, an ear, and a nose. To whom does this consciousness belong? Of course it does not belong to the nerves, the fat layer, and neurons comprising the brain. This is why Darwinist-materialists, who believe that everything is comprised of matter, cannot answer these questions.

For this consciousness is the spirit created by Allah, which needs neither the eye to watch the images nor the ear to hear the sounds. Furthermore, it does not need the brain to think.

Everyone who reads this explicit and scientific fact should ponder on Almighty Allah, and fear and seek refuge in Him, for He squeezes the entire universe in a pitch-dark place of a few cubic centimeters in a three-dimensional, colored, shadowy, and luminous form.

A Materialist Faith

The information we have presented so far shows us that the theory of evolution is a incompatible with scientific findings. The theory's claim regarding the origin of life is inconsistent with science, the evolutionary mechanisms it proposes have no evolutionary power, and fossils demonstrate that the required intermediate forms have never existed. So, it certainly follows that the theory of evolution should be pushed aside as an unscientific idea. This is how many ideas, such as the Earth-centered universe model, have been taken out of the agenda of science throughout history.

However, the theory of evolution is kept on the agenda of science. Some people even try to represent criticisms directed against it as an "attack on science." Why?

The reason is that this theory is an indispensable dogmatic belief for some circles. These circles are blindly devoted to materialist philosophy and adopt Darwinism because it is the only materialist explanation that can be put forward to explain the workings of nature.

Interestingly enough, they also confess this fact from time to time. A well-known geneticist and an outspoken evolutionist, Richard C. Lewontin from Harvard University, confesses that he is "first and foremost a materialist and then a scientist":

> It is not that the methods and institutions of science somehow compel us accept a material explanation of the phenomenal world, but, on the contrary, that we are forced by our a priori adherence to material causes to create an apparatus of investigation and a set of concepts that produce material explanations, no matter how counter-intuitive, no matter how mystifying to the uninitiated. Moreover, that materialism is absolute, so we cannot allow a Divine Foot in the door.[26]

These are explicit statements that Darwinism is a dogma kept alive just for the sake of adherence to materialism. This dogma maintains that there is no being save matter. Therefore, it argues that inanimate, unconscious matter created life. It insists that millions of different living species (e.g., birds, fish, giraffes, tigers, insects, trees, flowers, whales, and human beings) originated as a result of the interactions between matter such as pouring rain, lightning flashes, and so on, out of inanimate matter. This is a precept contrary both to reason and science. Yet Darwinists continue to defend it just so as "not to allow a Divine Foot in the door."

Anyone who does not look at the origin of living beings with a materialist prejudice will see this evident truth: All living beings are works of a Creator, Who is All-Powerful, All-Wise, and All-Knowing. This Creator is Allah, Who created the whole universe from non-existence, designed it in the most perfect form, and fashioned all living beings.

The Theory of Evolution is the Most Potent Spell in the World

Anyone free of prejudice and the influence of any particular ideology, who uses only his or her reason and logic, will clearly understand that belief in the theory of evolution, which brings to mind the superstitions of societies with no knowledge of science or civilization, is quite impossible.

As explained above, those who believe in the theory of evolution think that a few atoms and molecules thrown into a huge vat could produce thinking, reasoning professors and university students; such scientists as Einstein and Galileo; such artists as Humphrey Bogart, Frank Sinatra and Luciano Pavarotti; as well as antelopes, lemon trees, and carnations. Moreover, as the scientists and professors who believe in this nonsense are educated people, it is quite justifiable to speak of this theory as "the most potent spell in history." Never before has any other belief or idea so taken away peoples' powers of reason, refused to allow them to think intelligently and logically and hidden the truth from them as if they had been blindfolded. This is an even worse and unbelievable blindness than the Egyptians worshipping the Sun God Ra, totem worship in some parts of Africa, the people of Saba worshipping the Sun, the tribe of Prophet Ibrahim (as) worshipping idols they had made with their own hands, or the people of the Prophet Musa (as) worshipping the Golden Calf.

In fact, Allah has pointed to this lack of reason in the Qur'an. In many verse, He reveals in many verses that some peoples' minds will be closed and that they will be powerless to see the truth. Some of these verses are as follows:

As for those who do not believe, it makes no difference to them whether you warn them or do not warn them, they will not believe. Allah has sealed up their hearts and hearing and over their eyes is a blindfold. They will have a terrible punishment. (Surat al-Baqara, 6-7)

… They have hearts with which they do not understand. They have eyes with which they do not see. They have ears with which they do not hear. Such people are like cattle. No, they are even further astray! They are the unaware. (Surat al-A'raf, 179)

Even if We opened up to them a door into heaven, and they spent the day ascending through it, they would only say: "Our eyesight is befuddled! Or rather we have been put under a spell!" (Surat al-Hijr, 14-15)

Words cannot express just how astonishing it is that this spell should hold such a wide community in thrall, keep people from the truth, and not be broken for 150 years. It is understandable that one or a few people might believe in impossible scenarios and claims full of stupidity and illogicality. However, "magic" is the only possible explanation for people from all over the world believing that unconscious and lifeless atoms suddenly decided to come together and form a universe that functions with a flawless system of organization, discipline, reason, and consciousness; a planet named Earth with all of its features so perfectly suited to life; and living things full of countless complex systems.

In fact, the Qur'an relates the incident of Prophet Musa and Pharaoh to show that some people who support atheistic philosophies actually influence others by magic. When Pharaoh was told about the true religion, he told Prophet Musa to meet with his own magicians. When Musa did so, he told them to demonstrate their abilities first. The verses continue:

> **He said: "You throw." And when they threw, they cast a spell on the people's eyes and caused them to feel great fear of them. They produced an extremely powerful magic. (Surat al-A'raf, 116)**

As we have seen, Pharaoh's magicians were able to deceive everyone, apart from Musa and those who believed in him. However, his evidence broke the spell, or "swallowed up what they had forged," as the verse puts it.

> **We revealed to Musa, "Throw down your staff." And it immediately swallowed up what they had forged. So the Truth took place and what they did was shown to be false. (Surat al-A'raf, 117-119)**

As we can see, when people realized that a spell had been cast upon them and that what they saw was just an illusion, Pharaoh's magicians lost all credibility. In the present day too, unless those who, under the influence of a similar spell, believe in these ridiculous claims under their scientific disguise and spend their lives defending them, abandon their superstitious beliefs, they also will be humiliated when the full truth emerges and the spell is broken. In fact, world-renowned British writer and philosopher Malcolm Muggeridge also stated this:

> *I myself am convinced that the theory of evolution, especially the extent to which it's been applied, will be one of the great jokes in the history books in the future. Posterity will marvel that so very flimsy and dubious an hypothesis could be accepted with the incredible credulity that it has.*[27]

That future is not far off: On the contrary, people will soon see that "chance" is not a deity, and will look back on the theory of evolution as the worst deceit and the most terrible spell in the world. That spell is already rapidly beginning to be lifted from the shoulders of people all over the world. Many people who see its true face are wondering with amazement how they could ever have been taken in by it.

They said, "Glory be to You! We have no knowledge except what You have taught us. You are the All-Knowing, the All-Wise."
(Surat al-Baqara, 32)

NOTES

1. Bediuzzaman Said Nursi, *Risale-i Nur Collection*, The Sixteenth Flashes; Dhu'l-Qarnayn "Saw the sun setting in a spring of murky water."
2. Iskender Ture, *Zulkarneyn* (Dhu'l-Qarnayn), (Istanbul: Karizma Yayinlari, 2000), pp. 133-168.
3. Carl Sagan, *Cosmos*, Random House, New York, 1980, p. 199.
4. Omer Nasuhi Bilmen, *Kuran-i Kerim'in Turkce Meali Alisi ve Tefsiri* (Commentary of the Qur'an), Bilmen Publications, vol. 4, p. 1989.
5. Bediuzzaman Said Nursi, *Risale-i Nur Collection*, The Sixteenth Flashes; "Where is the barrier of Dhu'l-Qarnayn? Who were Gog and Magog?"
6. Ibn Kathir and Zamakhshari tafseers.
7. Bediuzzaman Said Nursi, *Risale-i Nur Collection*, The Twenty-Fourth Word, Third Branch.
8. Sidney Fox, Klaus Dose, *Molecular Evolution and The Origin of Life*, W.H. Freeman and Company, San Francisco, 1972, p. 4.
9. Alexander I. Oparin, *Origin of Life*, Dover Publications, NewYork, 1936, 1953 (reprint), p. 196.
10. "New Evidence on Evolution of Early Atmosphere and Life", *Bulletin of the American Meteorological Society*, vol 63, November 1982, p. 1328-1330.
11. Stanley Miller, *Molecular Evolution of Life: Current Status of the Prebiotic Synthesis of Small Molecules*, 1986, p. 7.
12. Jeffrey Bada, *Earth*, February 1998, p. 40.
13. Leslie E. Orgel, "The Origin of Life on Earth", *Scientific American*, vol. 271, October 1994, p. 78.
14. Charles Darwin, *The Origin of Species by Means of Natural Selection*, The Modern Library, New York, p. 127.
15. Charles Darwin, *The Origin of Species: A Facsimile of the First Edition*, Harvard University Press, 1964, p. 184.

16. B. G. Ranganathan, *Origins?*, Pennsylvania: The Banner Of Truth Trust, 1988, p. 7.
17. Charles Darwin, *The Origin of Species: A Facsimile of the First Edition*, Harvard University Press, 1964, p. 179.
18. Derek A. Ager, "The Nature of the Fossil Record", *Proceedings of the British Geological Association*, vol 87, 1976, p. 133.
19. Douglas J. Futuyma, *Science on Trial*, Pantheon Books, New York, 1983. p. 197.
20. Solly Zuckerman, *Beyond The Ivory Tower*, Toplinger Publications, New York, 1970, pp. 75-14; Charles E. Oxnard, "The Place of Australopithecines in Human Evolution: Grounds for Doubt", Nature, vol 258, p. 389.
21. "Could science be brought to an end by scientists' belief that they have final answers or by society's reluctance to pay the bills?" *Scientific American*, December 1992, p. 20.
22. Alan Walker, *Science*, vol. 207, 7 March 1980, p. 1103; A. J. Kelso, Physical Antropology, 1st ed., J. B. Lipincott Co., New York, 1970, p. 221; M. D. Leakey, Olduvai Gorge, vol. 3, Cambridge University Press, Cambridge, 1971, p. 272.
23. Jeffrey Kluger, "Not So Extinct After All: The Primitive Homo Erectus May Have Survived Long Enough To Coexist With Modern Humans", *Time*, 23 December 1996.
24. S. J. Gould, *Natural History*, vol. 85, 1976, p. 30.
25. Solly Zuckerman, *Beyond The Ivory Tower*, p. 19.
26. Richard Lewontin, "The Demon-Haunted World," 71 Malcolm Muggeridge, *The End of Christendom*, Grand Rapids: Eerdmans, 1980, p. 43.
27. Malcolm Muggeridge, *The End of Christendom*, Grand Rapids: Eerdmans, 1980, p. 43.

Also by Harun Yahya

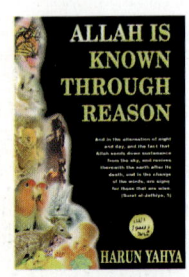

The plan, design, and delicate balance existing in our bodies and reaching into even the remotest corners of the iuniverse must surely have a superior Creator. Man is unable to see his Creator yet he can nevertheless grasp His existence, strength, and wisdom by means of his intellect.

When the events of "sickness" and "recovering" take place, our bodies become a battleground in which a bitter struggle is taking place. The body however has a mechanism that combats them. This system proves that the human body is the outcome of a unique design that has been planned with a great wisdom and skill.

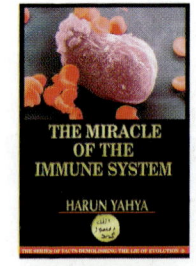

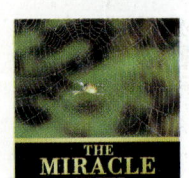

Just as a tiny key opens a huge door, this book will open new horizons for its readers. Relating the amazing and admirable features of spiders known by few people, this book reveals the excellence and perfection inherent in God's creation.

The purpose of this book is to display the miraculous features of plants and hence to make people see "the creation miracle" in things they often encounter in the flow of their daily lives and sidestep.

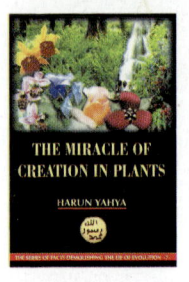

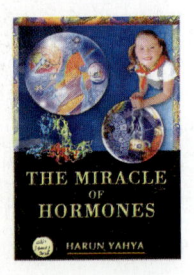

100 trillion cells in your body meet all your bodily needs thanks to a perfect communication system. This is carried out by your hormones. The main thrust of this book is to display the impossibility of the coincidental formation of the extraordinary systems in living things, and to show the perfection in the creation of Allah with examples.

The creation of man, who is endowed with a highly complicated body structure, from a drop of water, comes about through an extraordinary course of development. This development certainly does not happen as the result of an idle process, and random coincidences, but is a conscious act of creation. This book is about the details of the "miracle in man's creation."

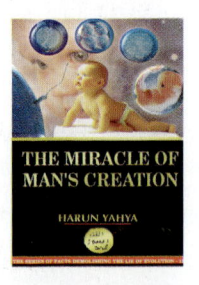

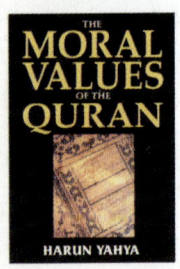

A study that examines and seeks to remind us of the basic moral principles of the Qur'an, particularly those that are most likely to be forgotten or neglected at times. This book is also available in Bengoli.

God, in the Qur'an, calls the culture of people who are not subject to the religion of God "ignorance." The purpose of this book is to take this comparison further, displaying the extent of the "crude understanding" of ignorant societies.

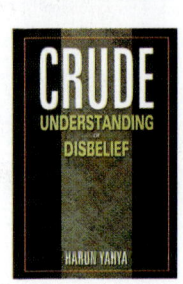